15 Dec 08

Unlocking Democracy

20 years of Charter 88

Unlocking Democracy

20 years of Charter 88

edited by
Peter Facey
Bethan Rigby
Alexandra Runswick

POLITICO'S

First published in Great Britain 2008 by
Politico's Publishing, an imprint of
Methuen Publishing Ltd
8 Artillery Row
London
SW1P 1RZ

10 9 8 7 6 5 4 3 2 1

A CIP catalogue record for this book is available from the British Library.

ISBN 978-1-84275-232-6

Set in Bembo by SX Composing DTP, Rayleigh, Essex
Printed and bound in Great Britain by
TJ International Ltd, Padstow, Cornwall

Contents

Acknowledgements

nlock Democracy would like to thank the following for their assistance with this book:

All current staff at Unlock Democracy, in particular those who worked in detail on the project – Peter Facey, James Graham, Bethan Rigby and Alexandra Runswick. Peter and Alex are grateful to James for providing additional material for their chapters. Bethan would like to thank Martin, Annwen and John for their support over the years. Alex would like to thank Elaine Ryder for all her support and Lindsey Graham for providing an exit strategy in 2003.

We would also like to thank our current council and management board; our advisers on this project, Stuart Weir and Anthony Barnett; our interns Josh Robson and Tom Cleaver; all previous staff, volunteers, council, activists, signatories and members of Charter 88; Debbie Chay for advice; Alan Gordon Walker and Jonathan Wadman at Politico's for kind and professional assistance; Paul Farthing and Keith Ablitt for archive help, as well as the library staff at the University of Essex; and Anne and Bob for putting Bethan up during her archive searches. Thanks also to Tim Sanders, David Shenton and Jane Monahan for their kind permission to reproduce their excellent cartoons, to the *New Statesman* for the use of their cover, and to Polity Press for permission to reproduce the cover of *Debating the Constitution*. We are grateful to David, Dolapo and Esther Tewogbade for the use of the photo of Esther which appears on the front cover of the book.

In particular we would like to thank the Joseph Rowntree Reform Trust for helping to make this book happen. Finally, a big thanks to all of our authors, who produced such interesting and vital work at short notice and at no charge – your interest, patience and co-operation have been very much appreciated.

There are instances where we have been unable to trace or contact the copyright holder of the material appearing in the Archive. If notified, the publisher will be pleased to rectify any errors or omissions at the earliest opportunity.

About the contributors

Anthony Barnett

Anthony Barnett was the first director of Charter 88. He is the author of *Iron Britannia: Why Parliament Waged Its Falkland's War* (1982) and the optimistically titled *This Time: Our Constitutional Revolution* (1997). He has also edited and co-authored a number of books, including *Aftermath: The Struggle of Cambodia and Vietnam* (with John Pilger, 1982), *Soviet Freedom* (with Nella Bielski, 1988), *Debating the Constitution: New Perspectives on Constitutional Reform* (with Caroline Ellis and Paul Hirst, 1992), based on the Charter 88 Manchester Constitutional Convention, *Power and the Throne* (1994), drawn from the Charter 88 monarchy debate, *Town and Country* (edited with Roger Scruton, 1999) and *The Athenian Option* (with Peter Carty, 2008). In 2001 he was a founder of openDemocracy and was its editor in chief until 2007. He now edits its British blog, OurKingdom, and is co-director of the Convention on Modern Liberty.

Geoffrey Bindman

Sir Geoffrey Bindman is a British lawyer specialising in civil liberties and human rights issues, media law, defamation, anti-discrimination and general litigation. From 1966 to 1976 he was legal adviser to the Race Relations Board and thereafter until 1983 to the Commission for Racial Equality.

Geoffrey is a visiting professor of law at University College London and at London South Bank University. He has received honorary doctorates from De Montfort and Kingston universities, and is chair of the board of trustees at the British Institute of Human Rights. He has won awards for a lifetime's achievement in human rights from Liberty (December 1999) and the *Law Society Gazette* (October 2003).

Geoffrey is co-author, with Lord Lester of Herne Hill QC, of *Race and Law* (1972), and has contributed chapters to several books, including *Halsbury's Laws of England* (4th edition). He has written many articles in legal journals and in the national press and broadcasts frequently on his specialist topics. He has represented the International Commission of Jurists, the International Bar Association, Amnesty International, and other bodies in human rights missions in many countries worldwide.

Gordon Brown

Gordon Brown was born in 1951 and educated in Kirkcaldy. He studied at Edinburgh University from the age of sixteen and graduated with an MA at nineteen with first-class honours, later gaining a doctorate of philosophy. He was elected rector of Edinburgh University by the student body and from 1972 to 1975 was chairman of the University Court. From 1976 to 1980 he lectured at Edinburgh University and then at Glasgow College of Technology, before taking up a post at Scottish TV.

From 1983 to 1984 Gordon Brown chaired the Labour Party Scottish Council and in May 1983 became MP for Dunfermline East. He was opposition spokesperson on Treasury and economic affairs (Shadow Chancellor) from 1992. With the election of the Labour government in May 1997, Gordon Brown became Chancellor of the Exchequer, and held the post for ten years, making him the longest-serving Chancellor for 200 years. Following the resignation of Tony Blair, he became Prime Minister in June 2007. Gordon Brown is married to Sarah Macaulay and they have two sons.

Gordon Brown's publications include *Civic Society in Modern Britain* (1987), *Where There Is Greed* (1989), *Constitutional Change and the Future of Britain* (1992), *John Smith* (1994), *Maxton* (2002), *Moving Britain Forward: Selected Speeches 1997–2006* (2006) and *Courage: Eight Portraits* (2007).

David Cameron

David was elected leader of the Conservative Party in December 2005, on a mandate to change the party and change the country. Before he was elected MP for Witney in 2001, he worked as a special adviser in government, first to the Chancellor of the Exchequer and then to the Home Secretary, and spent seven years at Carlton Communications. David, Samantha and their three young children live in London and west Oxfordshire.

Douglas Carswell MP

Douglas Carswell has been Conservative MP for Harwich since 2005. He previously worked in fund management and, before that, in commercial television. Immediately prior to the last general election, he worked in the Conservative Party Policy Unit helping prepare the manifesto.

In 2008, he sponsored a private member's Bill to allow parliamentary legislation to be tabled directly by members of the public through petitions. He has also led the campaign to replace the Speaker, Michael Martin. He has written for the *Daily Telegraph*, the *Financial Times*, the *Mail on Sunday* and the *Sunday Times*. His publications include *Direct Democracy* (2002), *Paying for Localism* (2004) and *The Plan: Twelve Months to Renew Britain* (2008). He blogs every day at www.TalkCarswell.com.

Louise Christian

Louise Christian is the senior partner of Christian Khan solicitors. She represented the victims of the *Marchioness* disaster for ten years and was the lead solicitor for the victims of the Paddington and Southall rail crashes in major public inquiries, successfully conducting compensation claims. Louise acts for all the bereaved families in the inquest into the Potters Bar rail crash, where Mr Justice Sullivan, sitting as coroner, has suggested a joint public inquiry which would also look at the recent Grayrigg train crash. She is also acting for Marina Litvinenko, the widow of Alexander Litvinenko, in a case against the Russian government at the European Court of Human Rights. Louise has dealt with many significant human rights cases, including the leading ECHR case of *Osman* and the case of *Abbasi* in the Court of Appeal, which considered the situation of UK citizens detained in Guantanamo Bay.

Louise was awarded the first LAPG/Independent Lawyer Legal Aid Personality of the Year Award in 2004. In the same year she received a special joint award from the Law Society, JUSTICE and Liberty for outstanding commitment to the rule of law in acting for persons detained in Guantanamo Bay. She is a senior fellow of the Association of Personal Injury Lawyers. She is named as a leader in the *Chambers UK* directory in the fields of administrative law and human rights. She is chair of Liberty and has an honorary doctorate from Staffordshire University.

Nick Clegg MP

Nick Clegg is MP for Sheffield Hallam and leader of the Liberal Democrats. He studied at Cambridge and Minnesota universities and at the Collège d'Europe before training as a journalist. Nick then worked as a development and trade expert in the EU, sat as an MEP (1999–2004), lectured at Sheffield and Cambridge universities, and was elected as an MP in 2005.

In Parliament Nick was quickly appointed Europe spokesperson and later shadow Home Secretary, a role in which he spearheaded the Liberal Democrats' defence of civil liberties and promoted a new approach to cutting crime. He was elected leader in December 2007 and has pledged to double the party's number of MPs within two elections. Clegg is married with two young children.

Deborah Coles and Helen Shaw

Deborah Coles is co-director of INQUEST. She chairs the board of trustees of the charities Women in Prison and the Buwan Kothi International Trust and she is a trustee of the Centre for Corporate Accountability. She is co-author of *In the Care of the State?* (with Barry Goldson, 2005) and *Dying on the Inside* (with Marissa Sandler, 2008).

Helen Shaw is co-director of INQUEST. She chairs the board of trustees of the charity British Irish Rights Watch. She is also a non-executive member of the non-departmental public body the Human Tissue Authority, which regulates the removal, storage, use and disposal of human bodies, organs and tissue from the living and the deceased.

Deborah and Helen are co-authors of the book *Unlocking the Truth* (2007) and joint editors of *Inquest Law*, the journal of the INQUEST Lawyers Group. They both undertake policy, research and consultancy work on the strategic issues raised by contentious deaths, their investigation, the treatment of bereaved people and state accountability. They are frequent media commentators and work closely with other leading agencies in the field of human rights and criminal justice, and they are regularly consulted by government agencies and non-governmental organisations.

Simon Davies

Simon Davies is one of the world's foremost privacy advocates and is a pioneer in the international privacy field. He is founder and director of the watchdog organisation Privacy International and for the past decade has taught at the London School of Economics, where he is visiting senior fellow. He is also chief executive of the new privacy consultancy 80/20 Thinking Ltd.

Brice Dickson

Brice Dickson has been professor of international and comparative law at Queen's University Belfast since 2005. In 1981 he helped to found the Committee on the Administration of Justice, a civil liberties group in Belfast. From 1991 to 1999 he was the foundation professor of law at the University of Ulster, and served during most of that period as a member of the Equal Opportunities Commission for Northern Ireland. From 1999 to 2005 he was seconded from the University of Ulster to serve two terms as the first chief commissioner of the Northern Ireland Human Rights Commission, a statutory body established as a result of the Belfast (Good Friday) agreement. He has written the standard textbook on the legal system of Northern Ireland (now in its fifth edition), as well as authoring or editing other books on French law, the European Convention on Human Rights, civil liberties in Northern Ireland, the House of Lords and judicial activism.

Peter Facey

Peter Facey is the founding director of Unlock Democracy. He became director of Unlock Democracy's predecessor organisation, the New Politics Network, in 2001 and was later made the final director of Charter 88, merging the two organisations in 2007.

Peter has worked in democratic reform, citizenship and

participation for more than thirteen years and was previously chief executive of the British Youth Council. He is recognised as an expert in democratic reform and comments widely in the UK media. He has given evidence to parliamentary committees on issues as diverse as devolution and decentralisation, lobbying and war powers.

Peter has established Unlock Democracy as the leading provider of interactive citizenship conferences for 16–19-year-olds. He has a particular interest in elections and how to get more people involved in the political process.

Zac Goldsmith

Zac Goldsmith was editor of the *Ecologist* for nine years. He stepped down last year after being selected as the Conservative Party parliamentary candidate for Richmond Park, but he remains director of the *Ecologist*.

In 2005 he was asked to oversee a wide-ranging review of environmental policy for the Conservative Party. The Quality of Life policy review was delivered to David Cameron in September 2007 and many of its recommendations have become party policy.

In 2003 Zac was one of two people awarded the Beacon Prize for Young Philanthropists. The following year he received the Global Green USA International Environmental Leadership Award.

Katherine Gundersen

Katherine Gundersen is the research officer for the Campaign for Freedom of Information, where she has worked since 1999. She joined the Campaign as the Freedom of Information Bill was being introduced into Parliament and was closely involved in the Campaign's efforts to improve the measure, for which it received the Liberty/JUSTICE Human Rights Award in 2000. She edits the UK Freedom of Information blog, advises requesters about their rights under the FOI Act and is responsible for much of the research that underpins the Campaign's work.

Katherine studied politics at the University of Bristol. Before joining the Campaign, she worked in the constituency office of Estelle Morris MP.

Nick Herbert MP

Nick was elected Conservative MP for Arundel & South Downs in May 2005. He was appointed shadow minister for police reform later that year and in 2007 joined the shadow Cabinet as shadow secretary of state for justice. Prior to his election Nick was the director of Reform, the independent think tank which he co-founded; chief executive of Business for Sterling, where he launched the successful 'no' campaign against the euro; and a campaigner with the precursor to the Countryside Alliance.

Simon Hughes MP

Simon Hughes is federal president of the Liberal Democrats. He is the longest-serving member of the Liberal Democrat shadow Cabinet and is currently shadow leader of the House of Commons.

Simon has roots in England, Wales and Scotland. He studied, trained and worked in Belgium and France before returning to London to work as a human rights lawyer in 1977. Simon joined the Liberal Party in 1971, inspired by the campaigns for justice in South Africa and Palestine. He was elected to Parliament in Bermondsey in 1983 as the youngest opposition MP on a record British parliamentary wing of 51 per cent. Simon was re-elected for the enlarged Southwark & Bermondsey constituency in 1983, 1987 and 1992 and for North Southwark & Bermondsey in 1997, 2001 and 2005.

Simon stood for the Liberal Democrat leadership in 1999 and 2005 and in 2004 was the Liberal Democrat candidate for London mayor.

John Jackson

John Jackson has been chairman of Mishcon de Reya since 1992. He was chairman of Active Citizens Transform until its merger with Charter 88; he then became one of Charter's two deputy chairmen until it joined with New Politics Network to form Unlock Democracy, of which he is a council member. He writes for openDemocracy (of which he has been a director since its inception) and its blog OurKingdom on constitutional matters.

John has served on, or chaired, the boards of a number of

companies in a wide range of industries including Hilton International, BHP Billiton, Celltech and WPP. He is currently chairman of the four Oxford Technology Venture Capital Trusts and Instore plc. He was chairman of the Countryside Alliance for seven years and has been chairman and part-owner of the magazine *History Today* since 1981.

Helena Kennedy QC

Helena is a leading barrister and an expert in human rights law, civil liberties and constitutional issues. She is a bencher of Gray's Inn and president of the School of Oriental and African Studies, University of London. She was the chair of Charter 88 from 1992 to 1997, the Human Genetics Commission from 1998 to 2007 and the British Council from 1998 to 2004. She also chaired the Power Inquiry, which reported on the state of British democracy and produced the Power Report in 2006. She has received honours for her work on human rights from the governments of France and Italy and has been awarded more than thirty honorary doctorates. She is currently acting in cases connected to the recent wave of terrorism and is a member of the House of Lords.

Helena is a frequent broadcaster and journalist on law and women's rights. Her publications include the widely acclaimed *Eve Was Framed: Women and British Justice* (1992, revised 2005) and *Just Law: The Changing Face of Justice and Why It Matters to Us All* (2004).

Helen Margetts

Helen Margetts is professor of society and the internet at the Oxford Internet Institute, University of Oxford. She joined the OII in 2004 from University College London, where she was director of the School of Public Policy. She is a political scientist of international standing in e-government and digital-era governance, investigating the nature and implications of the relationships between governments and the internet and related technologies in the UK and internationally.

Helen's publications include *Information Technology in Government: Britain and America* (1999), *Digital Era Governance: IT Corporations, the State, and E-Government* (with Patrick Dunleavy and others, 2006) and *The Tools of Government in the Digital Age* (with Christopher Hope, 2007). She has also published major research reports in this area for such agencies as the UK's National Audit Office.

Bhikhu Parekh

Lord Parekh, professor of political philosophy at the University of Westminster, is a fellow of the Royal Society of Arts, the British Academy and the Academy of Learned Societies. He was chair of the Runnymede Commission on the Future of Multi-Ethnic Britain (1998–2000), whose report, *The Future of Multi-Ethnic Britain*, was published in 2000. He is vice-chairman of the Gandhi Foundation and a trustee of the Anne Frank Educational Trust. His main academic interests include political philosophy, the history of political thought, social theory, ancient and modern Indian political thought, and the philosophy of ethnic relations.

Lord Parekh is the author, among many other works, of *Hannah Arendt and the Search for a New Political Philosophy* (1981), *Marx's Theory of Ideology* (1981), *Contemporary Political Thinkers* (1982) *Colonialism, Tradition and Reform* (1989), *Gandhi's Political Philosophy* (1989), *Gandhi* (1997), and *Rethinking Multiculturalism* (2000). He has received many awards throughout his career: the Sir Isaiah Berlin Prize for Lifetime Contribution to Political Studies from the Political Studies Association (2002), the Distinguished Global Thinker Award from the India International Centre, Delhi (2006), the Interdependence Prize from the Campaign for Democracy, New York (2006), and the Padma Bhushan honours in the 2007 Indian Republic Day honours list.

Trevor Phillips

On 8 September 2006, Trevor Phillips was announced as chair of the new Equality and Human Rights Commission, which took over the work of Britain's three existing equality commissions from 1 October 2007. Trevor had been appointed chair of the Commission for Racial Equality on 1 March 2003.

Born in London in 1953, Trevor attended secondary school in Georgetown, Guyana, and then studied chemistry at Imperial College, London. Between 1978 and 1980, he was president of the National Union of Students. He then went into broadcasting, becoming head of current affairs at London Weekend Television in 1992. He was elected as a member of the London Assembly in May 2000, and became its chair later that month.

Trevor is a director of Pepper Productions, founded in 1995, and was the executive producer on *Windrush* (which won the Royal Television Society documentary series of the year award in 1998), *Britain's Slave Trade, Second Chance* and *When Black Became Beautiful.* Trevor had previously received awards from the Royal Television Society in 1988 and 1993 and is currently a vice-president of the society.

At present, Trevor is a board member of the Almeida Theatre in Islington, Aldeburgh Productions and the Bernie Grant Centre in Tottenham. He is a patron of the Sickle Cell Society. Between 1993 and 1998, Trevor was chair of the Runnymede Trust.

In addition to many newspaper articles and comment pieces, Trevor has co-written *Windrush: The Irresistible Rise of Multiracial Britain* (with Mike Phillips, 1998) and *Britain's Slave Trade* (with S. I. Martin, 1999).

Alexandra Runswick

Alex is responsible for Unlock Democracy's parliamentary strategy and policy development work; she is the organisation's deputy director and its parliamentary and policy officer. She volunteered for a range of voluntary sector organisations, including Greenpeace and the Fawcett Society, while studying for an MA in social policy, and she joined Charter 88 in 2001.

Alex is the author of a number of policy briefings as well as two pamphlets on party funding reform. *Life Support for Local Parties* analyses the decline of local political parties and the case for state support, while *Party Funding: Supporting the Grassroots* (with James Graham) explores how party funding can be used to support grassroots activity and how the trade union link could be reformed.

Alex also specialises in participatory decision-making and how citizens can be involved in constitutional reform. She worked with the British Council to produce *People and Policy-Making: A Guide for Political Parties*, a resource for local political parties on how they can involve the public in policy-making. Her other interests include public participation in health policy and equalities issues.

Alex is a trustee of the Ryder Tremberth Trust and a member of the Electoral Reform Society's Council.

Trevor Smith

Lord Smith joined the University of Exeter as a lecturer in 1959, the same year he stood as unsuccessful Liberal parliamentary candidate in Lewisham West. In the 1960s he taught at the University of Hull and California State University, Los Angeles. In 1967 he moved to Queen Mary College in London, where he was promoted to professor and head of department, and then to vice-principal. In 1991 he was appointed vice-chancellor of the University of Ulster, a post he occupied with distinction until his retirement in 1999.

Lord Smith has authored or co-authored a large number of books and articles on British politics and society. These include *Town and County Hall* (1966), *Anti-Politics* (1972), *Direct Action and Democratic Politics* (1972), *The Politics of the Corporate Economy* (1979) and *The Fixers* (1996). Lord Smith was chair of the Political Studies Association from 1988–1989 and its president from 1991 to 1993.

Lord Smith was been a director of the Joseph Rowntree Reform Trust between 1975 and 2006 and was its chair between 1987 and 1999. He became a Liberal Democrat working peer in 1997 and is the party's spokesperson on Northern Ireland in the House of Lords. He is on the Lords Constitution Committee. He is an honorary professor at the University of Ulster.

Alan Trench

Alan is a research fellow in the School of Law at the University of Edinburgh, where he now works on financial aspects of devolution in the UK and in federal and regional systems of government elsewhere. He was formerly at the Constitution Unit at University College London.

He has edited and contributed to numerous books on aspects of devolution, including *Devolution and Power in the United Kingdom* (2007) and *The State of the Nations 2008* (2008).

Stuart Weir

Stuart Weir is the director of Democratic Audit, at the Human Rights Centre, University of Essex, and a visiting professor with the university's Government Department. Democratic Audit conducts research into the quality of democracy and human rights in the UK and internationally. He is author and editor of *Unequal Britain* (Politico's, 2006) and joint author of reports on the government's counter-terrorism laws and strategy, the politics of the BNP and power and participation in the UK. He is also joint author of three democratic audits of the UK, the latest being *Democracy under Blair* (Politico's, 2002), and of *The IDEA Handbook on Democracy Assessment* (2008) and *The State of Democracy* (2003). He has been an active facilitator for democratic reform in Macedonia, Malawi, Namibia, Nigeria and Zimbabwe.

Introduction

I think Charter 88 was a huge step forward in the political education of many people, myself certainly included, and possibly the long-term effects will be most marked, in fact, not in direct and measurable legislative consequences so much as in a gradual enlightenment among those who think about these things. Charter 88 made that enlightening a lot less gradual and a lot more focused, and that understanding hasn't gone away. It now serves, for me anyway, as a sort of litmus test of whether any proposed constitutional change is cosmetic or fundamental. The big idea was the revelation that such things as local democracy, the House of Lords, the voting system, devolution, party funding and so on are all connected.

Philip Pullman, author and former chair of Charter 88 Oxford

Charter 88 was written to mark the anniversary of two events – the 1968 'revolutionary wave' and the 1688 Glorious Revolution. It could equally have been published to mark the thirtieth anniversary of the life peerage system (which at least stalled the system of creating hereditary peerages even if it did not end patronage), the fortieth anniversary of the Universal Declaration of Human Rights, the sixtieth anniversary of universal suffrage (and the seventieth of the first women getting the vote) or the 150th anniversary of the Chartists (and their apex almost exactly ten years later). Scots will want me to mention the treaty of Edinburgh in 1328, whilst the Cornish will want me to mention the Charter of Pardon, establishing their own parliament, in 1508. John Milton, a republican and champion of freedom of speech, was born in 1608. There seems to be something cosmological about years ending in 8 and milestones in democracy.

To mark this latest step along the way, we approached dozens of campaigners, experts and politicians, from within the Charter 88 family and without, to contribute an article for this anthology. We gave them carte blanche to write on whatever they wanted related to the state of British democracy. The resulting book, I believe, is both a testament to the success of Charter 88 and a vivid illustration of the need for its campaign to continue (now as Unlock Democracy).

It was a success because it was largely responsible for creating the momentum behind the constitutional reforms that New Labour introduced in the late 1990s: the Human Rights Act (in 1998 – another 8), the Freedom of Information Act and devolution to Scotland and Wales. Despite media indifference, it has been successful in less tangible ways as well.

This book includes articles by all three main party leaders. In and of itself that shows how far we have come in twenty years. If we had been publishing a book on democratic reform in 1988, we would have struggled to get the leader of the then Social and Liberal Democrats to write (mainly because he, Paddy Ashdown, was in the process of being elected at the time). If we had been publishing this in 1998, we would almost certainly have had enthusiastic pieces by both Ashdown and Tony Blair, but William Hague would have been a struggle. Now we can boast an article by a Conservative Party leader claiming that 'if some of our prescriptions are different in important respects, our overall goals are remarkably similar to those of Unlock Democracy'. It may be tempting for some to dismiss that as empty rhetoric, but I believe it would be a profound mistake to do so. After eleven years in the political wilderness, the Conservatives have been forced to review their ideas about the nature of power.

Charter 88 has transformed our political discourse. Talk about a Bill of Rights and even hints of a written constitution have become mainstream. The Conservatives are now proposing to scrap the Human Rights Act (HRA). However, in a sign of how the debate has irrevocably shifted, at the same time they propose introducing a 'British Bill of rights and responsibilities'. Quite how exactly this could operate on a daily basis in a way that is substantially different from our current position under the HRA is unclear – Cameron has explicitly ruled out derogating from the European Convention on Human Rights and has even praised it.[*]

---

[*] David Cameron, 'Balancing freedom and security: a modern British Bill of Rights', speech at the Centre for Policy Studies, 26 June 2006.

If, as some suggest, Cameron's proposals are to make his new Bill non-justiciable, refusing most ordinary people recourse to the courts when their rights are denied and putting all decisions in a court in Strasbourg, he is unlikely to get his way without a fight. It would be an odd move for a first-term government to want to make.

The current government's position can be equally obfuscatory. From time to time, ministers tend to call for the HRA to be emasculated, usually when a judicial ruling goes against them.* Yet at the same time they are calling for a 'Bill of rights and duties' as part of the 'Governance of Britain' agenda. The government has explicitly stated that its version would build on the rights in the existing HRA rather than replace it. Going further still into Charter 88 territory, it even hints at the possibility of a new Bill of Rights being the first step towards a written constitution.† Once again this could just be words, but one has to ask why they are talking about this now when the public are hardly beating down the door demanding they do so (polling suggests that the public do broadly support a written constitution,‡ but it is not a priority for them).§

In this context we have brought together a number of Charter 88's leading figures to discuss the writing of the charter itself, the founding of the campaign organisation of the same name and the long-term impact of both in the opening History section. This is not intended to be a comprehensive history. For example, we have only touched lightly on the creation of Operation Black Vote (with the 1990 Trust) and NO2ID (with Liberty). I would like to thank all of Charter 88's past co-ordinators, directors,

---

* See for example Clare Dyer, 'Outrage at plan to end judicial review in asylum cases', *Guardian*, 11 December 2003; Ned Temko and Jamie Doward, 'Revealed: Blair attack on human rights law', *Observer*, 14 May 2006.

† Ministry of Justice, *The Governance of Britain* (Cm 7170, 2007), para. 212. See also Jack Straw, 'Modernising the Magna Carta' speech at George Washington University, 13 February 2008.

‡ See *State of the Nation 2006* (York: Joseph Rowntree Reform Trust, 2006), p. 1.

§ See *Audit of Political Engagement 5: The 2008 Report* (London: Hansard Society, 2008), p. 31.

members of staff, volunteers, local groups and council and executive members for carrying the flag.

Stuart Weir and Anthony Barnett give their own accounts reminding us of the huge range of different people from the political and arts spheres who came together to launch the campaign, the early struggles to capture the imagination of the political class and the campaign's tremendous success in mobilising grassroots support. If Stuart and Anthony were Charter's founding fathers, then Trevor Smith and his fellow Joseph Rowntree Reform trustees were its benevolent uncles. In his piece, Trevor talks about the Reform Trust's contribution to Charter 88, which as Anthony suggests was more than simply financial, and sets the organisation in the context of the wider democratic movement in the 1980s and 1990s.

Alexandra Runswick brings us bang up to date, by discussing Charter's period from the 2001 general election up to the present day, having now merged with the New Politics Network to form Unlock Democracy.

Finally, we have a piece from Helena Kennedy, the chair of Charter 88 in the mid-1990s and for many its public face. In her article she talks about her frustrations in attempting to get the New Labour government to grasp the wider constitutional implications of its democratic reform agenda. She goes on to talk about the Power Inquiry, another project funded by the Joseph Rowntree Reform Trust (along with its sister Charitable Trust) which helped to revive the debate on democratic reform.

One thing you will find that all the contributors to this first section agree on is that we cannot afford to rest on our laurels. Charter 88's success may have been tremendous, but its work is still not completed.

Our second section is a smorgasbord, a snapshot of the state of British democracy circa 2008. One thing it is not, and was never intended to be, is a coherent manifesto for change. We have put these in alphabetical order and they are not intended to be read in sequence – indeed we recommend that you do not do so. You will find that many of our contributors contradict and passionately disagree with each other; there are many things in this collection that Unlock Democracy itself would take issue with. You will find an essay about legal aid sitting alongside an impassioned plea for small government. This collection is intended to provoke debate, not provide definitive answers.

There is sadly another reason why such a wide spectrum of people can write so passionately about the need for democratic reform: necessity. The original Charter 88 was written at a time when the levers of power were working relatively well; a key premise on which it was built was that they were working too efficiently and leaving the people largely out of the equation. Twenty years on, there is a sense that while central government in some ways is more powerful than ever, its ability to effect meaningful change and legitimacy is open to question as never before.

Within this section there are broadly three types of contribution. The first comprises broad overviews of how the authors feel British democracy needs to be transformed. In this category I would include the pieces by the Prime Minister, Gordon Brown (actually a reprint of his 1992 Sovereignty Lecture, to which he has added a foreword linking it with his government's current programme for constitutional change); the Conservative leader, David Cameron, with the shadow justice secretary, Nick Herbert; and the Liberal Democrat leader, Nick Clegg. Douglas Carswell and Simon Hughes provide alternative visions of Conservative and Liberal Democrat constitutional reforms respectively.

The second type comprises pieces which examine the relative merits of specific mooted reforms. Bhikhu Parekh outlines how he believes the House of Lords should be reformed. Brice Dickson addresses the question of social and economic rights and argues how they could be incorporated into a future Bill of Rights without leading to the bugbear of 'judicial activism' threatening Parliament's legislative role. Deborah Coles and Helen Shaw write about how the current system of inquests fails to provide a proper system of accountability for deaths in custody and explore how this undermines basic human rights – a critical democratic issue. Helen Margetts discusses the debate surrounding electoral reform and the prospects of it being introduced in the House of Commons. Katherine Gundersen discusses the Freedom of Information Act, its positive impact and how it might be improved. Trevor Phillips discusses the equality and human rights agenda in his capacity as chairman of the commission of the same name. Zac Goldsmith proposes going one step further than the original charter by introducing more direct systems of democracy via citizen-led initiatives and referenda.

Finally, the third type of essay consists of warnings of crises ahead which future governments will have to deal with regardless of their political leanings. Alan Trench writes about the unintended consequences of Labour's devolution agenda and how it could now threaten the integrity of the United Kingdom itself. Geoffrey Bindman talks about the curtailment of the system of legal aid and how this is denying people on low incomes access to justice. Taking government proposals to extend pre-charge detention to forty-two days as an example, Louise Christian questions whether our current political system is capable of protecting basic human rights. Simon Davies discusses how our privacy has come under attack from the government in recent years and how this has undermined the public's trust. In a provocative piece which ranges from ancient Sumeria up to the present day, John Jackson explores the concept of the rule of law and how the Constitutional Reform Act 2005 established it as a constitutional principle for the first time in British law despite its failure to spell out the implications of this in a country which lacks a written constitution.

Unlock Democracy is the successor organisation to Charter 88, following its merger with the New Politics Network in 2007. Building on the original charter, we campaign for fair, open and honest elections; rights, freedoms and a written constitution; a stronger Parliament and accountable government; bringing power closer to the people; and a culture of informed political interest and responsibility.

In some of these areas we expect to make progress, while others remain frustratingly out of reach. We appear to have won much of the argument but vested interests conspire to prevent us from achieving the two most vital reforms: electoral reform and a written constitution. In my concluding chapter, however, I explain how our political system is inching into a period of crisis during which time vital aspects of our unwritten constitution will urgently need to be codified. Meanwhile, the decades-long trend towards multi-party politics is destabilising the first-past-the-post electoral system and it is no longer delivering what can be described as representative. If we are to ensure that our achievements such as the Freedom of Information and Human Rights Acts do not die deaths of a thousand cuts, we need to entrench them into a constitutional framework and rediscover our hunger for democracy. Fundamentally, it is time for us to rebuild a mass movement for reform.

I hope you find this book as interesting and provocative as we consider it to be. More than that, I hope you will be inspired to take action. Charter 88 was rooted in people power, both as a goal and as the means to that end. This philosophy has continued into Unlock Democracy today.

Peter Facey
Director, Unlock Democracy
September 2008

PART I

HISTORY

Tilting at windmills
The first years of Charter 88

Stuart Weir*

harter 88 began life fortuitously. I became editor of the *New Statesman* in 1987 intending to make democracy the magazine's outstanding editorial commitment. I felt strongly that I had to rescue the magazine from the drab hegemony of labourism (and an unhealthy degree of Labour Party influence) and create a more pluralist policy that might begin to create a proper balance between the front and back halves – that is, broadly, between political activists, most of them Labour, who read the first half (politics) and the too few people in the liberal intelligentsia who read the second half (arts and books). Couldn't we bring them together?

I gathered around me some like-minded contributors to the magazine, such as Anthony Barnett, Paul Hirst and Stephen Howe, and the new editorial stance did gradually attract attention. I remember Will Hutton being impressed by the Christmas 1987 editorial – which Anthony began and I finished – on the significance of 1988 being the twentieth anniversary of 1968 and the tercentenary of the Glorious Revolution. But the magazine's reputation was sadly diminished and I had no promotion budget to reach beyond the current readership to draw a wider public's attention to the change and to try and reverse damaging print media stereotypes. Some hope! Then in early 1988 I was discussing how best to support the dissidents in Czechoslovakia with the American academic Arthur Lipow, and he suggested that

* My thanks go to Anthony Barnett and Hilary Wainwright for their comments on the first draft of this chapter.

we issue a 'Charter 88' declaration, building on their celebrated manifesto, Charter 77. I saw the opportunity to apply the idea not to eastern Europe, but to life in Britain under Margaret Thatcher. The 1688 tercentenary was being smugly celebrated with no reflection on what progress or otherwise we had made in the following 300 years. If the magazine could draw up a democratic charter and persuade eighty-eight of the widest possible spectrum of eminent people to sign, they could secure a place in public debate that the *Statesman* alone could not achieve. We could publish the charter in the magazine and as an advertisement in the *Guardian*, at once striking a blow for democracy and civil liberties, publicising our new politics and re-establishing communion between the magazine's political and cultural halves.

The *Statesman*'s chief executive could not find the money to invest in the idea. Fortunately, the board of directors included Trevor Smith, who as chairman of the Joseph Rowntree Reform Trust was pressing forward with a democratic agenda. Trevor is the unsung hero of Charter 88 (and many other democratic initiatives): he secured us a £5,000 loan from the trust, later transmuted into the first of a succession of grants for the organisation.

I assembled a small group to draft the charter (Anthony, Hilary Wainwright, Ursula Owen, Francis Wheen, Ben Whitaker and others) in January. I asked Anthony to write a first draft. By now it was obvious to Hilary and me that Charter 88 could become a campaigning organisation in its own right. Everyone warmed to that idea and decided to keep the option open. Anthony refused to have anything to do with an organisation. He was too busy and he was able only to write a partial draft. I wrote a first paragraph that slid down to the last lines of the second paragraph. Gradually a draft emerged, written mostly by Jolyon Jenkins from the magazine, Anthony and me, that combined radicalism with the moderation I believed we needed to win over a wide range of signatories. The draft called for a new constitutional settlement, based on ten demands, the most important of which was for a written constitution.

I had now to build a small consensus around the document to determine a final draft, one that we would not amend at the request of people we asked to sign. Otherwise the process would be chaotic. If I remember correctly, I began with Richard Holme, who chaired the Constitutional Reform Centre (CRC). He was an established and moderate democratic figure. If I could secure his backing, then he would assist me in recruiting the 'great and good' members of the centre, retired civil servants and the like, who were essential ballast to give legitimacy to a venture that began in the *New Statesman*. Richard became integral to the project, co-operated from the start and was closely involved in drafting the document. He and I began a series of negotiations, one a group meeting in a private room of the Reform Club (where ties had to be worn and documents could not be openly produced), another at dinner with David Marquand at a Social and Liberal Democrats conference, several over breakfast at the Waldorf Hotel.

The main sticking point was the demand for a written constitution. While Richard was committed to the principle that we should be citizens, not subjects, he was alarmed by talk of a written constitution and advised us in his silky, rather pedagogic, way that we should drop it. (It is I think to Charter's credit that talk of a written constitution – just talk, mind – is now more or less routine. Then it was positively revolutionary.) However, by now I had asked Lord Scarman, the law lord and a member of the CRC, to vet the draft, and he was absolutely for a written constitution. That swung it. Scarman was quietly and wonderfully radical. He asked us to incorporate 'social rights' gently into the text and added a touch of iron to the last sentence, arguing that while only people themselves can ensure freedom, democracy and equality before the law, they can more effectively guard and obtain such ends once they have constitutional protections that 'belong to them by inalienable right'. I also incorporated suggestions from Marquand and Salman Rushdie.

We were supposed now to be ready to go, but the business of revising and negotiating over the text went down to the wire. In October I asked John Hoyland, who had formerly worked with Hilary Wainwright in the Popular Planning Unit at the Greater London Council, to join us in the *Statesman*'s office in Perseverance Works, Shoreditch, to organise the four months of labour at the end of which Charter 88 was to be born. For by now we knew we were on the brink of creating a new movement for democratic change. John was soon plunged into the sometimes angry and very precise debates over the wording of the document itself. His diary records one such debate, probably on Tuesday 25 October 1988:

> *Tuesday.* I got shouted at on the phone by both Anthony Barnett (in America) and Richard Holme. I was the intermediary in an argument they were having about Scotland in the Charter. Anthony wanted 'In Scotland, democracy has become a travesty' while Richard Holme wanted 'In Scotland, government from Westminster seems more imported than representative'. They both refused to talk to each other about it, but shouted at me instead ... Stuart, the next day, managed to negotiate a compromise: 'Scotland is governed from Whitehall like a province'.

John's first task was to assist us in recruiting eighty-eight people from all walks of life to sign the charter and make a donation. We would then publish the charter in the *Statesman* and the *Guardian* advertisement, with a coupon inviting people to 'Add Your Name to Ours' and to make a donation. I assumed that we would need to ask 150 people or so to be sure of obtaining 88 signatures. John brought with him a contact book full of the names of people who had supported the fund-raising campaign run from the GLC Popular Planning Unit with Women against Pit Closures, raising over £500,000 for the devastated mining communities. It was this campaign that inspired our celebrity-led approach.

Those weeks were exhilarating. A glittering array of people signed at once and made donations. A cheque from Harold Pinter arrived with his signature the next day. Simon Rattle faxed his response from the United States. Billy Bragg called from a telephone box in Scotland. Emma Thompson rang me to reassure herself that she was dealing with rational people, signed and said she would ask Kenneth Branagh to sign as well (he didn't). It was obvious now that we had caught the mood of the time and that we would receive far more than eighty-eight signatures. So we went all out to recruit as wide and diverse a group of signatories as we could. It was remarkable how many people we asked John

to approach actually signed up, or meant to. The theatrical agent
Jan Evans circulated our request for signatories to all her clients;
Ray McNally, who was something of a hero after playing a
Labour Prime Minister, Harry Perkins, on television in *A Very
British Coup*, signed as a result. I think she took him for lunch. By
our deadline in November a diverse and celebrated cast of 348
people had signed up (only well-known Conservatives were
missing, though many Conservatives did sign later); quite a few
famous people who agreed to sign, like the novelist Angela Carter,
missed the first cut.

Very few people we approached refused to sign the charter.
The most obvious group who did refuse were prominent Labour
Party loyalists, such as John Mortimer, Ben Pimlott, who was
publishing his own reformist magazine, *Samizdat*, John Lloyd, my
predecessor as editor of the *New Statesman*, and Baroness
Blackstone (who said no rather apologetically). The intellectual
left split: Edward Thompson (to my regret), Tariq Ali and Eric
Hobsbawm were refuseniks, while Ralph Miliband, Robin
Blackburn and the socialist feminists Sheila Rowbotham and
Lynne Segal signed. Many left-wing lawyers, like the *Statesman*'s
voluntary libel lawyer, Andrew Nicol, also refused to sign. They
were hostile to the idea of a Bill of Rights, because it would
empower unelected judges at the expense of an elected Parliament
(through which the government was endlessly shunting through
policies restricting liberties). The playwright Edward Bond spent
nearly an hour on the telephone to me, trying to persuade me to
drop the demand for a Bill of Rights so that he could sign up.

I asked Keith Ablitt to design the charter and the advertisement,
which he did beautifully. He created a striking Charter typeface of
people in silhouette, carrying letters and numbers on placards; it is
used for the initial letter of each chapter in this book. (One of
them is a silhouette of the Queen; good to have her on board.) In
contrast, the actual charter, which we presented as a petition to
Parliament, was inelegant and very fragile. To encourage people
not to petition, Parliament insisted on absurdly restrictive rules.
The charter had to be hand written on a single sheet of paper. Can
this possibly be right, I ask myself now. Anyway, that is what we
did. As it happens, the charter document fell apart while we were

sitting in a local caff across the road from Big Ben, waiting to give it to the MPs Robin Cook and Archy Kirkwood for presentation to the Speaker. We had to stick it together with Sellotape, prompting a mocking article in the *Independent* the next day by a journalist who had been sitting nearby.

It was the only press coverage that we got that day. We had around eight people at the table for the press conference in the House of Commons. Cook took the chair; Salman Rushdie was with us, as were I think Ian McEwan, Ursula Owen and Sarah Spencer. Rick MacArthur, the publisher of *Harper's Bazaar*, flew over from New York and joined us to protest about the ban in Britain of the latest edition of the US magazine that had run up against our primitive libel laws. We outnumbered the listless journalists who actually turned up, none of whom wrote anything that I saw. It was as though we were tilting at windmills. The news desks were simply unable to appreciate a new phenomenon. The publication of the charter itself, with articles by David Puttnam, Sarah Benton and Ed Pearce among others in the *Statesman*, and as a handsome full-page advertisement in the *Guardian* (at a discounted rate), soon changed that.

The columnists took over. I do not have the cuttings, but my recollection is that the likes of Peter Kellner, Peter Jenkins, Martin Linton and Bruce Anderson saw the charter in conventional two-party terms. They wrote of us as part of a co-ordinated nexus of Labour reformers rather than as the independent-minded and various group of people we were. They were, I think it fair to say, as unconscious of the strength of the new phenomenon as were the newspapers' news desks, and on the whole they were hostile. Kellner was especially cross about the charter's advocacy of proportional elections for Westminster, and accused us of being hidden anti-monarchists. Still, he also observed that any gathering that brought together Bruce Kent, Rabbi Julia Neuberger, Michael Meadowcroft, Andrew Phillips, Sir Sigmund Steinberg and Benton must have something going for it. They had all been guests at Kellner's recent wedding.

Ferdinand Mount, writing in the following week's *New Statesman* (9 December 1988), professed himself as being 'panic-stricken' by one omission from the list of signatories: why wasn't

Mortimer, 'the Fat Owl of the Remove, blinking amiably down upon the proceedings'? Mount was a great deal more perceptive than the pack. He saw the charter as a 'standard manifesto of the liberal left', but stated firstly, that its aspirations differed markedly from the kind that a similar cast would have subscribed to at any time during the past thirty years; and secondly, that the names less often to be found on such lists, such as Lord Scarman, 'only emphasise the sea-change'. Mount correctly identified the difference between the charter, with its demands for a Bill of Rights, written constitution and 'settled and equitable distribution of power between local, regional and national government', and the Labour Party's traditional goal of a powerful unrestrained Labour government representing 'the General Will of the march'. He scorned the demand for electoral reform, as did many of those with affiliation to either the Conservatives or Labour, for whom first-past-the-post elections to Westminster kept a permanent place in or near government.

The distance between the charter's aspirations and the Labour Party's position was soon to be made evident by the reactions of both Neil Kinnock, who described us as 'whiners, wankers and whingers', and Roy Hattersley, his deputy, who denounced the charter as 'a charter of despair'. (On the other wing of the party, Tony Benn had declined to sign, though quietly.) Hattersley's response is illuminating. 'Hope' for him lay with a Labour government able to use a parliamentary majority won on a minority of the vote as a battering ram for change. The idea that the party's agenda had to be argued for and won within a pluralist political environment and that government might be restrained by rules was anathema. As it happens, Kinnock eventually signed the charter, some time after his wife Glenys.

But we were accused across the political spectrum, and not just by those in the Labour Party, of making a fuss when not much was really wrong. The self-interested complacency of the political class amazed me then, and twenty years later, it does still. Of course, part of the incomprehension derived from the centuries-old tradition of 'strong' government, reinforced by the experience of imperial rule. As we have seen, this tradition continues to this day and should not be mistaken for 'effective' government. Indeed, it

makes policy disasters possible, from fiascos such as the poll tax
and rail privatisation to the brutal decision to invade and occupy
Iraq. But there is another element, too – the belief that the two
main parties and their interests take precedence over any
interference with the political process. As I write, David Davis has
renounced his seat and post as shadow Home Secretary to fight
and win a by-election in his constituency over the June 2008
House of Commons vote for up to forty-two days' detention
without charge for people suspected of terrorist offences. He has
attracted vicious opprobrium from politicians in both major
parties and very many figures in the political class. It seems to be
inconceivable that a leading politician might put the hard-won
principle that individuals in custody should be informed of the
charge against them above party calculation.

The accusation against us was sharpened by the title we had
chosen. We were accused of taking advantage of the dissidents
who had published Charter 77 in Czechoslovakia, where
freedoms were seriously denied. We had of course not only
foreseen this line of argument, but declared in the charter itself our
solidarity with them and others campaigning for freedom in
eastern Europe. We had out of courtesy asked Václav Havel and
our friends among the Czech dissidents if they objected to the
echo of their Charter 77 in our title; and Jan Kavan, who was in
exile in Britain, was one of our signatories. They were, of course,
pleased. They said our campaign would only strengthen the case
for democracy and freedom there and around the world. Havel
came later to England and said much the same thing once again.

By then the reaction of the political class, which is made up not
only of party politicians but also of the London-oriented media
commentariat, was irrelevant. Their reaction was drowned by the
reaction of the public. We had asked people to 'add their names
to ours'. And they did, in their thousands. We had struck oil. We
took successive advertisements in the *Guardian*, the *Independent*
and the *Observer* (after Anthony Barnett and I personally
persuaded editor Donald Trelford, himself a signatory, to give us
a cut-price double spread on which we could list the names of all
signatories thus far). John Hoyland now had to deal with the
thousands of names and donations that poured in, making sure

that each new signatory was named in one of the advertisements. After January 1989, John went on to organise the public defence of Salman Rushdie after the *fatwa* was pronounced on him. We at the *Statesman* had begun a vigorous campaign in Britain to get the political and literary establishments to rouse themselves and act on his behalf, with articles and a delegation to 10 Downing Street of Harold Pinter, Hanif Kureishi, Liz Calder, Salman's publisher, Anthony and me.

Meanwhile we were now a campaign with no organisation and no home (apart from a spare space at the *Statesman*). The first task was to appoint a director. Several people assumed that I would take this on, but I had had my fill of pressure group life previously at the Child Poverty Action Group and Shelter. Besides which I had a magazine to edit. I felt that Anthony had the right mixture of principled understanding and political nerve to take the adventure further. There was some alarm at the idea of handing Charter 88 on to him, but I was unmoved and he became, initially at least, 'co-ordinator' rather than director, and Richard Holme and I became joint chairmen. We took advice on how we should organise and agreed that we would not become a membership organisation. We believed that such a body would soon be reduced to an active core with a neglected membership and might then be vulnerable to the kind of infighting that had disabled other political bodies. We took Greenpeace as a model: we would keep in regular touch with, inform and consult the signatories and 'make waves' on their behalf, and they would keep the organisation going through donations.

Anthony and I recruited a varied group of signatories to form an executive committee: Paul Hirst, Richard Wainwright, Marina Warner, David Marquand... It was a joy to attend the meetings. Anthony also formed a wider council of invited members, to whom he added a jury of twelve signatories, chosen by lot from all those who had signed the charter, to represent the signatory body; and he also developed the marketing strategy that was the vital element behind Charter's success. The initial advertisements, and then more targeted ones highlighting issues of the day, enabled Charter to build a strong and continuing financial and signatory base while still campaigning. There were also intense negotiations with the Joseph Rowntree Reform Trust over longer-term funding, which Anthony resolved by asking trustees to provide 'matching funding' of up to £100,000 for every pound that the signatories raised. They gave us the £100,000 in a matter of weeks. Charter 88 was well on the way to achieving both a signatory base of more than 80,000 and, for more than a decade, a level of political influence unprecedented for a body outside the political class.

Why did Charter 88 take off as it did? Conventional wisdom was that it simply filled a political vacuum. A triumphalist Margaret Thatcher was at her zenith. She had just driven the poll tax, like Boadicea's chariot, through a Parliament where her own party had severe misgivings about its effects. The Labour Party was weak and unconvincing and not good at opposing; Tory ministers had been relieved at its ineffective opposition to the poll tax in the House of Commons. The Liberal Party and the Social Democrats were stumbling towards union. Charter 88 was therefore a rallying point for opposition. There is truth in this analysis, but it is only half the truth.

The conventional analysis projected only a Westminster view: the short-sighted conventional mantra 'if it ain't broke, don't fix it'. Well, it certainly wasn't 'broke'! Thatcher's runaway progress showed how well the still-entrenched ideal of 'strong government' could be made to work. But it badly needed fixing nevertheless, as people outside the Whitehall village were able to see more clearly than the insiders. The truth missing from the conventional analysis is that a significant number of people were increasingly intolerant of the weaknesses in governing structures that Thatcher had exploited to brush aside the conventions of good government. She ignored the understandings and customary self-restraint of previous governments to create an overweening central state, to put civil liberties at risk and to erode the autonomy of independent sources of power within civil and civic society. The shabby deceptions of the *Belgrano* sinking, Westland and Zircon were in people's minds. There was a general, but diffuse, feeling of dissatisfaction with the way Britain was governed and a profound unease about what was being lost under Thatcher's permanent revolution. It seemed as though the state bore down directly on people; and there was a residual and widely held sympathy for mining families and their beaten communities after the miners' strike was broken.

Particular campaigns had also begun to identify the need for reforms in a variety of forms and different settings. The Campaign for Freedom of Information (CFOI), established earlier in the 1980s by Des Wilson and Maurice Frankel, became the most conspicuous of these campaigns, with private members' Bills in Parliament, skilful media-friendly argument and meticulous analysis. The cause of electoral reform had moved beyond the confines of the long-established Electoral Reform Society and the Liberal Party and was taking root in the Labour Party and among Social Democrats. The new left had taken up the cause of both electoral reform and a Bill of Rights. A Labour Rights Group had been campaigning through the policy-making processes of the Labour Party to make the demand for a Bill of Rights party policy. Richard Holme's Centre for Constitutional Reform worked at an elite level to combine such proposals with reform at Westminster. In Scotland, enraged by the early introduction of the poll tax, demands for devolution were becoming irresistible. On civil liberties, there was, it is true, a vacuum to be filled, for the National Council for Civil Liberties (now known as Liberty) was then bitterly divided over the idea of a Bill of Rights.

What Charter 88 did above all was firstly to give voice to a general sense that government was out of control – in a crude sense, it embodied a general desire to keep Maggie in order. But it did so in a declaration that argued from both principle and a history of hard-fought freedom that there were systemic and long-term problems that should and could be solved. The charter showed that the apparently unrestrained powers at the disposal of the executive were linked to the reduction of the liberties of ordinary people; and that the protection of those liberties depended on reforms that would curtail those powers through a written constitution, a Bill of Rights and proportional elections to Parliament. Thatcher's impatient rejection of constitutional convention was a symptom of a long-term illness. The charter also provided an overarching argument combining and giving coherence to the individual reform campaigns and an organisation that was capable of following the argument through.

Anthony Barnett's account of his time as director is included in this collection. Here I will merely say that he realised the potential of Charter 88 through high-profile campaigning with an acute grasp of the constitutional issues at stake. He organised vigils, demonstrations and major conferences, including the Manchester Constitutional Convention and another on the monarchy; he published advertisements, press releases and pamphlets on issues of the day; and he highlighted individual injustices. At the 1992 election, Charter members around the country held some 100 Democracy Day meetings involving parliamentary candidates from all parties. Anthony made significant progress within the higher ranks of the Labour Party, establishing the Sovereignty Lectures, which were given by Gordon Brown, Lord Scarman, Ferdinand Mount, Shirley Williams and John Smith (at his own request) when he became Labour Party leader. Brown's lecture is reprinted in this collection. Charter framed democracy as a major issue for Labour and the Liberal Democrats.

Smith had a commitment at least to some of the reforms we were advocating, but unfortunately, and for more reasons than simply the quality of our democracy, he died of a heart attack in 1994. He was replaced by a leader with agendas of his own and no interest in democratic reform nor even in social justice. Reformers within his Cabinet, the Cook–Maclennan constitutional agreement (made before the 1997 election and for him a fail-safe device) and the power of the demand for devolution all obliged Tony Blair to take on a large programme of democratic reforms. But he did so under the rubric of 'modernisation', which leached out the principles of accountable, devolved and rule-based government on which Charter 88 had campaigned for nearly ten years. Blair, just as much as the old Labour politicians he so despised, was determined to retain all the flexible and unaccountable powers that a Prime Minister inherits along with large and unrepresentative parliamentary majorities. The programme of reforms was thus fatally flawed. Another ten years later, his successor has set out an apparently strong set of 'governance' proposals to rebalance power between central government, Parliament and local councils. But they are equally flawed due to a similar determination to preserve executive power in his hands.

Every organisation that seeks to achieve change, or to hold it back for that matter, has to make choices between broad-brush campaigning in public and detailed lobbying on key policy issues. Naturally most organisations try to achieve a balance between the two. At its inception, Charter 88 had no choice. There was no way in which politicians in the major parties would sit down to thrash out the details of policies that would deny them unearned majority power at Westminster, restrain them in their use of that power and oblige them to share that power with institutions and people outside. It was only funk that led Blair and Peter Mandelson to sanction the talks on reform that led to the Cook–Maclennan agreement. Charter had to build up intellectual and public support for change across the board in its drive to oblige Labour politicians in power to accommodate its demands. Its momentum as well as its ethic also depended on engaging the public, not least to maintain its fund-raising. Yet Charter 88 was often criticised for not consolidating Anthony Barnett's considerable successes in public debate with the kind of policy prescriptions that they and officials could translate into action when they came into office.

This seems to me to be a very simplistic view. Firstly, others were already in a position from which they could enter into the detail of policy. The Scottish Constitutional Convention had a worked-out policy with considerable political backing from the Scottish Labour Party and the Scottish trade unions. The CFOI had draft legislation in hand from a series of private member's Bills; and after 1997 James Cornford was in place to brief David Clark, the Cabinet minister who was charged with introducing the government's Freedom of Information Bill. Francesca Klug, who had developed the case for a Bill of Rights while at Liberty and had been active in the Labour Rights Group, became a key adviser to ministers, ultimately coming up with the means by which the Human Rights Act reconciled parliamentary sovereignty with judicial rulings on human rights.

Secondly, lobbying invariably takes place on the government's terms. The British government is in a very powerful position with regard to reform proposals that it doesn't like. The majoritarian constitution, which embeds the Prime Minister's party in near-absolute power, is (as the late Richard Crossman once wrote) like a 'rock' against which the waves of popular emotion or opinion generally break, allowing the government time to wait for the tide to go out. Which is just what Blair, with his gift of manipulative ambiguity, did on several significant reforms. He took the heat out of pressures for electoral reform by establishing the Jenkins commission, but then sat on its recommendations and delayed and delayed again the referendum he had promised. And, as Clark's fall from grace over his radical White Paper proposals on freedom of information showed, even the best-informed lobbying does not necessarily secure its goals. Jack Straw took over and slowly and deliberately produced a highly restrictive Act. And when Charter 88 did change course and gave more emphasis to lobbying, the campaign lost its momentum and did not make any significant gains.

In my view, Charter made a fundamental mistake in accepting the government's modernisation label. It above all others ought not to have derogated from the essential principles and traditions of democracy on which its success was founded. The right course would have been to detail the deliberate weaknesses in the government's reforms through forensic analysis, and to expose both in public and in Parliament the essential purpose of these weaknesses — that is, to preserve the overweening powers against which Charter 88's thousands of signatories had protested. I cannot say that this strategy would have succeeded. The Blair government was riding its own popular wave; it had the protection of a large parliamentary majority; and it would have been very difficult to penetrate the rhetoric of substantial reform and expose the self-interested realities of the detail. There is also the issue of the ambiguity at the heart of the Charter campaign itself. I have no doubt that it was right to choose the signatory structure over a membership organisation. But the essence of this arrangement was that a very few people would make the waves on behalf of the vast majority of supporters without necessarily mobilising their energies. The Democracy Day events at election time were the only occasions on which signatories were mobilised in numbers. Nevertheless, the reform programme that the Blair government undertook has a dynamism that cannot easily be checked. The Human Rights Act has not so far proved able fully to protect essential liberties against recent counter-terrorism laws, but the potential is there; and it is certainly the case that, thanks to the Act, the dignity and rights of people who receive public services are far better protected. The Freedom of Information Act is opening up government in manifold and unexpected ways, as people learn to make use of it. Devolution to Scotland and Wales is producing regimes and practices that offer progressive alternatives to the ways of Westminster; and there are demands for further devolution. The unacceptably obsolete nature of first-past-the-post elections to Westminster is starkly revealed by the elections for the Scottish Parliament and the National Assembly of Wales (though these are not fully proportional), for the European Parliament (using the party list system), and for local authorities in Scotland (using the single transferable vote). We may even get a second chamber wholly or largely elected by a proportional system, though not soon. The inertia and self-interest of the political class, however, remains a substantial obstacle to reform. Yet the strength of dissatisfaction with the essentially unreformed state is evident in the high proportion of the initial signatories who continue, twenty or so years later, to support Charter in its new manifestation as Unlock Democracy. The new Charter 88 is a well-led, well-organised and well-informed membership organisation. I trust that its staff and board will stick to the overarching view of democracy that holds together the various single-issue campaigns that form different parts of the overall fabric; and never lose sight of the truth that 'only people themselves can ensure democracy, freedom and equality before the law'.

The rise and fate of
Charter 88

Anthony Barnett

'Ah yes, Charter 88, a seminal moment.'
The words were those of Charles Kennedy. I was nearly twice his age, yet he spoke to me as if he was reminiscing to a youngster about the distant past.
It was September 1999. Kennedy had just become leader of the Liberal Democrats as the successor to Paddy Ashdown. We were meeting privately in a room in the House of Commons thanks to Richard Wainwright. Wainwright had been a Liberal spokesman on economic affairs (characteristically he had refused a peerage when he retired as an MP). Lively, generous hearted, with sharp judgement and formidable experience – outside politics he was a successful accountant – he remained a respected figure in his party. He had been an important and generous member of Charter 88's original executive, saving it at a critical moment in its early growth. I suspect that he had helped fund research for his new party leader.

Wainwright had arranged the meeting for a purpose. My mission was to enquire whether, as a fresh force in British politics, Kennedy would like to gather around him an informal group of interested, reform-minded thinkers and writers – public intellectuals if you will. Some would be Liberal Democrats, some Labour supporters, some independents like myself. The aim would be to carry forward the loose progressive alliance that Charter 88 had stimulated, with Kennedy – young, bright and charismatic – providing the pole of attraction. Labour had pushed through its extraordinary first wave of reforms. But Tony Blair was clearly pulling back from orchestrating a full-throated democratisation of the British state by allowing the reforms to release public energy. New thinking and a new approach were needed.

As you can sense, these were still positive and confident times. In 1999 the recently created devolved institutions in Scotland, Wales and London were uncertain but possibly exciting experiments. Lords reform, with its potential for providing a unifying institution, lay ahead. The voting system was tagged for consideration. It remained a moment – probably the last moment – when UK-wide reform could still be discussed in good faith from the centre alone. As his memoirs recount, Ashdown, advised by Richard Holme, had attempted to shape this by seeking to influence Blair and Gordon Brown and fell victim to their good-cop, bad-cop routine. Ashdown saw that there was no constitutional rewriting on the wall for him, and withdrew from our parochial affairs. Blair had embraced 'corporate populism' rather than democratic renewal.* There was an opportunity for the Liberal Democrats under their new leader to take the intellectual and cultural high ground vacated by Downing Street and its derisory 'third way' (that being somewhere between the second coming and the fourth dimension, as Francis Wheen once memorably observed). There was a chance to shape the political agenda. However, the Liberal Democrats could not do this on their own within the confines of party politics and a media spun by Alastair Campbell. On the other hand, if they could spark back into the life the boldness and openness of Charter 88, in which they had been key players, but this time with Labour in government...

Kennedy did not for a second seek to explore the suggestion or probe how it might work. I was given a friendly smile and handshake after an audience long enough not to appear rude. I wouldn't say he tried to hammer a nail into Charter 88's coffin; exertion was to be avoided and anyway it would have been a form of engagement. Rather he waved it goodbye. No curiosity as to the reasons for its impact was demonstrated. No possibility of lessons that might be of relevance was entertained. Thank you, but if he had anything to do with it, there would be no further seminal moments.

* Anthony Barnett, 'Corporate Control', *Prospect*, February 1999.

Instead, he kindly explained that he had had excellent talks with Roy Jenkins. The aroma of lubrication hovered over his smile as he passed on the privilege gained by such guidance. Jenkins had advised him against any precipitous action, or indeed, Kennedy implied, any bold action at all. He should wait for events to happen, not risk unnecessary measures that might prove damaging. If this was indeed Jenkins's advice, it proved insightful in time. The Iraq War happened and put the Liberal Democrats in a hugely strong position. At the 2005 general election, with the Tories onto their third leader (and Michael Howard at that!), a strong, well-founded Liberal Democrat strategy could even have pushed the Conservatives into third place. But you need to prepare in depth if you are ever to take a commanding role when the opportunity comes. I suspect Jenkins had an altogether tougher understanding of his seemingly bland approach than Kennedy, and was counselling caution, not passivity. But Kennedy's interpretation was that he had been the beneficiary of the best possible strategy, to sip and wait.

The rise of Charter 88

Looking back it seems to me that this small, unpublicised episode provides a neat point for assessing the influence and frustration of Charter 88. Why was it seminal? What was the nature of its impact? Can this be exercised again by its successor organisation, Unlock Democracy, or any other alliance? Why, despite its influence, was it unable to take things forward on its own terms?

It is perhaps especially useful to ask these questions through the optic of the Liberal Democrats. They were always at least as important as Labour in Charter 88. But because it was Labour that needed persuading; because, arguably, it was indeed persuaded when John Smith was at the helm and gave his Charter 88 lecture that committed the party to a Bill of Rights and a new settlement; because the spirit of democratic constitutional reform was then doused by Tony Blair, Gordon Brown and Peter Mandelson as they seized power, most of the story focuses on Labour. This permits the Liberal Democrats to get away with it, so to speak.

When challenged they swirled their cloak to show they agreed completely, and remained untouched as the bull rushed past, unable to take them with it.

Some Liberal Democrats worked mightily to make the Charter a success, most notably Trevor Smith in his position as chair of the Joseph Rowntree Reform Trust and a close, practical adviser. Perhaps Lord Scarman, with whom I always sounded out in advance anything I thought might prove controversial, should also be regarded as an honorary Liberal, and like Smith he had mettle. (It was not generally known that, as well as being a retired law lord, Leslie Scarman had been a young staff officer planning and implementing Operation Overlord, the Allied invasion of Normandy, and was present at the German surrender in Berlin.) Our collaboration began when I invited him to London to launch Charter's ten-year strategy at the start of 1990. He declined. Then he rang the office to tell me he had now read the document carefully and had changed his mind, saying simply by way of explanation: 'This is very ambitious.'

Even for Scarman almost no press turned up and, more seriously, there was little media recognition of the problem we were trying to address. But I am jumping ahead.

To say that Charter 88 was an accident would be most unfair to the tremendous effort and resources Stuart Weir invested in it from the *New Statesman* and the work of John Hoyland. But Charter 88 as an organisation was not to my knowledge intended or planned. Stuart's initial ambition was to make a mark for the magazine. It grew as the quality of the names willing to sign the statement widened its potential appeal. Later he told me he felt a sense that it would be something big. He made one of what were a number of master-strokes by commissioning Keith Ablitt to design the charter, and Keith created its trademark 'folk alphabet'. Perhaps the fact that a new typeface had been designed should have signalled to me that something unusual was stirring. But this was 1988, the zenith of Thatcherism and the Lawson boom, and a nadir for the left and for liberals, among whom there was a pervasive sense of hopelessness. (Personally, I had decided to emigrate if my companion was offered a position in the United States, as indeed she then was.)

I recall a weird atmosphere at the final pre-launch meeting in the Reform Club in November 1988, where we were guests of Richard Holme. It was explained to me that it was forbidden to bring out a piece of paper or be seen to do any 'work' until safely in the small room reserved for this purpose. Richard had had the idea of adding a coupon to the charter requesting money. We discussed whether its wording should include 'Add your name to ours'. I thought we could hardly appeal for democratic support without giving people the chance to sign. 'What if they do?' Richard wondered with a worry. But no-one suggested they would. It was, I felt, in a sombre mood that Charter 88 was waved down the slipway.

There would have been no 'seminal' impact without the document, of course, its design and its initial well-known signatories. But what we think of as Charter 88 today was primarily created by a hunger and a demand for it. Five thousand added their names 'to ours' between the first full-page ads appearing in the *New Statesman* and the *Guardian* at the end of November 1988, followed by the *Independent* on 10 December, and the New Year. Many sent money. I can see them now, strangely shaped grey Post Office sacks full of envelopes.

People embraced the charter for a variety of reasons but the most important for me was the way it brought separately needed reforms into a connected programme for a new constitutional settlement. This may be familiar to us now. Then, it appeared like a bolt from the blue. It was Liberal Democrat policy but they never highlighted it. Up and down the land, *Independent* and *Guardian* readers opened their papers and said, often out loud, some combination of 'Of course!' and 'At last!' and reached for their pens.

Charter 88 based its case for change in history and included a menu of demands, many tendentious and in need of unpacking. But two things were at the heart of its appeal. First, its simplicity, captured by Ian McEwan, who asked: 'If we in Britain are the proud possessors of fundamental freedoms, what can be the possible objection to writing them down?' Second, its opposition to Thatcherism. The Prime Minister had proclaimed the quality of her conviction in contrast to the rottenness of consensus politics. But a society needs to share a consensus on how it should be governed. Charter 88 proposed this: it was clean, principled and also full of conviction but with a tone that was generous, inclusive, pluralist, tolerant and, if I may say so, intelligent.

Thatcher famously protested, if half in jest, that she was not against consensus, provided everyone agreed with her! Now there was an alternative. Not in terms of socio-economic policy or party policy but in the sense of an alternative way of being governed, hence a different sense of direction for the country.

It does not matter how small the flame; if there are more than embers, if fuel can be provided, then a good blaze can be brought to life. I tended the fire and did my best to shovel in fuel, but the flame had a life of its own. This was its attraction, for me. In the past, I had been associated with a number of what I thought were worthy causes. They had all failed to make an impact, usually because of well-meaning inefficiency laced with self-indulgent sectarianism. I am putting it briefly and politely. Now here was something that was genuinely wanted. Never underestimate the motivating force of shame, or rather the fear of shame. I could not bear the humiliating prospect of people saying 'What a missed opportunity'.

Stuart had booked a 1½-page advert in the *Observer* where the plan was to publish those who had added their names. This too was a bold stroke. But he had a weekly magazine to edit and it was proving a struggle to pull it off. Having sworn I'd not have anything to do with the organisation I offered to do the *Observer* ad. Guy Boanas entered the names on an early computer database. Josephine King worked as a volunteer with business experience. Jane Powell, who would later join and organise Democracy Day, told me: 'You don't realise how exceptional this is' – pointing to the sacks of envelopes that were filling a cave-like corner of the *Statesman*'s office.

We delayed the *Observer* ad by a week, enlarged the space to a two-page spread and the editor agreed to run an article by Lord Scarman in its support. I was very conscious of the cruelty of the British system and the way that the impetus of the great Chartist petition of 1848 had been smashed by scorn and ridicule when, despite vast numbers signing it, some names were shown to be duplicates, or people who had signed as Mr Punch. It wasn't fair, but there you are. To make a public display of named support we had to be accurate as well as fast. Get the names right and we might still be ignored; get them wrong and we'd be destroyed.

On Sunday 22 January 1989, not only did we publish all the thousands of names accurately in alphabetical order (with Eric and Phyllis Cleaver coming between Angela Carter and John Cleese) but also as important, and unseen to the public, we wrote to them all by first-class post on the Thursday telling them that their names would appear in Sunday's *Observer*, asking those who had given money to continue their support and those who had not donated to do so. Not only had they signed, we had also added their names to a vast public advert across two pages of a major newspaper *and* we had written to thank and inform them in advance. Nearly 5,000 more people added their names in response to the *Observer* appeal, while many of the first wave were bonded to become committed supporters.

We had proposed a democratic constitution for Britain. Now the proposal was backed by lots of people and it could become a focus of influence.

Perhaps I should add here that it was only just in time. One of those who helped with the final drafting was Salman Rushdie, and he joined the delegation Stuart led to present the charter to Robin Cook in the House of Commons. *The Satanic Verses* had just been published with its gripping argument about migration personified in its two heroes (the book's core theme being the struggle between those who say one is true to oneself by moving and leaving, and those who hold that one is true to oneself by staying and remaining). In January, the book was burned in Bradford due to its meditations on the historic Muhammad. Stuart asked me to write a *Statesman* editorial warning that this was a serious outrage. On 14 February 1989 the fatwa sent a shock wave through British public life, political and cultural. I drafted a statement that Harold Pinter read out to the media before handing it in to No. 10. It seemed to me that standing firm for Rushdie's free speech and human rights was a natural extension of the values expressed by Charter 88. But

Britain's liberal public was alarmed. Progressive sentiments suddenly had consequences; simplicity was not quite so simple after all. Throughout this period, the *New Statesman* had been carrying weekly adverts for the charter. I'm sorry to say that after the fatwa new signature support diminished almost overnight. Within ten weeks of the birth of public debate over whether post-war Britain should have a democratic written constitution, the fight against fear and phobia and the contest with terrorism and fundamentalism became intertwined with the reshaping of the UK, and have remained so.

Nonetheless we had the basis for an organisation and a campaign. We created a council and executive and applied to the Joseph Rowntree Reform Trust for matching funding to launch a ten-year strategy, 'Prospects and Plans for the Nineties', which set out a 'two-winged' approach: 'The Charter's strategy is to combine a popular, non-party citizens' movement outside traditional politics with an influential, all-party lobby within the old doors.'* As the song goes, 'It ain't what you do, it's the *way* that you do it'. Over the next five years until Tony Blair's takeover of the leadership of the Labour Party, you can see Charter 88 as:

- **A marketing campaign** run by Paul Farthing and guided by Tim Miller and George Smith. Between 1988 and 1993 we put forty advertisements in the *Guardian*, most of which were full page, also six in the *Independent*, eight in the *Observer*, and others in the *Independent on Sunday* and the *Sunday Times*, almost all of which paid for themselves off the page and drove membership towards 50,000, reinforced by a brilliant direct mail operation.
- **A press campaign** run by Pam Giddy, who also edited *Violations of Rights* (which linked both marketing and ideas) and forced Charter 88 into the print media despite the gritted teeth of philistine sub-editors.
- **A league of dedicated supporters**, with local groups and monthly vigils held on the steps of St Martin-in-the-Fields in Trafalgar Square to provide photo opportunities and a visual means of linking to special campaigns.

* *We Can Make It Happen in the Next Ten Years*, January 1990.

- **A battle of ideas**, which started with 'Make a Date with Democracy' on 14 July 1990, expanded to the Manchester Constitutional Convention in November 1991, co-ordinated by Caroline Ellis and attracting more than a thousand people, continued with the Sovereignty Lectures, notably launched by Gordon Brown in 1992, and culminated in the Monarchy Conference at the Queen Elizabeth II Conference Centre and the resulting book *Power and the Throne*.
- **A campaign to convince Labour**, which involved hand-to-hand lobbying, provocation and persuasion but also offered to its modernisers a sense of energy and a forward-looking perspective as well as a framework for a 'progressive alliance' with the Liberal Democrats.
- **An opportunity to legitimise the national question**, more for Wales than Scotland, with the latter being a source of energy and inspiration.
- **An expression of the European spirit**, from Beverly Anderson, the first chair of the council, presenting the charter to Václav Havel, to Giddy and me questioning Thatcher as to why she backed a 'Magna Carta of rights' for Europe but wouldn't permit one in Britain, at a rare press conference in Paris a week before she was toppled.

The high point of Charter 88's direct impact was Democracy Day. Held on 2 April 1992, a week before the general election, it had been conceived eight months before to take place on the Thursday prior to the election. A hundred meetings took place across the UK with thousands attending. Nothing like it had been done before. To get round the legal restrictions on influencing voters they were designed to educate candidates on the opinions of citizens! Marketing, campaigning, press coverage, lobbying the parties and local group organisation came together. Neil Kinnock scheduled the possibility of proportional representation into his party's campaign that morning while Paddy Ashdown opened his press briefing with 'Welcome to Democracy Day'. We had set ourselves the objective of forcing party politics to address the constitution as an election issue. And we succeeded.

Er, hem, they made a hash of it. Roy Hattersley even blamed

Charter 88 for losing Labour the election, which was a bit desperate. But I think it is fair to say that we made constitutional reform – if, alas, not a new constitutional settlement – an issue of election politics, which it has remained ever since. This created the possibility for voters to decide *how* they are governed as well as by whom.

The fate of Charter 88

Many have tried to shake the bars. At the launch of Charter 88 as thousands started to sign, we were told that issues of principle about how we govern ourselves were not a matter of concern to the ordinary man and woman and that the 'punters' (itself a dreadful and demeaning term) would never be interested. A well-known left-of-centre columnist who is now a distinguished expert on British government and public opinion, went out of his way to come up to me and say: '*C'est magnifique, mais ce n'est pas la politique.*' The French made it all the more of a historic put-down. Its origins lie in a famous remark made by a witness to the charge of the Light Brigade in 1854, when it launched a disastrous frontal attack on the Russian cannon in the Crimean War. Tennyson memorialised the moment:

Into the valley of Death
Rode the six hundred.
Cannon to right of them,
Cannon to left of them,
Cannon in front of them
Volley'd and thunder'd;
Storm'd at with shot and shell,
Boldly they rode and well,
Into the jaws of Death . . .

You get the point. It is heroic, even magnificent to storm the great cannon of British establishment with banners calling for a Bill of Rights, freedom of information, accountable government and a written constitution, but... futile. For centuries the bodies of radical martyrs were strewn among the cannonball and shot, as they died gasping for breath, crying out 'Electoral reform!', 'Save our liberty!' or 'Power to local government!'. Few recall their names, none their successes, apart from the suffragettes. 'You do democracy if you want to,' was the message. 'We know better, and we have the cannon.'

This is still the establishment view and even language. This year the *Spectator*'s political editor, Fraser Nelson, blasted David Davis after he walked out of the Commons and forced a by-election on the 'slow strangulation of our freedom'.* Nelson perfectly reproduced the revulsion of Westminster at Davis's action, then he concluded:

> There is something undeniably inspiring about Mr Davis forsaking his career to protest against the increasing power of the state. For the millions who despise the Westminster system, it is an encouraging gesture and it will help the Tories that the maverick in question is wearing a blue rosette ... but [this is] a one-man Charge of the Light Brigade. Westminster's reaction is the same as General Bosquet's at Balaclava: *C'est magnifique, mais ce n'est pas la guerre.*

When journalism becomes a cliché machine, thought evaporates in the service of the phrase. At one moment – and this is the very big, perhaps decisive, change from twenty years ago – 'millions ... despise the Westminster system'. Here we see casually registered a degree of popular revulsion which alone should be enough to cause a crisis in a healthy polity. But the contempt of voters for Westminster is regarded as a normal phenomenon remote from the affairs of real power and politics. Here, Davis is a mere 'one-man charge'. Rarely can the condescension of our elite and the gap between it and the people have been so succinctly if inadvertently exposed.

And this is how 'they' want to keep it. It is presumed that the millions will despise the Westminster system. It is also presumed that such popular cynicism and disengagement will in fact shield

* Fraser Nelson, 'Poor, brave David Davis has become the Eddie the Eagle of Westminster', *Spectator*, 18 June 2008.

the state, ensuring that *citizens* never demand such basic rights as fair voting or habeas corpus.

The point I am trying to register briefly is the stifling nature of resistance to democratic constitutional reform by what can be termed the 'political class'. I use the term in the full sense that Peter Oborne has developed, meaning the media, political advisers, think tanks, leading civil servants, business and trade union lobbyists, as well as politicians.* Despite honourable exceptions, taken as a whole it will do everything it can to prevent its monopoly on power from being broken by democracy.

The best way it can do this is by asphyxiating the hope of change. It is a ductile and duplicitous elite in Britain, pliable and polite in its manners, clever (it thinks) in its assessment of the main chance, cold and unrelenting in its love of power. Faced with calls for the need for reform, its first line of defence is to respond by agreeing to the argument in the abstract, 'I am sure you are right but...', while insisting on its irrelevance as a matter of fate. It is 'marvellously sincere of you' that you should be concerned about liberty/democracy/fair elections/injustice (tick as relevant) but it isn't 'wanted', it will be scorned, the people are indifferent.

The process can be observed in the *New York Times*, which sent James Atlas to London in the spring of 1989 to find out what was going on. Capturing the growing anxiety and the atmosphere of resistance and opposition to Thatcher, to which Charter 88 gave a programmatic expression, he opened his long survey as follows: 'Charter 88 arrived on the newsstands of Britain with the rhetorical force of a Tom Paine tract. "We are losing our liberties − because they do not belong to us as citizens," read the text in colorful bold print on the cover of the *New Statesman* last December.'† Atlas was unaware perhaps that Paine was much disliked in his home country. He reported that when he went to No. 10 'a Thatcher spokesman', whom he asked about Charter 88, responded: 'I think there'll be massive

* Peter Oborne, *The Triumph of the Political Class* (London: Simon & Schuster, 2007).

† James Atlas, 'Thatcher puts a lid on censorship in Britain', *New York Times Magazine*, 5 March 1989.

public indifference and ridicule to the whole thing.' He spoke to
Max Hastings, then editor of the *Daily Telegraph*, who told him:
'Thatcher is an extremely shrewd judge of what the public cares
about and what it doesn't. These are issues it doesn't care about.'

Twenty years later just such phrases are being rolled out with
respect to David Davis. Only this time a prime source is a Labour
government. In an article in support of Davis, the Labour MP Bob
Marshall-Andrews recounted how a former government chief whip
had told him: 'People in my constituency don't give a damn about
civil liberties.'* Marshall-Andrews explained how it was clear *she
didn't want them to*. Our rulers know that the people would prefer a
better system and could make good use of it. It is hard to over-
estimate, however, the effort the political class puts into making sure
that the voters themselves think they don't care about how they are
governed and agree that there is nothing they can do about it.

But now our understanding of the true nature of public opinion
has advanced in three important respects since Charter 88 began.

First, while voters are sceptical of offers of power from politicians,
polling evidence shows that, asked if they would like to have the
constitution written down, between 70 and 85 per cent say 'yes'. At
the time I analysed one such poll at some length, the MORI/Joseph
Rowntree Reform Trust *State of the Nation* poll of 1995. Its detail
shows that support for a written constitution is higher among the
poorer than among the better off. Actual opposition to a written
constitution, though low everywhere, was twice as high among ABs
and those who read broadsheets as it was among C2s and those who
read popular papers.† I concluded: 'It is the proponents of the status
quo who are a small ... upper middle-class, broadsheet-reading,
London-based minority ... Across the land almost everyone else,
from 65 per cent of Conservative voters to 75 per cent of skilled
workers, would be happy to have a written constitution.'‡ It may not

---

* Bob Marshall-Andrews, 'We should all back this fight against an out-
rageous assault on our liberty', *Yorkshire Post*, 9 July 2008.
† See *State of the Nation* (York: Joseph Rowntree Reform Trust/London:
MORI, 1995).
‡ Anthony Barnett, *This Time: Our Constitutional Revolution* (London:
Vintage, 1997), pp. 112–13.

be top of people's list or even perceived as a practical option, but nonetheless a written constitution would be overwhelmingly welcomed.

Second, while passively at ease with the idea of constitutional reform, the public has become increasingly disaffected with Westminster politics. The Power Inquiry probed the extent of people's revulsion at and distrust of Britain's ancient parliamentary system. It was chaired by Helena Kennedy, who had been an outstanding advocate for Charter 88 as chair of its council, and was run by Pam Giddy. The inquiry mapped the extent to which Westminster is indeed 'despised'. This was an important deepening of the understanding of the need for reform. Charter 88 faced towards Westminster and argued that democracy is essential to rescue the British state. The Power Inquiry looked the other way, into the depths of voters' feelings and concerns, and concluded that reform of the state is essential to rescue British democracy.

Third, we now have the evidence of ten years of significant reforms. From Scotland to the Human Rights Act these get disdainful coverage from the London media. But this is because they work. Wales voted for an assembly by a slim margin with widespread abstention; now Cardiff Bay is prized and autonomy has popular momentum. To go to Holyrood is to feel the confidence in Scotland's parliament. In London most did not bother to vote on the referendum for a mayor, but just try to take away their right to have one now! The same goes for reforms that offer more accountability: the Freedom of Information Act and the Human Rights Act are much used. Official displeasure is a sign of their success. Today we can say with confidence that should Parliament ever agree to a popular convention to draw up a new constitutional settlement, the people would rise to the occasion.

Reflecting on this one can see the pity of it all. Tony Blair put through the great reforms he did because he had inherited the commitments from John Smith. He didn't think they mattered; he didn't want them to matter; he tried, with blatant disregard to their nature, to fiddle the outcomes of the Labour Party selection processes for who would run London and Wales. He and his team refused to tie the reforms together into a new settlement.

But Britain could have moved to a federal democracy in 1997 and it would have worked.

The nature of Charter 88

Perhaps the best way of seeing what happened is by looking at the offer that the supporters of Charter 88 made to the political class. We proposed that the United Kingdom should become a modern, democratic country. The 1970s had been a decade of crisis and breakdown saved by Margaret Thatcher. Her coffers fuelled by North Sea oil, she broke the closed shops of the trade unions and the City of London, opening the latter to its 'big bang' globalisation in a formula that can be summed up as combining economic freedom, social division and authoritarian government. Charter 88 offered an alternative way forward: a democratic solution for the national question inside the UK; a means of becoming a European country with our own constitution protecting us from the Continental behemoth; a solution to the growing disengagement by creating a genuine framework for citizenship. We offered an economy where everyone had a stake, a case made by Will Hutton; a legal system that worked for all; a culture that was open, not fustian, and could celebrate incomers who made a claim on it.

It was an offer the political class was reluctant to buy. So we pitched. Charter's supporters campaigned in public and lobbied in private to show that what we proposed was practical and could be popular. In the end the offer was rejected. But the route to its acceptance was via Labour (with the Liberal Democrats, especially their members, in strong agreement). When John Smith replaced Neil Kinnock as leader of the Labour Party after the 1992 election, he did indeed embrace the idea of a new constitutional settlement. His office asked me if he could give a Charter 88 speech and on 1 March 1993 he said:

> I am arguing for a new constitutional settlement, a new deal between the people and the state that puts the citizen centre stage. A deal that gives people new powers and a stronger voice in the affairs of the nation. And a deal that restores a sense of cohesion and vitality to our national life.

I want to see a fundamental shift in the balance of power between the citizen and the state – a shift away from an overpowering state to a citizens' democracy where people have rights and powers and where they are served by accountable and responsive government.

In the following Labour Party conference Kinnock signed Charter 88 at a small ceremony hosted by Helena Kennedy.

But there was another view inside the Labour Party at the time. Tony Blair was Smith's shadow Home Secretary, assisted by the energetic Graham Allen MP, who had the brief for constitutional reform. Allen organised a special meeting to discuss how to make Smith's new policy of a Bill of Rights attractive to voters. Blair opened the proceedings with an account of the way he had been converted in one of those 'this House believes' debates, when he had found himself convinced by his opponents. We broke up into smaller groups with instructions to brainstorm ideas on how best to present a Bill of Rights to the public. I found myself in the same group as Peter Mandelson. He took the lead and suggested that the line should be 'a Bill of Rights means better government'. After some discussion I observed that politicians are always offering 'better government'; wouldn't it be more attractive to say that codifying our rights would give us 'a better system of government'? 'System?' Mandelson queried. 'That sounds like Grosvenor Square.'*

---

* A reference to the 1968 demonstrations outside the US embassy in London. Mandelson knew me well enough to know that I'd been there in spirit and indeed I was there in fact. Later I published an account of this episode in 'Corporate Control', *Prospect*, February 1999 (which he certainly saw, it carried the large picture of Mandelson posing with a bulldog that had marred Labour's 1997 election campaign). His remark was not just a casual example of Labour sectarianism against someone who was not a party member. At my suggestion, he and I had co-operated successfully in a Charter 88 operation to secure Smith's agreement on a referendum on PR, as I described in the article. It was not that I was not *partiinyi* (Mandelson was in the Young Communists while 1968 was an anti-Stalinist movement). Rather, his remark expressed the fact that he didn't want to change the system – and saw no electoral advantage either in pretending that he did.

Smith died. Mandelson helped Blair seize the leadership of the party in partnership with Gordon Brown. Brown always insisted that he would have taken a unified approach to their constitutional reforms but he certainly didn't persuade his colleagues. The rest, you might say, is history. They decided that they would continue to run the state on the lines pioneered by Margaret Thatcher even when they implemented different policies.

Which leads to the larger point about the political class. Who else argued that Labour should make a proper fist of their reforms and be more sweeping and radical, rather than less? Where were the party members, the Labour pressure groups, the trade unionists, the 'business community', the far-sighted financiers, the wealthy entrepreneurs, the newspaper editors and proprietors, the independent think tanks and policy specialists, the powerful legal specialists, the long-range historians and political theorists, the forward-looking members of the political class? Where, indeed, was the *New Statesman* after Stuart Weir stopped being editor? Why, in short, was no-one else saying to the leaders of New Labour, who were desperately sensitive to demand, 'Britain does indeed need a new constitutional settlement'?

A new friend has just emailed me, saying: 'I have come to realise that the establishment is smug and conceited. It not only has an inbuilt inertia born of its own self-conceit, it is inherently conservative and incapable of reform unless it is under threat itself.' But couldn't any of them see that they *were* under threat, not only from the long-term consequences of EU membership, but also and more important, if Scotland got its own parliament? A threat isn't only something you wait for until it ambushes you. There was an opportunity to see it coming, seize the initiative and make a better country. There were individuals who did see this, such as Jeremy Hardie, Marina Warner, David Marquand, Carole Tongue, Stephen Howe, Jean Lambert, Neil Belton and Paul Hirst. Otherwise it was pass-the-parcel and wait-and-see.

This brings me to the Liberal Democrats. They too, in effect, were made the offer. The party hierarchy has a network of wealthy business supporters and excellent organisers, as well as strong local parties and millions of votes. It always backed Charter 88. But while its members were often our greatest enthusiasts, its

leadership, with few exceptions like Shirley Williams, backed
Charter 88 as an army supports a battering ram, hoping it would
breach Labour's walls in a way that they could not.

The challenge Charter 88 posed to the Liberal Democrats was
that it suggested their core values could be popular! That there
was a world to win, that proportional representation could follow
from a new settlement rather than be gained within the old one.
Apart from the trustees of the Joseph Rowntree Reform and
Charitable Trusts, with their larger realism, the leaders never saw
us as pioneering a better way of succeeding. Instead they viewed
Charter 88 in an instrumental fashion.

No doubt as part of the traditional political class, Liberal
Democrat leaders disliked Charter 88 because it was born in the
bowels of the *New Statesman*. But its leftist agenda could be
summed up in a phrase of Neal Ascherson, that 'you can no more
get socialism from the British state than milk from a vulture'. You
could say the same for democracy and, indeed, for liberalism. The
means shape the end. You might want equality, but first there
needs to be a fair and democratic system of government. It
followed that this would not guarantee any outcome – for left or
right. As Charter's founding director, I always insisted on this. Its
proposition had to remain open minded and be made in good
faith. It was for rights-based democracy. Then let the best
arguments win.

Perhaps it suffered from the weaknesses of my impatience as
well as gaining from its energy. The aim was not a rooted
movement arming itself for a 25-year campaign. It was to
persuade the current leaders of the whole political class to do the
plain obvious and give us a chance to create a 'new deal between
the people and the state'. John Smith was apparently persuaded.
The rest let the moment pass them by. Charles Kennedy spoke for
the lot of them.

Britain is now a changed country. Outside Whitehall and
Westminster, in Scotland, Wales and Northern Ireland, there are
new democracies with different parliaments. For those of us still
governed directly by the dead hand of the 'two Ws', the stifling
gloom of the database state threatens, a modernised form of the
authoritarianism that Charter 88 originally protested and organised

against. The extent and seriousness of the hi-tech state is only now being understood. Twenty years ago we also offered a democratic way forward for Britain as a whole when it could have been implemented. Whatever the way forward now, the spirit of refusal that Charter 88 rekindled and invigorated still flickers in the darkness.

The first decade of Charter 88

Fruitful interaction with the Joseph Rowntree Reform Trust

Trevor Smith

ord Falconer of Thoroton, when Lord Chancellor, would pepper his speeches on the constitution with reference to the Burkean notion of gradual reform that he claimed had historically informed changes made to the UK's system of governance. Such a view, at best, is a nineteenth-century hangover; he used it as an excuse to disguise the lack of progress in undertaking further principled reform during the second and third Blair administrations. It is true, of course, that in 2005 the government made provision for the complete separation of the law lords from Parliament by creating a Supreme Court. However, the manner in which this was achieved – a covertly contrived concordat between Falconer as Lord Chancellor and Lord Woolf, the Lord Chief Justice – was hardly an exemplar of open, democratic constitutional deliberation. The second and third Blair administrations, then, contrasted starkly with the dramatic reform initiatives taken during the first.

The nature of constitutional change in the UK

In fact, there was little reason to invoke Burke regarding the developments in government that occurred between the 1911 Parliament Act and the Bills that created devolved legislatures in Scotland and Wales at the end of the twentieth century. With the exception of the 1958 Life Peerages Act, all the major changes that took place in the intervening decades were confined exclusively to the executive branch of government. They were administrative responses to perceived political needs and, as such, could in no way be seen as ongoing constitutional renewal. That would have required setting them in a wider context. Such a context would have had to place changes in the executive in the light of possible or necessary consequential reforms to the legislative and judicial branches of government – and the 2005 creation of a Supreme Court did not fulfil these requirements. Furthermore, movements in public opinion and central–local relations would also have had to be taken into account.

The truth is that major constitutional change in the UK occurs in fits and starts with very long intervals in between. Such interest as there was in matters constitutional – which was not much – was largely confined to parties in opposition at Westminster. This indifference was undoubtedly due to the predominance of England in the UK polity, as greater interest was to be found in the topic in the kingdom's other nations: Northern Ireland, Scotland and Wales were – and are – much more prone to discuss aspects of constitutionalism as, for example, was reflected in John Smith's commitment to devolution.

The evolution of constitutional campaigns after 1968

Les Evènements of 1968 came and went leaving an iconic memory rather than having any practical effect. In due course, however, the lack of constitutional change throughout the middle years of the last century did provoke a revival in ideas in the 1970s which gained considerable momentum over the two succeeding decades. The Scottish Constitutional Convention was a significant manifestation of this. Think tanks were also formed to prosecute the constitutionalist cause. The Outer Circle Policy Unit, directed by James Cornford, existed between 1976 and 1980. The Centre for Constitutional Change was the brainchild of Richard Holme and lasted from 1984 to 1993. In 1984 the Campaign for Freedom of Information was formed under the direction of Maurice Frankel. In 1988 the Institute for Public Policy Research started up with Cornford as its first director. Democratic Audit, directed by Stuart Weir, was created in 1991, while Demos appeared in 1993 with Geoff Mulgan as its director. The last four are still going strong.

Allied to this cerebral activity was the formation of a plethora of pressure groups aimed at promoting the cause of constitutional reform. Tactical Voting '87, rebranded as Common Voice in the following year, sought to advance anti-Conservative electoral pacts, as did the Voter Reform Group, which was created in 1993. They later merged, becoming Make Votes Count. *Samizdat* magazine, edited by the late Ben Pimlott, was launched in 1988 to inspire a 'popular front' of the centre-left to oppose the prolonged period of continuous Tory rule. The same year saw the birth of Charter 88, inspired by Weir, the then editor of the *New Statesman*, and with the ingenious Anthony Barnett as its first director. Its remit was to advance the general cause of constitutional reform, forcefully and coherently. It attracted a wide variety of well-known signatories from all walks of life, to which were added many thousands more concerned citizens. Through its network of local groups, the 1991 Manchester Constitutional Convention (held in collaboration with the *Independent* in the city which had spawned the Anti-Corn Law League), and the staging of Democracy Days, it established itself as the major vehicle for promoting constitutional reform. One of its main tactical successes was to orchestrate a series of Sovereignty Lectures arranged in memory of John Smith. Until his premature death, Smith had been an advocate of Scottish devolution and his conviction was so strong that the momentum of his legacy ensured that the policy had to be adopted by his successor, Tony Blair. There is no evidence, however, that the new leader was at all convinced of the need for significant constitutional change. In fact, the evidence points to the reverse. For example, he disparagingly referred to the prospect of a future Scottish Parliament as being 'little more than a parish council'. Equally, by watering down the provisions of the Freedom of Information Bill, he reneged on his commitment to the more robust version he had accepted before being elected. Similarly, his half–hearted approach to electoral reform (proportional voting for everywhere but Westminster) suggests he was a reluctant rather than an ardent reformer. The point is that by being the first Sovereignty lecturer (Gordon Brown and Mo Mowlam were among others), Blair had been skilfully manoeuvred by Barnett into appearing to subscribe to the programme of Charter 88.

The Joseph Rowntree Trusts and reform

The Joseph Rowntree Reform Trust Ltd, being incorporated as a tax–paying limited company, was able to finance many of the campaigns that sought to promote constitutional change. Indeed, to a greater or lesser extent, it supported almost all of them from time to time. Through its charitable wing, the Joseph Rowntree Social Service Charitable Trust, it could help finance much of the educational research of the various think tanks in the field. In 1991 it launched a regular series of *State of the Nation* surveys, which sought to gauge public attitudes to a variety of constitutional questions, including fixed–term parliaments, voting reform, rights and duties, and parliamentary reform. The aim was to measure changes in public attitudes over time and to provide essential data for the media, pressure groups and think tanks.

In all its undertakings the Reform Trust was in the unique position of being able to cover both thought and action. It could do this corporately in a way that, for example, Stuart Weir, Anthony Barnett and others could do as individuals. They possessed both the intellectual imagination and the promotional and marketing skills that are the prerequisites of political entrepreneurs; they were the 'spin doctors' working for democracy as opposed to those justifying the control–freakery of government.

Charter 88 and beyond

I was privileged to have a ringside seat during these heady days of constitutional agitation and dissemination. As chair of the Reform

Trust, I was in communication, at times almost daily, with Anthony Barnett. Charter 88 became the flagship of the trust's grant-making: it was the main recipient, being given more than £1.3 million in its first ten years. Even the *Daily Telegraph*, never an ardent supporter of constitutional change, had reluctantly to acknowledge that Charter 88 was the foremost pressure group of the 1990s.

Charter 88 had a real impact on the public agenda and helped to create the climate for change that culminated in the devolutionary settlement created by the first Blair government. The rhetoric is still called in aid from time to time, most recently by Gordon Brown in his first weeks as Prime Minister. The subsequent publication of his Green Paper *The Governance of Britain* offers the prospect of further reform to make government more accountable and democratic. It has induced a degree of consultation over House of Lords reform among other issues, but little is likely to happen in the near future and, despite occasional nods in favour of an elected Upper House, any future Conservative government is unlikely to make this more of a priority than the present Labour one. Proportional representation seems equally far away. It is time to mobilise the spirit of Charter 88 once more.

Power to the people

Helena Kennedy

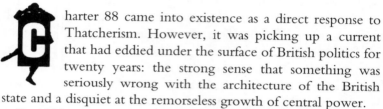

harter 88 came into existence as a direct response to Thatcherism. However, it was picking up a current that had eddied under the surface of British politics for twenty years: the strong sense that something was seriously wrong with the architecture of the British state and a disquiet at the remorseless growth of central power.

By 1988 voters in Scotland and Wales were feeling completely alienated from the Westminster parliament and wanted decision-making powers closer to home; parliamentary structures were outmoded and we still had a House of Lords overwhelmingly filled with hereditary peers; the secrecy which surrounded the working of government made it difficult to hold politicians to account; and when citizens' rights were trammelled by the state, it took six long years for cases to journey to the European Court of Human Rights to seek recourse. And then there was the issue of unfairness when it came to voting, whereby the first-past-the-post system privileged the two main parties. Proportional representation was a recurring theme on the wish-list of many seeking reform. In there too were demands for a written constitution, a Bill of Rights, a Freedom of Information Act, reform of the House of Lords and reform of the judiciary.

The Charter 88 campaign felt fresh and empowering. It brought together people from all parts of the political firmament, apart from establishment Labour and the Conservative Party. Even then, a few enlightened Tories such as Richard Shepherd MP and Ferdinand Mount either supported the campaign or agreed with the direction of travel. And we all knew, to quote Lord Hailsham, that 'an elected dictatorship' was bad for democracy. New checks and balances had to be created.

I was a member of the Charter 88 council from the outset and was its chair from 1992 until the 1997 election. Since 1992 a lot has happened but not enough has changed.

After Labour lost the 1992 election and John Smith was elected leader of the party, Charter 88 knew it had a sympathetic ear for its campaign issues. Smith was a lawyer who understood the value of the European Convention on Human Rights and he agreed to give a lecture for us on the subject of creating a Bill of Rights for the United Kingdom. Gordon Brown also gave a lecture for Charter 88 which touched on the subject of Scottish devolution and we suddenly felt that the tectonic plates of the Labour Party were shifting. When Smith died tragically and New Labour was invented, it was Peter Mandelson who saw the force of embracing the constitutional agenda as part of Labour's modernising project. After a series of negotiations we had the breathtaking excitement of seeing our whole platform absorbed into the New Labour manifesto for government. For many of us the 1997 victory for Labour augured the building of a new relationship between citizen and state. I was appointed to the House of Lords to help champion the constitutional reform agenda through Parliament, and that first term of Labour in office produced more far-reaching reforms than anything seen since the Great Reform Act of 1832.

However, I soon realised the changes did not spring from a coherent vision of a pluralist democracy. The shallow nature of the commitment became apparent very quickly. Real reform required a deep understanding of how the individual changes articulated one with the other but the government was frequently schizophrenic: so while we had devolution to Scotland and Wales we saw increasing centralisation in England; while we had an innovative Human Rights Act we also had a raft of deeply authoritarian legislation, which reduced civil liberties, attacked the right to jury trial and expanded the state's capacity to intrude into the lives of citizens. The reforms should have meant giving power away. However, as our new masters found, power is profoundly seductive.

The will for deep constitutional reform was soon lost once Labour was settled in office. The benefits of patronage became all too clear and executive power too delightful. On virtually every constitutional front, reform was trimmed or delayed. When senior judges delivered judgement against the government on their treatment of asylum seekers, the Prime Minister himself suggested that legislation might be needed to curtail judicial power. When a mayor was being selected for London and a leader for the Welsh Assembly, Downing Street sought to parachute into office its own hand-picked candidates. When reform of the House of Lords was in train, Tony Blair machinated for a wholly appointed chamber rather than one that would be democratically elected. Secrecy was almost as rampant as before.

It was with a sense of déjà vu that I found myself in 2004 chairing an independent inquiry into Britain's democracy, called the Power Inquiry, and revisiting so many of the issues and governmental failures that existed under Margaret Thatcher. The inquiry was the centenary project of the Joseph Rowntree Charitable Trust and the Joseph Rowntree Reform Trust and the question we were set was: why are we seeing such a decline in voting and a haemorrhaging of membership of political parties?

We called our report *Power to the People*, because we wanted to emphasise the need to shift away from the old pre-democratic constitutional settlement, where the people have incidental roles and government is at the centre of the drama, to a stronger sense that the state belongs to the people.

There were good historical reasons why we have become stuck in this pre-democratic model. When challenged, the powers of the monarch had simply shifted to his or her ministers in government – the executive. And while this locus of power has been somewhat eroded by an ad hoc mix of conventions, practices, precedents and occasional enactments, there is still too much power in the hands of central government. One of the strongest recommendations in our report was to empower the people at a local level and the Commons at the centre to hold the executive to account. It became clear that representative democracy needed to be enriched and new ways found to engage the electorate on important issues between elections.

The 'C-word' is not one that captures the public imagination. Constitutional change is one of those subjects that can easily invoke groans. Yet it is the way to give people real influence over bread-and-butter issues which affect their lives. As we went around the country taking evidence over a period of a year – in community centres and town halls and sports grounds – it was clear that the disengagement from politics could not be dismissed as the preoccupation of the few. The substance of our findings was found in the voices of thousands of people who felt depressed about politicians and alienated from the processes. When it came to politics they felt they were eating stones. Yet when people moved beyond the first round of criticism, which usually centred on perceptions about politicians' self-interest and lies about what they would do to get your vote, a very different complaint surfaced. The disquiet was about having no say.

Again it became clear that our democracy needs revitalisation and a review of our constitutional arrangements. A constitution for the twenty-first century would say that sovereignty belongs to the people, instead of the Crown in Parliament. There would be a clear and simple written constitution expressed in accessible language. The royal prerogative would be abolished. Ministers and civil servants would be servants of Parliament or the people, not the Crown. The House of Lords would become an elected second chamber with representation on a national and regional basis. Devolution from the centre to local and regional level would create new sites for civil engagement, and place a check on the centralising tendencies of government. A Bill of Rights would retain and enhance the Human Rights Act by establishing certain guarantees such as habeas corpus, trial by jury for serious crime, due process before loss of liberty, freedom of expression and the right to protest. Electoral reform would make the House of Commons democratically legitimate and introduce new parties into its fold. Unlock Democracy, Charter 88's successor organisation, has its work cut out in continuing to campaign on these issues.

However, such significant constitutional reform has to be the creation of the people. When considering the content of a Bill of Rights, the nature of electoral reform or the content of the written constitution, some sort of nationwide convention would have to be the engine. It cannot be the product of any one political party or a stitch-up by the great and the good behind closed doors. For reform to have legitimacy and for people to feel it was their creation, there would have to be a deliberative process to produce it. But just think what an invigorating thing that could be – with citizens' juries and congresses, evidence-gathering sessions and debate; the impact on political awareness and ownership would be huge. The Charter of Rights in Canada came out of just such a process. All the parties responded with interest to our report. All have cherry-picked their way through our recommendations but we have yet to see whether the political class have really understood the depth of the distrust that has been sown. Only a radical remedy will fix it but that involves giving away power. Power: the very reason for winning elections. Who would be so bold?

Dissolution and reformation
From Charter 88 to Unlock Democracy

Alexandra Runswick[*]

This is based on the text of a speech given on 4 July 2008 at the conference 'Charter 88 and Constitutional Reform 1988–2008: A twentieth anniversary retrospective'.[†]

his anthology celebrates the twentieth anniversary of Charter 88 as well as exploring the future challenges in democratic reform, but I want to start by painting a picture of a period when it was far from clear that there would be an organisation left to celebrate this anniversary.

The year 2003, Charter's fifteenth birthday, was very turbulent for us and could easily have seen the end of the organisation. I was working as a policy officer at Charter 88, and following a period of redundancies and resignations I was the most senior member of staff left. Financially, Charter was in serious difficulty and there was no easy way out. At the beginning of December that year I had the dubious honour of being told that Charter was being evicted from its offices. Now that's what I call a bad day at work!

[*]This chapter is dedicated to the memory of my step-father, Neil Ryder. My involvement with Charter 88 is partly due to Neil, who when I turned sixteen dug out his signatory pack, sat me down and told me about this really important movement that I should join.

[†] Additional research by James Graham.

This chapter explores how Charter got to the point of being evicted and then examines its merger with the New Politics Network and how it has begun to be reinvigorated as Unlock Democracy. Needless to say, these reflections give my personal view of events – others will have different interpretations.

1997 and all that

In many ways 1997 appeared to be Charter 88's moment – skilful campaigning and lobbying meant that the new Labour government was committed, formally at least, to many of the proposals in the charter. However, the shallow nature of the promise became apparent very quickly,* and the government's approach to reform created a number of challenges for Charter as a campaigning organisation.

No-one would dispute that the Labour government has significantly changed the UK constitution, but its approach has been half-hearted and chaotic. Where the 1997 government fell down was not so much in the ingredients of constitutional reform, but in failing to make any sense of them. It singularly failed to create a strong democratic narrative. Because its heart wasn't in it, its reforms have often disappointed in the detail.

How do you keep funders convinced of the urgency of reform when the government appears to be delivering it for you? Having manoeuvred the government into appearing to adopt your policy agenda, how do you say that you want reform – just not this version of reform? And how do you keep activists and supporters enthused when you appear to be having to compromise at every stage? These were the challenges that Charter faced in the late 1990s – trying to encourage further reform and to improve what was already on offer, while maintaining campaign momentum.

* This period has been covered by a number of other contributions to this anthology. See in particular the chapters by Helena Kennedy and Stuart Weir.

Inherent conflicts

One of the central tensions within Charter 88 was the charter itself. More specifically, there was conflict between the longer narrative of the charter and the list of demands at the end. While the narrative remains, in my view, very relevant and persuasive, the fact that the charter includes a list of specific demands has led some supporters to be dogmatic in their approach to campaigns. There are people for whom, if it is not specifically listed, and preferably in bold type, in the original charter, then Charter 88 should have nothing to do with it. This was particularly evident when Charter 88 first became involved in the campaign against identity cards. Charter 88, with Liberty, played a key role in this campaign,* bringing together a coalition that ultimately led to the creation of the NO2ID campaign. Some supporters left the organisation because they felt ID cards were not a constitutional issue. But Charter's campaign against ID cards has always been about the fact that without a written constitution our basic rights, including the right to personal privacy, are unprotected in the UK. We are the only organisation that has made that specific case.

When you consider the breadth and radicalism of the agenda outlined in the charter it is easy to have some sympathy with this fundamentalist approach. There are more than enough battles to face – House of Lords reform, proportional representation and a Bill of Rights, to name just three – without seeking out new ones. Yet this approach detaches the call for institutional reform from the wider, and far more challenging, narrative about where power lies in the UK and why change is needed. It also implies that the charter should be preserved in aspic, even while the political situation continues to evolve and develop. Sacred texts are for religions, not pressure groups.

There is also a key difference between Charter 88, the organisation, and the charter itself. The organisation has always

---

* See www.unlockdemocracy.org.uk for more information about Charter 88's involvement in the campaign against ID cards and for the 2001 pamphlet *ID Cards: Arguments Against.*

been about the process of politics and decision-making and not just the outcome. In calling for a Bill of Rights, for example, Charter 88 didn't start drafting the legislation. Instead we outlined the citizen-led process that we wanted to result in the creation of a Bill of Rights. We certainly suggested what could be included but we were clear that our role was to create the activism that would lead to the Bill of Rights, rather than drawing it up ourselves.

The charter was an assessment of the state of the nation at a moment in time. While much of the analysis in the full charter is remarkably current today, to be successful in the future, the organisation has to be able to adapt to the circumstances it finds itself in, and must recreate narratives showing why constitutional reform matters. A dogmatic approach to the charter can also lead to the tick-box approach to reform adopted by Labour in government. Devolution to Scotland, Wales and Northern Ireland has been achieved; there is a Freedom of Information Act and a Human Rights Act (HRA). But each of these reforms was abandoned almost as soon as it was passed. In stark contrast to Ron Davies's vision of ongoing and evolving decentralisation, Whitehall has treated devolution as an event, and not a process. It certainly didn't lead to decentralisation in England. The failure to engage citizens in implementing the HRA means that rather than being proudly championed as one of the greatest achievements of the Labour government, it has become a tabloid punchbag – the so-called 'criminals' charter'.

From the Pinocchio campaign to the Future of Democracy, 2001–3

Our disintegrating relationship with the Labour Party and its model of reform became public with the Pinocchio advertisements, run during the 2001 general election campaign. The images, displayed on a barge around central London and in national newspapers, showed Tony Blair with a Pinocchio nose alongside a series of manifesto commitments that had not been delivered, including 'We will have a referendum'.* It prompted Trevor Kavanagh, then the political editor of the *Sun* and certainly not one of Charter's usual supporters, to ask about the ads during a press conference. Unfortunately he thought they referred to the referendum on the euro, not the promised referendum on proportional representation. There was a clear sense with the Pinocchio campaign that Charter felt there was no longer anything to be gained from working as an insider organisation.

However, there were deep divisions within the supporter base over this campaign. For some it showed Charter 88 returning to campaign on its core issues. But there were a number of Charter supporters and donors who were also Labour Party members, who felt the adverts went too far. They effectively resigned from the organisation. In some ways they were the right adverts but used during the wrong election. The New Labour honeymoon was continuing in 2001 and the campaign failed to capture the public mood or to relaunch the organisation as a popular mass movement. Ironically, by 2005 the Pinocchio image was everywhere. It had been used by the Conservatives to highlight tax increases, and by the anti-war movement to draw attention to the invasion of Iraq,† but in 2001 it was seen as going for the jugular too early. Charter may have seen itself as 'Jiminy Cricket to Tony Blair's Pinocchio'‡ but for many within the Labour Party it seemed that Charter was seeking to be a puppet master,

---

* The three manifesto commitments that appeared in the adverts were 'We will have people's peers', 'We will have a referendum' and 'We will have a new relationship between people and government'. See www.unlock democracy.org.uk for more information.

† See 'Tories' "Pinocchio Blair" campaign', Mail Online; Jennifer Whitehead, 'Tories brand Blair a Pinocchio in new DM push', Brand Republic website, 8 July 2003; 'Blair lied – thousands died', press release, Stop the War Coalition, 13 July 2004. Some anti-war organisations also suggested 'nose-in parties', where activists dressed up as Tony Blair with Pinocchio noses; see 'Ideas for Local Action', *Voices Newsletter*, August 2003.

‡ Pam Giddy, quoted in 'End cynicism – embrace democratic reform', Charter 88 press release, 24 May 2001.

dictating the government's programme. It certainly made my first Labour Party conference in 2001, representing Charter 88, interesting!

Charter had a mini-revival in November 2002, organising the successful 'Future of Democracy' conference, with Robin Cook as the keynote speaker,* and once again it made the case both for the need for reform and for the creation of a new coalition for democracy. This was to include anti-racist groups, trade unionists, anti-globalisation protestors, women's groups, environmentalists, the rural lobby and human rights activists.† But financially, the organisation was unviable and all this positive energy soon came to a crashing halt.

In June 2003 Paul Hirst died very suddenly. Paul was the chair of the executive committee and was immensely important not only to the intellectual rigour of Charter 88 but also to the management of the organisation. The executive committee was divided about the way forward and Paul had been both able and committed to keeping the organisation together. A kind and highly intelligent man, he often managed to bring committee members, passionately divided over current issues, back to focusing on the shared commitments that had brought them to the organisation in the first place. In many ways his death was the final straw. There were no easy answers to Charter's predicament and things came to a head by the end of the year.

Reformation, 2004–7

So how did Charter 88 emerge from its troubled teens? Its salvation came in the form of the New Politics Network (NPN), which allowed Charter to operate out of its offices rent free for a period, gave it a bridging loan so that it could recover financially,

---

* For the text of Cook's speech see 'The Future of Democracy Conference', Office of the Leader of the House of Commons website.

† For more information about the Future of Democracy conference see Tom Bentley, 'The Future of Democracy: You Can't Impose Democracy from Above', Unlock Democracy website, accessed 19 August 2008.

developed a joint working programme and, in November 2007, merged with Charter to form Unlock Democracy. The NPN was a think tank formed in 2000 which was committed to embracing the 'new politics' being espoused by Tony Blair at the time. Ironically the NPN stopped using the term 'new politics' just at the time that it was embraced by Gordon Brown, Nick Clegg and David Cameron.* The fact that it has been bandied about with such enthusiasm does suggest that it may have lost some of its ideological moorings.†

The NPN was formed following the winding up of Democratic Left, which itself emerged out of the ashes of the Communist Party of Great Britain (CPGB). That latter fact tends to cause rather more excitement than the prosaic reality justifies. By the time it ended in December 1991, the CPGB was avowedly euro-communist and Democratic Left was a herald of New Labour. Disgruntled members had been leaving the party since 1956 in opposition to euro-communism, the last of these splits forming the Communist Party of Britain in 1988. But while it was not the fifth-columnist front of conspiracy theory, there is no denying that the NPN was, like Charter 88, a creature of the left. One of its highest-profile initiatives was the anti-Conservative tactical voting campaign in 2001, although this was no longer associated with the NPN by the time the relationship with Charter began.

The *Observer* columnist Nick Cohen was, inadvertently, a midwife of Unlock Democracy. He predicted that Charter 88 and NPN would eventually merge in a *New Statesman* column as far

---

* See Gordon Brown's speech to the National Council for Voluntary Organisations, 3 September 2007; Nick Clegg's speech on becoming leader of the Liberal Democrats, 18 December 2007; David Cameron, 'Fixing Britain's Broken Politics', speech to the Welsh Conservative Party conference, 1 March 2008.

† 'New politics' is a term which has always had leftist connotations. In the United States, the New Politics movement in the 1950s called for a softer line against the Soviet Union, while the socialist *New Politics* magazine was first published in 1961. In the UK *Marxism Today*, published by the Communist Party of Great Britain and edited by Martin Jacques, published a series of

back as 2000,* but the truth is this was far from inevitable. It was certainly not the intention of some of the NPN's founding members, who at the annual general meeting in 2003 attempted to make it explicitly in favour of social democracy. If that move had been successful, the NPN would have been firmly rooted as a centre-left, social democratic think tank whose primary focus was influencing the Labour Party. It may well have ended up part of the Labour-supporting pressure group Compass.

In rejecting this move the NPN was free to become explicitly non-aligned and genuinely pluralist, without which a formal partnership with Charter would not have been possible. Just a Google search away, Cohen's piece was being read by a number of key players at this time with wry amusement. To some it was a source of inspiration.

Nor was the relationship between the NPN and Charter initially welcomed by all those who had remained with Charter. In 2004 there were two distinct schools of thought, one supporting a formal relationship with the NPN, the second in favour of a partnership with an organisation called Active Citizens Transform (ACT), which had just been established by Ron Bailey and Charles Secrett.† ACT was explicitly about making the links between the environmental and democracy movements and mobilising grassroots support for the concept of local sustainability. This became moot when ACT was merged with Charter in 2006. At that point the advantages of a formal merger with the NPN became clear and the formal process that resulted in the creation of Unlock Democracy began.

The NPN's contribution to Unlock Democracy was more than financial. While the ten-point charter is explicitly

Gramsci-inspired articles in the 1980s about the need for a 'new politics for new times'. Jacques's thinking proved to be influential in Labour circles during the development of New Labour. The phrase 'new times' went on to be used as the title of the magazine for Democratic Left in the 1990s.

* See Nick Cohen, 'Up for grabs: £3.5m of Stalin's gold', *New Statesman*, 23 October 2000.

† For more information on ACT see Paul Kingsnorth, 'Can "active citizens" transform British politics?', OpenDemocracy website, 14 July 2004.

concerned with institutional change, the NPN's vision of democracy was more focused on individuals and pluralism. The organisation's strap line was 'connecting people and politics', and that ethos has been retained in the new organisation. One of its sub-groups was Citizens for Europe, set up with the support of the late *Guardian* journalist Hugo Young, which was specifically concerned with how to develop a European 'demos'.* ACT may have been short lived as an organisation but it had a significant impact on Unlock Democracy, taking it back to its roots of enthusing people about change and seeking to create a mass movement.

The Sustainable Communities Act

Charter 88 has a proud history of being instrumental in the passage of key pieces of legislation – the Freedom of Information Act and the HRA, to name just two. The Sustainable Communities Act (SCA) stands out as a useful case study not just because it is one of our most recent achievements, but because it was passed on the back of a mass mobilisation campaign. It represents not just a highly desirable institutional reform but also an example of the way we want to achieve change.

It is not always immediately obvious to those interested in constitutional reform what sustainability has to do with them. In the case of the SCA, the short answer is: everything.

The Act was masterminded by Ron Bailey, now Unlock Democracy's campaigns director, who has been responsible for bringing together mass movements and coalitions that have been key to the passage of more than twenty-five pieces of legislation

---

* At the time of writing, Unlock Democracy continues to honour this relationship by helping to organise the annual Hugo Young Memorial Lectures. Past speakers of this series have included Philip Stevens (associate editor of the *Financial Times*), Gordon Brown, José Manuel Barroso (president of the European Commission) and Bill Keller (executive editor of the *New York Times*). The 2008 lecture is to be given by Peter Mandelson.

on a wide range of issues.* It gives new powers to communities and their elected councils to direct government policy to tackle local economic, social and environmental issues. Rather than being just another consultation exercise, or recycling tired rhetoric about community empowerment, this Act gives local communities real influence over what happens in their area.

For democratic reformers, this piece of legislation has two major appeals. Firstly, it is rooted in the very democratic notion that local people are the experts on their own areas and are liable to be able to come up with solutions that are far more practical and workable than anything Whitehall might want to impose on them. Secondly, the legislation is also concerned with the wider aspects of 'social wellbeing' and defines this to include 'participation in civic and political activity'. For reformers, this means that we now have in place a government process to argue for changes such as electoral reform at a local level.

The Act is not intended to deliver democratic renewal in one fell swoop, but it provides a mechanism for delivering real change. It is up to campaigning organisations like Unlock Democracy to motivate people to transform their communities by using the Act. It is all too easy to be cynical about these things and assume that people simply don't care. But, as the launch of Charter 88 demonstrated, the truth is that people do care and do take action when they believe that it will make a real difference. The SCA would never have been passed if tens of thousands of people hadn't cared enough to donate money, write to their MPs, persuade their councils to become involved, hold public meetings in their area to spread the word as well as attending rallies in, among other places, Dorset, London and Bolton.

The campaign was supported by 80 national organisations, 300 local organisations, more than 1,000 parish and town councils and tens of thousands of individuals. It united the Campaign for Real Ale (CAMRA) and the Women's Institute but, more significantly, it led to organisations like CAMRA sending out leaflets on the importance of local democracy and how to encourage

---

* See the early day motion EDM 1735 tabled by David Drew MP on 10 June 2008 for more information.

democratic participation. Like Charter 88, the SCA campaign went far beyond the usual suspects and engaged people in campaigning for democratic renewal who previously had not seen it as a priority.

The birth of Unlock Democracy, 2007

In the autumn of 2007 Charter 88 and the NPN formally merged to become Unlock Democracy. The name, chosen after extensive consultation and a ballot of all members, deliberately echoed Charter's earlier Unlocking Democracy campaign. Why drop the -*ing*? In part to give the name a sense of urgency, but also to be upfront about the need to take action. The NPN was a think tank; Unlock Democracy is not. The British state won't reform itself; we as citizens have to demand change. The role of Unlock Democracy, as spelled out in its constitution, is an attempt to marry Charter's hunger for institutional reform with the NPN's passion for popular participation. While the organisation's fundamental aim remains the achievement of a written constitution, in place of the list of specific reforms are broader calls for fair and open elections, transparency, empowerment and accountability.

Unlock Democracy has three main roles for the foreseeable future: to bridge the gap between democratic populists and democratic constitutionalists; to put pressure on the government for further reform as and when opportunities arise; and to continue to build support for more fundamental reforms such as a written constitution and proportional representation. By 'democratic populists' I mean those who are concerned that our present system does a poor job of representing the will of the people and who see anything that gets in the way as part of the problem (such as the judicial system and the 'accursed' HRA). By 'democratic constitutionalists' I mean those who seek to preserve and entrench rights and other limits on the state and are suspicious of popular opinion.

Back when Charter was first formed, the gulf between populists and constitutionalists either did not exist or was not apparent. The organisation embraced both aspects of democracy. The current political situation is vastly different. In the late 1980s, after a decade in power, the Conservatives were uninterested in any kind of democratic reform. Now they have embraced localism and more direct forms of democracy, while retaining their hostility to entrenched human rights and other constitutional artefacts.

Meanwhile, the human rights movement, battered by tabloid and political attacks and aware of post-9/11 anxieties, has spent most of the recent past defending what it has won rather than calling for further reforms. This is for entirely understandable reasons, but it has at times unfolded into suspicion of any suggestion of public engagement. For example, Liberty has argued against government plans to involve the public in drawing up a new British Bill of Rights, claiming that it would lead to a weakening of the protection currently provided by the HRA.*

Unlock Democracy is the only organisation in the UK that attempts to bridge that gulf. We remain fundamentally committed to human rights. Any Bill of Rights must include and preferably build on the HRA/European Convention on Human Rights. But we will continue to insist that the Bill of Rights must be owned by the people. We are keen to explore radical decentralisation and more direct forms of democracy while remaining clear that to avoid such measures from being abused we would need a codified constitution.

Opportunism in action

In 1997, one party swept into office with a large majority, seemingly poised to deliver our entire agenda. This is not likely to happen again soon. If we are to make progress, we will have to be opportunistic and prepared to work with people from across the political spectrum. This approach has already delivered significant

---

* 'Liberty is concerned that moves towards a new Bill of Rights for Britain would, in the current climate, be dominated by public, media and political pressure to weaken the protection currently provided by the HRA.' (Jago Russell, *Liberty's Response to the Joint Committee on Human Rights: 'A British Bill of Rights'* (London: Liberty, 2007), p. 4.)

results. In 2003 the opportunity to reform the House of Lords appeared to have been lost for a generation. In a confusing debacle of democracy, MPs rejected all seven options that they were offered. If it weren't for the persistence of individuals such as Billy Bragg and key reformers such as Robin Cook,* it is likely that all attempts at reform would have been abandoned. Charter 88 and the NPN launched the Elect the Lords campaign in 2004. While Bragg deserves great credit for keeping the issue alive within the Labour movement, without the cross-party support built up by Elect the Lords, it is distinctly possible that the 2007 House of Commons vote for Lords reform would have ended up a repeat of the 2003 fiasco.

During 2007–8 we have engaged fully with the Ministry of Justice's Governance of Britain programme up to and including the much-derided 'statement of values' project. It is understood that this is intended to form the preamble to the new Bill of Rights proposed by the government. We agree with the government that this is worth exploring. Preambles to declarations of rights, particularly those that explore the universalist values rooted in our shared humanity, are often more memorable and culturally significant than the wording of the individual declaration articles themselves. It is to be welcomed that the government is seeking to involve the public in this process. There are risks in this approach, as public involvement done badly can be very damaging, but it is all too easy to dismiss brave attempts to change the way we do politics as gimmicks. Unlock Democracy will work with the government to try and ensure that the public are meaningfully involved in the process.

At the same time we are actively seeking working relationships with Conservatives and exploring what might be achieved under

* It is impossible to reflect on the impact of Charter 88 and democratic reform in this period and not to recognise the influence of the late Robin Cook. For a tribute to Cook see Greg Power, 'Robin Cook and Constitutional Reform', *Citizen*, Spring 2008. Cook's analysis of the impact of the Cook–Maclennan agreement can be found in Robin Cook and Robert Maclennan, *Looking Back, Looking Forward: The Cook–Maclennan Agreement, Eight Years On* (London: New Politics Network, 2005).

a future Cameron-led government. The SCA was the result of a cross-party campaign over a five-year period, but the support of Nick Hurd, Oliver Letwin and David Cameron in passing the Act was vital. While the Liberal Democrats have always shared our belief in the need for radical constitutional change, they have often been shy about it. We were delighted therefore that Nick Clegg endorsed Unlock Democracy's call for a citizen-led constitutional convention as soon as he became party leader, and that he continues to make democratic renewal a key theme of his leadership.

Looking to the future, 2008 onwards

We may never have another moment like 1997 but what we do have for the first time is recognition from all three main political parties that there is a need for democratic renewal. Democracy is no longer just a centre-left issue and, notwithstanding the continual threats to human rights and civil liberties, that can only be a good thing for the future of the UK's governance.

Ultimately, however, it is crucial that while looking out for opportunities we do not lose sight of our fundamental goals. The reforms which would most improve British politics – electoral reform in the House of Commons and a written constitution – are the ones that will be most strongly resisted by the British political class. These reforms will not be given, only taken. This was Charter 88's greatest challenge, and it remains Unlock Democracy's. We have to build a strong grassroots movement and be prepared to go out and make the case for why these issues matter to every one of us. And we have to seize on controversial and topical events to show how the lack of a written constitution undermines the way we do politics.

That is why Charter 88 became involved in the campaign against identity cards, arguing that without a written constitution, UK citizens have insufficient protection against the progressive infringement of our liberties and rights by governments. Other countries that have identity cards, such as France and Germany, have this safeguard in place and are more cautious about the idea of building a database state.* We also intervened in the debate about whether there should be a referendum on the Lisbon treaty, arguing that it should not be up to the government to decide if a proposed law has constitutional implications or not, as such a decision will always be open to the charge of self-interest. Constitutional law should not be treated like standard legislation. Most EU countries insist on either a super-majority in Parliament or a referendum to ratify constitutional change.†

It is also why we took the decision to campaign in the Haltemprice & Howden by-election in July 2008. While we agree with David Davis that the erosion of civil liberties has gone too far,‡ for Unlock Democracy there is a more fundamental problem – the way in which the decision was taken. Even if you agree with extending pre-charge detention, you should be unnerved by the ease with which our rights and freedoms can be traded away on the floor of the House of Commons, in the face of such widespread opposition. The House of Lords would not be able to block this reform in the face of a determined government prepared to use the Parliament Act. These are the systemic problems that Unlock Democracy exists to highlight and ultimately to help the people of the UK solve.

---

* In Germany, for example, the Federal Constitutional Court ruled in 1983 that each individual had the right to 'information self-determination'. Data protection commissioners were therefore able to argue that the introduction of a unique identity number system would be incompatible with this right. As a result, the German ID Card Act of 1987 was obliged to contain detailed provisions to this effect.

† See Vaughne Miller, *European Union (Amendment) Bill (Bill 48 of 2007–08)*, Research Paper 08/03, House of Commons Library, 15 January 2008, pp. 20–28.

‡ On 12 June 2008 the Conservative MP David Davis, then the shadow Home Secretary, resigned his seat in protest at government plans to increase the time people suspected of involvement in terrorism offences could be detained without charge from twenty-eight days to forty-two. He did this in an attempt to start a national debate about what he saw as the erosion of civil liberties in the UK. Davis was re-elected as MP for Haltemprice & Howden on 11 July 2008. His resignation speech can be found on the Conservative Party website.

PART II

CURRENT ISSUES

Devolution in Scotland and Wales

Muddled thinking and unintended results

Alan Trench[*]

evolution was not central to the main thrust of Charter 88 when it was set up in 1988. Indeed, to today's readers the original charter has a very centralist, or Westminster-focused, feel. Although one of its demands was to 'guarantee an equitable distribution of power between the nations of the United Kingdom and between local, regional and central government', it was (and is) far from clear what that means. In hindsight, this approach is quite comprehensible – Charter 88, like many constitutional reformers, saw a different approach to territorial politics and relationships within the UK as part of the overall constitutional resettlement that was needed in the face of the centralisation and concentration of power which had taken place under the Thatcher governments. Its main focus, though, was on London institutions, and the work of Charter 88 developed largely separately from what was happening in Scotland (notably the Scottish Constitutional Convention, which first met in 1989) and Wales.[†]

---

[*] Research fellow, School of Law, University of Edinburgh; honorary senior research fellow, Constitution Unit, University College London.

[†] This chapter is concerned only with Scotland and Wales, not Northern Ireland, where devolution is only part of the institutional arrangements put in place as a result of the 1998 Good Friday Agreement and has had an interrupted history since then. Both the causes and development of devolution in Northern Ireland are significantly different from those in Great Britain.

Among the major shifts in political opinion in the 1980s was the conversion of many Scottish and Welsh Labour politicians to embrace devolution, when they had been neutral or hostile before – one of many changes wrought by the experience of the extended period of Tory rule. This was accompanied by a shift in the Scottish National Party (SNP) towards a 'gradualist' position away from seeking immediate outright independence, with devolution regarded as a helpful step along that path. The Liberal Democrats had long supported home rule in various forms too, so the result was that by 1997 there was a strong consensus of support for devolution among the main non-Conservative parties.

Any overall assessment of constitutional reform over the last twenty years would conclude that devolution for Scotland and Wales (and Northern Ireland) is one of the most significant areas where the Labour government has delivered constitutional change. In principle, devolution should have extended to England too – whether by elected regional government or some other change. But that did not materialise, and what we are left with is acutely asymmetrical. Despite the consensus that had formed behind devolution during the 1990s, devolution for Scotland and Wales has to be regarded as primarily a Labour project – and its strengths and weaknesses derive from how Labour conceived it and made it work. I shall argue that the confused understanding within Labour of what it was doing then has had serious consequences. I shall also suggest that if devolution is to deliver its promise, of enabling Scotland and Wales to have self-government within the United Kingdom (which is what people there appear to want), considerable changes in the institutional structure of devolution are needed, and needed urgently. These changes have been avoided up to now and seem very radical, but in truth they are not. They are simply the minimum needed to achieve what devolution was meant to accomplish, for the UK as a whole as well as for Scotland or Wales on its own.

Does devolution achieve what it was meant to?
Four conceptions and the reality

Devolution had a remarkably smooth ride when it came to be put into place in the late 1990s. Labour had a huge parliamentary majority, considerable public support and an extended honeymoon both in public opinion and from the mass media (and consequently high expectations). It also had a good deal of goodwill from the civil service, because it was offering them new things to do and had political energy – both of which had been lacking under the last years of the Major administration. But there were also tight limits on how much the new government could spend, thanks to its acceptance of Conservative spending plans. This meant that devolution became one of the main visible activities of government as a whole in its first few months in office – and the momentum it acquired meant that the underlying flaws in what was being proposed were never identified or resolved. Nor had they been picked up during the previous months and years, when the political struggles to secure devolution had focused on establishing an adequate sphere of devolved autonomy (in Scotland) and building support within the Labour Party and between Labour and the other opposition parties (in Wales). That meant that wider questions about the proposed changes for the working of the UK as a whole, or even bilateral relations between UK-wide and devolved institutions, were never considered. By the time devolution became a matter for the UK government machine, the only issues that it could engage with were technical. These were resolved (and generally rather well); but the underlying conceptual difficulties were not.

Chief among these were what devolution was meant to do and how it was intended to work on a UK-wide basis. With hindsight, one can discern four distinct purposes. These were seldom all discussed at the same time – no-one ever said 'this is what devolution was meant to achieve', not least because these purposes appealed to very different audiences and were not entirely consistent with one another. The first two were public and official, and can be seen in documents such as the devolution

White Papers.* The others were formulated and discussed more privately but clearly were factors for politicians in inducing them to support devolution.

First, devolution would create a **distinct democratic voice for Scotland and Wales**, through the new parliament and assembly. This would, in principle, redress the 'democratic deficit' that had arisen under Conservative rule, but which had vanished as most Scottish and Welsh MPs were now part of the governing majority at Westminster. It would also bring government closer to voters in a way that could be connected to other aspects of New Labour's 'modernising' agenda.

The second purpose was about the practice of government, by providing for **local control of public policy**. This took two forms. For economic matters, there was a limited conferral of powers for economic development, but within a single UK-wide economy. Macro-economic (interest rates, taxation, currency decisions) and micro-economic policy (business regulation, the labour market, employment law) were reserved to Westminster, and so devolved powers amounted to an exhortation to try to do better than the UK as whole, not a licence to use devolved institutions to create a distinctive Scottish or Welsh economy. For functions such as health, education or housing, this control was supposed to operate within a UK-wide welfare state, which would imply the different administration of common (UK- or Britain-wide) policies. So Scotland or Wales could run its National Health Service in a different way, with political account-ability to its own legislature and ministers, not Westminster or UK ministers – but there would still be a recognisable cross-UK NHS.

The third and fourth purposes were more nakedly political, and taken together their aim was to entrench Labour's political position – a strategy that could recruit support from other parties too, for different parts of it. The third gained support chiefly from the Liberal Democrats, and was to **undermine political nationalism** by satisfying the demand for self-government. As George Robertson once brutally put it, the aim was to 'kill

* Scottish Office, *Scotland's Parliament*, Cm 3658, 1997; Welsh Office, *A Voice for Wales: The Government's Proposals for a Welsh Assembly*, Cm 3718, 1997.

nationalism stone dead' and strengthen the Labour Party in Scotland and Wales at the respective expense of the SNP and Plaid Cymru. This would help Labour tactically, as well as in the larger goal of keeping Scotland in the Union (vital if Labour were to be able to win UK elections, for which it needs a substantial number of Scottish and Welsh seats).

The fourth goal embraced many supporters of nationalist parties as well as Labour and Liberal Democrats: to **create a bulwark against the return of a Conservative government**, so that a repetition of the situation of the 1980s and 1990s would not be possible. Devolved government would serve as a barrier to the imposition by Westminster of Conservative policies that did not attract support in Scotland or Wales, because the devolved institutions would have responsibility for many aspects of policy that mattered most on the day-to-day level.

The problem was that the institutional design of devolution did none of these things – and its main shortcoming was not how radical it was, but how timid. While devolution created elected legislatures for Scotland and Wales and gave them a good deal of power, it did not give them exclusive powers. Devolution as put in place in 1997 was not in any sense a form of federalism, with two distinct orders of government each having its own powers and being constitutionally and practically able to act independently of the other. Nor does it involve a system of delegated decision-making and limited authority, with Westminster setting a broad framework within which each part of the UK has authority to develop more detailed approaches. (That might have made sense in policy terms, but not politically – it would have been unacceptable to much of public opinion in Scotland or Wales, not least because it failed to create a bulwark against a future Conservative government.) Instead, Westminster remained formally and legally sovereign, and has continued to have a huge influence over politics across the whole UK. This is partly a result of England's size and importance, with 85 per cent of the UK's population and slightly more of its gross domestic product. But it also reflects a degree of institutional overlap and interpenetration between devolved and non-devolved functions. Finance remains in the UK government's hands, and although block grants give the devolved a great deal of spending autonomy, they also remain tied in to UK funding decisions and the UK public finance system. Then there are interactions between the social security system and devolved functions such as health or education, where, for example, Scottish policies for long-term care for the elderly have already caused problems and plans for a local income tax to replace council tax would cause more (because of uncertainty over continued funding for council tax benefit – see below). And in any case Westminster remains active as a legislature, for devolved as well as non-devolved functions: for all parts of the UK, thanks to the Sewel convention, which provides for Westminster to legislate for devolved matters provided the devolved legislature consents, and as the only legislature for Wales until May 2007 (and even since then it has been responsible for deciding, on a case-by-case basis, whether legislative powers should be conferred on the National Assembly). The system created by devolution was one of many overlaps and shared policies, where it was necessary for governments to get and to find ways of working with, or around, each other.

That was relatively easy (perhaps too easy) while Labour was still in office across Great Britain. Common Labour interests meant they found ways to resolve problems, and Labour politicians in one government were usually keen to avoid embarrassing their counterparts in another if they possibly could. But that ceased to be the case in May 2007; worse yet, an SNP government in Scotland is simply not interested in the common unionist outlook that Labour shares with the Liberal Democrats and Conservatives, while Plaid Cymru's presence as the junior partner in coalition with Labour means that many in Welsh Labour feel they have lost a good deal of power even while they remain in office.

But it is hard to see how devolution could succeed in attaining any of those four initial objectives. Giving Scotland and Wales a voice of their own was (and is) important. It was a way of acknowledging their distinctive nature, to be sure, and that recognition in, and for, itself is valuable. But its value is abstract, not tangible, and it does not achieve the more immediate political goals that underlie devolution. Albert Hirschman has compellingly showed, in a wide range of contexts, the importance of 'voice' – the sense that one can express views and have them taken into account by decision makers. But voice is important more because of what it is linked to than in itself. Views given voice can breed loyalty, and cement a damaged relationship, if those giving voice feel they have been heard and the organisation has responded, or at least sought to respond. If their views are rejected, the outcome is likely to be 'exit'.* In this context, the question is: what ensures that the voice is heard? For voice to breed loyalty would imply taking steps to ensure that the voice was heard at UK level and had an influence there. As I shall argue later on, that appears to be what public opinion wants too. In practical terms, that would mean ensuring links between the UK government and the devolved administrations so that they could speak up for Scotland or Wales. Westminster's shortcomings in playing this role were already apparent. But the new inter-institutional relationships were only thought about late in the process of making devolution happen, and were limited and only lightly institutionalised when they emerged. Links, whether between governments or legislatures, remained informal and largely ad hoc or personal. In practice most of these institutional mechanisms quickly fell into disuse, with most functional formats of the Joint Ministerial Committee (JMC) ceasing to meet after 2001 (the Europe format is the main exception), and no meetings of the plenary form of the JMC from October 2002 – despite a formal requirement for it to meet annually. The Scottish Parliament and the National Assembly for Wales may be voices for Scotland and Wales – but only in those nations, not on a broader UK stage, and without acting on that broader stage as well they cannot have the political impact they were meant to.

That is not the only way devolution has not worked as intended. Unsurprisingly, the devolved institutions have used their policy-making powers to develop distinctive approaches to policy. So far, these remain largely variations on a UK-wide theme, but the variations are growing and the theme becoming

---

* Albert O. Hirschman, *Exit, Voice, and Loyalty: Responses to Decline in Firms, Organizations, and States* (Cambridge, MA: Harvard University Press, 1970).

more indistinct. We do not have 'common services differently administered' but different services that resemble each other less and less. The scope of devolved powers, the political restraints that stop the UK government using its powers to constrain them and a permissive financial environment have led Scott Greer to dub this arrangement a 'fragile divergence machine'.* In the area of health services, Greer has found that even by 2003 there were in effect four different health services across the UK, each making policy in very different ways that were starting to have appreciable effects on how they worked on the ground as well. Those differences in policy have become more dramatic as time has gone by: long-term care for the elderly in Scotland, and grants to cover a large part of fees for Welsh-resident students going to university in Wales, are just two examples. (Ironically, the extent to which services do resemble each other also means it is easy for citizens to see the differences between them and draw adverse comparisons, for example about different treatments available on the NHS depending on where one happens to live. That makes the political implications of differentiation even harder to manage.)

The constraints on divergence are important, however. They are partly financial (important as growth in public spending has slowed), partly legal and administrative (devolved action can be blocked, not just for exceeding devolved powers but for being contrary to various, mainly security-related, UK-wide interests), partly party political. The overall impact, however, is that social and domestic policies vary, in ways that only make sense to those with a detailed knowledge of the constitutional and administrative framework of devolution. That is fine for academics and civil servants, but to the general public, journalists and indeed politicians outside government, it is unclear why some areas of government activity are devolved and others are not. The explanations are convoluted and technical, not rooted in general

---

* For a brief discussion, see Scott Greer, *Four Way Bet: How Devolution Has Led to Four Different Models for the NHS* (London: Constitution Unit, University College London, 2004); for a longer one, see Scott Greer, *Territorial Politics and Health Policy: UK Health Policy in Comparative Perspective* (Manchester: Manchester University Press, 2004).

principles. A general consequence has been the haphazard fragmentation of a sense of UK-wide social citizenship, but without any adequate replacement by Scottish, Welsh or English equivalents.*

Despite all this, devolution fails to act as a bulwark for the welfare state in Scotland or Wales against a possible Conservative government in London. The limitations on the powers of the devolved governments and legislatures mean that there are many things they might want to do but cannot, at least not on their own – they need co-operation from the UK government and parliament if they are actually to be able to shape policy.† The dependence of Scotland and Wales on the UK level is simply too great. Finance is particularly important here. As changes to the block grants for Scotland or Wales are determined by changes in spending on 'comparable functions' for England, significant changes in English public spending feed through to Scotland and Wales. This is pretty benign when spending grows (as it did in the early 2000s), but less so if growth in spending stalls, let alone if it is reversed. And if the balance of spending in England were to change significantly – if private funding came to assume a greater role in health or education, for example – the size of the devolved block grants would again be affected.‡ The devolved governments would have to face hard choices: either largely to follow the English policy, however much they might dislike it, or to make serious cuts elsewhere to protect social programmes. If London fails to co-operate with proposed changes in policy from Scotland or Wales, it can also seriously disrupt devolved policy-making

---

* This is discussed at greater length in Scott Greer (ed.), *Devolution and Social Citizenship in the UK* (Bristol: Policy Press, forthcoming).

† This is explored in detail in Alan Trench (ed.), *Devolution and Power in the United Kingdom* (Manchester: Manchester University Press, 2007), particularly chapters 3 and 8.

‡ An area where this is already happening is higher education, thanks to the increased resources flowing to universities in England, Wales and Northern Ireland but not Scotland. This is due to the UK government's policy of deferred variable fees – a flow that may increase considerably if, or when, the fees cap is raised.

when there is an interaction with non-devolved matters, most notably social security. The row in the spring of 2008 about council tax benefit in Scotland (and whether the funds that underpin the benefit would be available to the Scottish government if the Scottish Parliament were to replace council tax with a local income tax) vividly illustrates the sorts of problems that can arise.

When it comes to its political aims – to keep nationalists out of power generally, and to limit the impact a Conservative UK government might have – devolution similarly does not do what was expected. The goal of undermining support for nationalism was only achieved at the 2003 devolved elections, but Labour's poor showing in the 2007 elections would appear to be the first step in a more serious decline. In Wales, Labour has few ideas that distinguish it from the other parties there (as not many object to 'progressive universalism', the position it sought to embrace when Rhodri Morgan decided to put 'clear red water' between Welsh Labour and UK Labour). During 2009 it will also have to find a new leader, and new energy. In Scotland, there was no serious attempt to set out what Scottish Labour was for until November 2007, and what was proposed then by Wendy Alexander in her St Andrew's Day lecture was underdeveloped in both political and policy terms, and profoundly contentious within the party (whether within Scotland or at Westminster).* Despite its flaws and her resignation, it still offers the clearest idea of what the progressive brand of unionism could look like, recognising Scottish distinctiveness within the UK. The party also faces the challenge of losing its electoral and institutional bases in local government, following the introduction of single transferable vote for council elections – a change that will also have an impact on local party organisation.

Despite their longstanding support for devolution, the Liberal Democrats have not been able to take advantage of the opportunities it offers either, thanks partly to deliberate choices and partly to some poor internal decision-making. One of the

---

* Wendy Alexander, 'A New Agenda for Scotland', speech at University of Edinburgh, 30 November 2007.

ironies of devolution is that the parties to have benefited from it most are the two nationalist parties and the Conservatives. Both Plaid Cymru and the SNP struggled for a few years to make sense of how to operate in the new political environment, reflected in their comparatively poor showings in the 2003 elections. This is not surprising; they had, after all, each achieved a major medium-term goal, and that called for a tactical if not strategic rethink which then needed to be communicated to the public. With time, problems in each set of devolution arrangements started to become apparent, and dissatisfaction with Labour grew. As the second-largest parties in the Welsh Assembly and the Scottish Parliament, it is not surprising that Plaid Cymru and the SNP were poised to become beneficiaries of Labour's decline when that happened.

What is surprising is that Labour appears to have been unaware that sooner or later it would lose an election and the nationalist parties would be the most likely winners when that happened. With hindsight, this is a strategic blunder for Labour of staggering proportions. It failed to prevent defeat by a party that sought to undermine its fundamental interests. Instead, its only response (manifest in the 2007 election campaigns) was negative: to try to stigmatise the nationalist parties, especially in Scotland, as divisive and not committed to the best interests of people in Scotland or Wales – arguments which at best halted growth in public support for nationalist parties, but certainly did not reverse it.* The upshot was that Labour lost office in Scotland and was forced into coalition in Wales, with the parties it least wished to see gain at its expense – and in doing so it lost authority, and to a significant degree control of events.

Underlying this is a major difference in perspective about devolution. One of the most quoted sayings about devolution is

---

* I have argued elsewhere that the redefinition of politics as 'Scottish' or 'Welsh' also structurally advantaged the nationalist parties as those best able to stand up for Scotland or Wales. See Alan Trench, 'Scotland and Wales: The Evolution of Devolution', in Robert Hazell (ed.), *Constitutional Futures Revisited: Britain's Constitution to 2020* (Basingstoke: Palgrave Macmillan, 2008).

that of Ron Davies, former secretary of state for Wales, that 'devolution is a process, not an event'. For Scotland as well as Wales, that has been true – devolution has been about developing institutions and patterns of self-government where none had existed for a very long time, and by its nature it has been evolutionary. But for UK institutions, it was the other way round, an event, not a process. Devolution 'happened' in 1999, and by 2001 the UK government and parliament had stopped dealing with territorial issues on any but the most technical of levels. Warnings that further action was required, and that Westminster and Whitehall needed to engage in this process of change, went unheeded.*

Because the purpose of devolution was not clear at the outset, and that design was not related to the institutional design, devolution has changed the UK state much less than anyone might have expected in late 1980s or early 1990s. It is one of the ironies of fate that the main victim of this, in both the short and the long term, is the Labour Party. Devolution may be a Labour accomplishment, but its failure to be rooted in a broader strategic vision for the UK as a whole has meant that its delivery was incomplete and in some cases half-hearted. From a Labour point of view, it is a story of missed opportunities to entrench gains that had been made, or to confront difficult choices. And the consequence of that is that Labour is out of office in Scotland, on the back foot in Wales, and looking at a serious loss of power bases if, or when, the Conservatives regain office in London.

What the public want

The best public opinion data we have derives from academic surveys carried out for Scottish Social Attitudes in Scotland and a number of similar organisations in Wales, which have been

---

* Two notable Parliamentary examples are House of Commons Select Committee on Procedure, *The Procedural Consequences of Devolution*, fourth report, Session 1998–99, HC 185; House of Lords Select Committee on the Constitution, *Devolution: Inter-Institutional Relations in the United Kingdom*, second report, Session 2002–03, HL 28.

conducted regularly in both countries since 1997 (see Tables 1 and 2). For both Scotland and Wales, these surveys show a strong preference for those nations having extensive self-government within the United Kingdom, preferences which have if anything become stronger since 1999 – but with only limited support, even in Scotland, for independence.

Other survey evidence suggests that people in England are happy for Scotland and Wales to have devolution without seeking it for England.*

Table 1: Constitutional preferences in Scotland, 1999–2007 (%)

Scotland should ...	... be independent, separate from UK and EU or separate from UK but part of EU	... remain part of UK with its own elected parliament which has some taxation powers	... remain part of the UK with its own elected parliament which has no taxation powers	... remain part of the UK without an elected parliament
May 1997	28	44	10	18
Sep 1997	37	32	9	17
1999	28	50	8	10
2000	30	47	8	12
2001	27	54	6	9
2002	30	44	8	12
2003	26	48	7	13
2004	32	40	5	17
2005	35	38	6	14
2006	30	47	7	9
2007	23	55	8	10

The two independence options, one where Scotland remains within the European Union, and one where it does not, were offered to respondents separately. The first row of the table shows the combined total choosing either option.

Source: Scottish Election Study 1997; Scottish Referendum Study 1997; Scottish Social Attitudes Survey 1999–2007. Data for 2007 is provisional. Published in Charlie Jeffery (ed.), *Scotland Devolution Monitoring Report, January 2008* (London: Constitution Unit, University College London, 2008), p. 40.

---

* See generally John Curtice, 'Public Opinion and the Future of Devolution', in Alan Trench (ed.), *The Dynamics of Devolution: The State of the Nations 2005* (Exeter: Imprint Academic, 2005), particularly Table 6.12.

Table 2: Constitutional preferences in Wales, 1997–2007 (%)

Wales should ...	... be independent, separate from UK and EU or separate from UK but part of EU	... remain part of UK with its own elected assembly which has some law-making and taxation powers	... remain part of the UK with its own elected assembly which has limited law-making powers only	... remain part of the UK without an elected assembly
1997	14.1	19.6	26.8	39.5
1999	9.6	29.9	35.3	25.3
2001	12.3	38.8	25.5	24.0
2003	13.9	37.8	27.1	21.2
2006	11.5	42.1	25.0	21.3
2007	12.2	43.8	27.5	16.5

Source: Welsh Referendum Study 1997; Welsh Assembly Election Study 1999; Welsh Life and Times Survey 2001, 2003, 2006; Welsh Election Survey 2007; published in Richard Wyn Jones and Roger Scully (eds), *Wales Devolution Monitoring Report, January 2008* (London: Constitution Unit, University College London, 2008), p. 68.

But devolution has also, clearly, not gone far enough for people in Scotland or Wales. This is clearly shown in another set of questions from the same surveys, which seek to relate the level of government that people think should be most powerful with the one that they think actually is. These results are shown in Tables 3 and 4, and indicate a considerable disparity for both Scotland and Wales, about 40 percentage points, between the two levels. In each case the respondents thought that devolved government should be most important but that in fact the UK government is most important.

What we therefore now face is a situation where the original design of devolution has not done what it was intended to on a UK-wide basis, and fails to deliver what the people of Scotland and Wales have clearly said that they want as well. Such a situation cannot carry on indefinitely – especially when the Scottish government is keen to seek independence and has conducted itself skilfully in advancing its objectives. People want more influence for the devolved bodies, not less, and if the union is to succeed, the UK institutions need to respond by working out how to

**Table 3: Who ought to have most influence over the way Scotland is run?
Who actually has most influence over the way Scotland is run? (%)**

	Who ought to have...?				Who actually has...?			
	European Union	UK government	Scottish Parliament/ Executive	Local councils	European Union	UK government	Scottish Parliament/ Executive	Local councils
2000	1	13	72	10	4	66	13	10
2001	1	14	74	8	7	66	15	9
2003	1	20	66	9	5	64	17	7
2004	1	12	67	17	6	48	19	19
2005	1	13	67	15	8	47	23	15
2006	1	11	64	19	11	38	24	18

Source: Scottish Social Attitudes surveys, 2000–2006, published in Charlie Jeffery
(ed.), *Scotland Devolution Monitoring Report, January 2008* (London: Constitution
Unit, University College London, 2008), pp. 45–6.

**Table 4: Who ought to have most influence over the way Wales is run? Who
actually has most influence over the way Wales is run? (%)**

	Who ought to have...?				Who actually has...?			
	European Union	UK government	National Assembly for Wales	Local councils	European Union	UK government	National Assembly for Wales	Local councils
2001	1	26	56	17	3	64	17	16
2003	1	29	56	14	5	58	22	15
2007	0	18	74	8	6	53	36	5

Source: Welsh Life and Times Survey 2001, 2003; Life in Wales Survey 2007;
published in Richard Wyn Jones and Roger Scully (eds), *Wales Devolution
Monitoring Report, January 2008* (London: Constitution Unit, University College
London, 2008), p. 69.

deliver that – and to do so within a UK-wide framework, not one
that responds bilaterally to concerns from Scotland or Wales.

Instead, we now find ourselves in the midst of a sequence of
fragmented constitutional reviews of limited scope. In Wales, the
All Wales Convention, chaired by Sir Emyr Jones Parry, is to
consider whether a referendum should be held to bring in the
'primary legislative powers' set out in Part 4 of the Government
of Wales Act 2006, and what further steps might be needed if that
were to happen. The One Wales coalition agreement between

Labour and Plaid Cymru commits the assembly government to seeking a referendum by 2011 at the latest, however. In Scotland, the Scottish government's National Conversation on constitutional options, including independence, has failed to develop much beyond a blog.* The unionist parties have responded by setting up the Commission on Scottish Devolution, chaired by Sir Kenneth Calman, under the aegis of both the Scottish Parliament and the UK government. The commission's remit expressly excludes independence and its composition suggests it will be very hard for it to reach any sort of consensus.†
The Calman commission is expected to produce an interim report by November 2008 and a final one around May 2009. But only when that report is passed to the UK government will a UK-wide view of the issues intrude, and only in Wales (where the All Wales Convention is seeking to engage with the public in a number of interesting ways) is there a serious and imaginative attempt to involve non-party interests in the process. And there is a timing issue too: if the UK government starts to consider its response in the summer of 2009, once the Calman commission has reported, it will have no more than a year to decide what to do and act on it before the next UK general election. One has to question whether that can be done – so either the UK government will have made its mind up before Calman reports, or the report is likely to be for an incoming (and quite possibly Conservative) government to deal with.

It is a sad comment on Labour's constitutional management that what should have been one of its crowning, if slow-developing, achievements may have failed to deliver any of its expected political benefits. It is worse that this failure should also have put the union (which it was meant to preserve) at risk, and with it Labour's ability to win Westminster elections.

A further irony is that tackling these problems would be unlikely to trigger much by way of English hostility – or even promote demands for a similar response from England. The British Social Attitudes surveys have consistently found that

---

* See www.scotland.gov.uk/topics/a-national-conversation.
† See www.commissiononscottishdevolution.org.uk.

Table 5: English views on devolution for Scotland and Wales, 1997–2003 (%)

	Scotland should…				Wales should…			
	…be independent, separate from UK and EU or separate from UK but part of EU	…remain part of the UK with its own elected parliament which has some law-making and taxation powers	…remain part of the UK with its own elected parliament which has no taxation powers	…remain part of the UK without an elected parliament	…be independent, separate from UK and EU or separate from UK but part of EU	…remain part of the UK with its own elected parliament which has some law-making and taxation powers	…remain part of the UK with its own elected assembly which has limited law-making powers only	…remain part of the UK without an elected assembly
1997	14	38	17	23	13	37	18	25
1999	24	44	10	13	20	34	22	15
2000	20	44	8	17	17	35	17	20
2001	19	53	7	11	17	39	19	14
2003	17	51	9	13	16	37	20	15

Source: British Social Attitudes Survey 1997–2003, reported in Curtice, 'Public Opinion and the Future of Devolution,' in Alan Trench (ed.), *The Dynamics of Devolution: The State of the Nations 2005* (Exeter: Imprint Academic, 2005), Table 6.12.

people in England are happy about devolution for Scotland and Wales but have little interest in it for themselves (see Tables 5 and 6). While there is some (slowly growing) support for change (whether for regional government or an English parliament), that support remains limited and divided.

Table 6: Constitutional preferences for England, 1999–2006 (%)

Respondents were asked: With all the changes going on in the way different parts of Great Britain are run, which of the following do you think would be best for England?

	England should be governed as it is now, with laws made by the UK parliament	Each region of England should have its own assembly that runs services like health	England as a whole should have its own new parliament with law-making powers
1999	62	15	18
2003	55	24	16
2006	54	17	22

Data for some years (2000, 2001, 2002, 2004, 2005) omitted.

Source: British Social Attitudes, 1999–2006, abstracted from John Curtice, *Where Stands the Union Now? Lessons from the 2007 Scottish Parliament Election* (London: Institute for Public Policy Research, 2008), Table 7.

What does this mean now?

This suggests that it is now urgent for supporters of the union to think fast, and act intelligently, if a reformed version is to survive into the second decade of the twenty-first century. This applies whatever complexion of government is in London – but UK institutions in London need to understand how much, and how rapidly, the situation has changed and is changing in Scotland and Wales, and how little control London now has over events. This problem arises partly because the UK government has stubbornly pursued a strategy that does not actually work. Simple confrontation with the SNP will not succeed, because the SNP government is regarded in Scotland as pretty popular and effective – and even more important, it is the government that the people voted for as recently as May 2007.

So what should London do now if it wishes to preserve the United Kingdom as a whole while delivering on the promise of devolution to improve accountability and democratic control of government across all parts of the UK? Sorting out the government of England is hard, not least because it is hard to know what form of government the English really want that they do not have (although there are clear demands for more local control of government, which might provide a partial answer). But as far as relations between the UK institutions and Scotland and Wales are concerned, my suggestions are these:

- London – the UK government and parliament – needs to take the lead. Westminster and Whitehall need to do so carefully and thoughtfully, to be sensitive to the interests and concerns of all parts of the UK. They cannot be driven by considerations of party political advantage. The pursuit of party advantage, whether under the Conservatives between 1979 and 1997 or Labour since 1997, has led to where we are now.

- UK institutions must take on a conscious and active role in managing the territory of the UK as a whole, rather than trusting to inertia or luck. Taking on such a role does not mean trying to assume central control of the UK – in fact it means the opposite: central institutions need to accept and embrace devolution as a means of recognising the national and territorial diversity of the UK, not try to impose a uniformity that is not desired and which would prompt a huge counter-reaction. Devolution is an attempt at a halfway house to preserve the UK. The continued existence of the UK cannot be taken for granted nor achieved by practising crude partisan politics.

- UK institutions need to accept that there are many worse things than a peaceful break-up of the union. The union is simply not worth defending as an absolute good. To preserve a reluctant union by use of institutional power would be worse than dismantling it. That would end up undermining the legitimacy of government in all parts of Great Britain. If the union is not based on the consent of its members, freely given, it has lost not just its legitimacy but also its *raison d'être*.

If it exists, it must be because its members are better off together than they are apart. A reform plan needs to be rooted in asking the question 'what is the union for?' and finding sensible and convincing answers.

- Those answers need to relate to the institutions of the union and to be embodied in institutional form. So far, the position of both main parties has been that the union has to survive because the union has to survive – which intellectually is nonsense. Accompanying this with rhetoric about 'British values' is little better, not least because there is nothing uniquely British about a belief in free speech, fair play or the rule of law. These are common to all meaningful democracies, including many that once were (but no longer are) governed from Westminster.

- Delivering all this will require an energetic programme of institutional reform. Such reforms have been ducked up to now, because they are somewhat inconvenient. If they had been taken up, life would now be easier. Avoiding them is no longer an option if the union is to survive. Such reforms will need to include:

  > Reconstructing the financial system, to ensure that the funding of the devolved governments is not dependent on spending in England but is a separate stream. Such a reform should also give meaningful (but not absolute) fiscal autonomy to the devolved governments, in a framework that also seeks to balance UK-wide interests of equity with devolved autonomy.

  > Reforming the division of powers, so that devolved and non-devolved functions do not get in each other's way. That will also necessitate extensive reorganisation and procedural reform in Whitehall, to ensure that departments and officials know which matters are devolved and where. The UK government has created a convoluted system, a confusing division of powers and an informal and uninstitutionalised way of making that work. It cannot combine that with preserving the union.

> Reforming procedures at Westminster, again to distinguish between devolved and non-devolved business. The introduction of proportional representation would be advisable too; it offers the best hope of minimising the impact of the 'West Lothian question' in a union parliament that must, by definition, represent all parts of the union.

Reforming the House of Lords

Bhikhu Parekh

Being an integral part of our constitutional structure, the House of Lords is bound up with its other institutions in highly complex ways. Its reform therefore cannot be discussed in isolation from their powers and functions, especially those of the House of Commons, its legislative twin. The latter has since the early twentieth century enjoyed pre-eminence, primacy or superiority in the sense that the government of the day is appointed from and removable by it, and that it alone has the power to levy taxes and decide financial matters. Its pre-eminence is even embodied in our language. Though Parliament includes both Houses, only a member of the House of Commons is called a member of Parliament, a symbolic but eloquent linguistic legacy.

The pre-eminence of the House of Commons

It is widely argued that the House of Commons should continue to enjoy its current pre-eminence for at least two important reasons. First, it is a precipitate, a hard-won achievement, of our democratic struggle, is deeply woven into our political culture and habits of thought, and lies at the basis of our political system. Unscrambling it would cause considerable dislocation and disorientation, and would virtually amount to radically redesigning our political system. Such an exercise would take decades to secure consensus, and would in the meantime create great political uncertainty.

Second, it is argued that the pre-eminence of the Commons

has also much to be said for it. Unlike the presidential and symmetrically bicameral systems of government, it simplifies the political system by locating ultimate political authority in a single body. It also ensures transparency and accountability in the sense that we know who is in charge of making public policy and governing the country, and who is to blame if things go wrong. The electorate is in no doubt what to expect if it elected a particular political party, and is able to make clear choices.*

Although these arguments are not conclusive and one can in theory make out an equally good case for the parity of powers between the two Houses, they are not devoid of merit. Constitutional decisions do not occur in a historical and cultural vacuum. We must start from where we are and take full account of the country's history, traditions and political culture. The pre-eminence of the Commons is not only a historical fact but also has some of the advantages claimed on its behalf, and is no worse than its alternatives. The fact that the bulk of the British public opinion values it and does not wish to replace it provides a further reason in its favour. Any politically realistic and historically sensitive discussion of the reform of the House of Lords must therefore begin by accepting the pre-eminence of the Commons as its basic and currently non-negotiable premise.

Since this pre-eminence is so central to the debate, we should be clear about what it means and implies, as otherwise we remain vulnerable to the manipulations of those who use it to impose arbitrary or ideologically convenient limits on the reform of the Lords. As I observed earlier, it basically means three things. First, the government of the day must enjoy the confidence of the House of Commons, and the latter alone has the power to remove it. Second, the Commons alone has the final legislative authority, which is derived directly from the British people. The Lords may not altogether reject, or delay indefinitely, legislative measures initiated by the government, especially those for which it has a popular mandate, a practice safeguarded by the Parliament Act and the

---

* See Philip Norton, 'Adding Value? The Role of Second Chambers', *Asia Pacific Law Review* (2007), vol. 15, pp. 3–18. I thank Prof. Norton for discussing with me some of the basic arguments of this paper.

Salisbury convention. Third, the Commons alone has the authority to levy taxes and determine the allocation of public resources.

All this requires that the Prime Minister and other senior ministers should belong to the Commons so that they can be questioned, asked to explain their policies, chastised and, if necessary, denied its confidence. The pre-eminence of the Commons does not mean that senior ministers and even the Prime Minister may not appear regularly in the Lords to answer questions, as they do in India and several other parliamentary democracies, that the Lords may not express its views on financial matters, or that it may not enjoy powers unavailable to the Commons. We may or may not introduce these and other practices. But if we decide to do so, it is not ruled out by the doctrine of the pre-eminence of the Commons.

The question, then, is what we want the House of Lords to do, subject to the pre-eminence of the Commons; that is, what its role, powers and functions should be such that it does things the latter does not do, or does not do well, on its own. Some of its functions are the same as those of all second chambers, others are necessitated by the distinct character of the British political system.

The role of the House of Lords

The House of Lords obviously scrutinises and revises legislation, and ensures that the laws passed are carefully thought through, mutually consistent and procedurally proper; that they conform to human rights and other basic constitutional norms; and that they represent effective and proportionate ways of realising clearly stated objectives. Since MPs have heavy constituency duties and are subject to populist pressures, they are unable to give legislation as much careful and detailed attention as it deserves, and that increases the responsibility of the Lords. The House, for example, spent fifty-three hours considering the Anti-Terrorism, Crime and Security Bill in November–December 2001, and made substantial and important amendments many of which were accepted by both the Commons and the government alike. The House of Commons has select committees that cover government departments. By contrast the House of Lords' committees cover broad issues that cut across departmental boundaries, notably science and technology, economic affairs and the constitution. This enables it to take a different and broader view of the subject in question.

The Lords also holds the government accountable and critically examines its actions and policies. Since the partisan character of the Commons ensures that the official opposition does this job rather well, the role of the Lords in this respect is largely secondary but no less important. During the past ten years it has blocked plans to restrict jury trials, to create a new offence of incitement to religious hatred and to reorganise local government. It has forced defeats on the government on important issues, and nearly a third of these, which related to policy matters, were accepted by the government in whole or in part.

Weaknesses of the House of Commons

Although, and partly because, the Commons is democratically elected, it is not representative of the full range of views, voices and interests. Political parties put up candidates who are likely to win elections, and tend to select those who are safe and acceptable to both the party hierarchy and the electorate. As a result, women, ethnic and religious minorities, the disabled and others do not find their way into the Commons in numbers corresponding to their presence in the country at large. Their presence in Parliament is important to protect the interests and express the views of the minorities concerned, and their number should be broadly pro-portionate to ensure a critical mass and to reflect their strength in the country. Since the Commons suffers from this representa-tional deficit, the Lords attempts to redress it. While the Commons, for example, has fifteen members from ethnic minorities, mostly Labour, the Lords has more than twenty, distributed among all three parties and on the crossbenches.

Many men and women have a great contribution to make to political life by virtue of their expertise in different areas, public standing, proven record of public service, or their reputation for courage, integrity and judgement. Our political life would be infinitely poorer without them, especially as it sometimes has a tendency to attract the opposite kinds of people. Such men and women are often unlikely to brave the hassle of elections and, if they do, they are unlikely to win. The Lords is their ideal home. It is true that experts can be brought in as witnesses or employed as ministerial or departmental advisers, but they are likely to carry more weight and exercise greater influence if they are also members of the Lords and able to shape the thinking of their peers through formal and informal interactions.

The Upper House and devolution

The House of Commons is largely preoccupied with matters of immediate importance or those that catch media headlines. It does not have the time or the inclination to deliberate on long-term trends in British society or the larger implications of government policy. We need a structured space where deliberation rather than debate, rational reflection rather than political polemics, is prized, and where members patiently explore where British society is going, what problems it is likely to throw up in the future, and how best to tackle them. The House of Lords provides such a space. Even when it has fewer constitutional powers, it can wield the far more important power of ideas. It is difficult to think of any second chamber in the world that can boast more than a dozen distinguished and currently active academics, as many scientists, four former Chancellors of the Exchequer, five former chiefs of staff, and four former chief secretaries to the Treasury, as the House of Lords does, even with its current far-from-ideal composition. The quality of its debate as a result is exemplary in its wisdom, insight, dignity and expertise, not to mention the elegant use of the English language.

Being structurally partisan, the House of Commons is largely concerned to sustain or embarrass the government of the day and to score political points. While this has a legitimate place in political life, we also need a place where party loyalties are less demanding and allow for a relatively non-partisan and disinterested discussion of public issues. Since the House of Lords has no role in sustaining the government and loyalty is not crucial to it, it can offer this. We reinforce its relatively non-partisan ethos by requiring that no single party should command a majority in it, and that a significant number of its members should be independent of political parties. The latter has been the case since the 1960s, and the former since 2000, with the result that no political party in the House today can get its way without securing a cross-party consensus and rising above narrow partisan considerations.

Britain's membership of the European Union and the devolution of power to three of the country's four nations, namely Scotland, Wales and Northern Ireland, have added a new dimension to its political life and have made unprecedented demands on the House of Lords. EU legislation is highly technical, extremely detailed, stands in a complex relation to domestic legislation and requires a most careful examination. The Commons has not been terribly good at this task, largely for lack of time, interest and expertise. The Lords is free from these constraints and has built up an enormous Europe-wide reputation for its thorough scrutiny of EU legislation. Its regular reports are widely read and consulted by other EU members, and have saved both Britain and the EU from many a mistake. Its EU committee is the largest in the House, larger than its counterpart in any other EU member country, and includes as many as seventy members, divided into seven sub-committees.

Although devolution has not made Britain a federal state, it has taken it further in that direction than ever before. Each of the three devolved nations has common interests and concerns and faces common problems. They seek and need collective representation at the UK level, and only the Lords can meet their aspiration. The case of England is complex. Some of its areas have a strong regional consciousness, others do not. In many cases, regions based on administrative boundaries do not necessarily correspond to the 'real' or historically self-conscious ethno-cultural regions or areas with which people identify. It is not, however, necessary that administrative regions should all be equally self-conscious or be 'real' regions. In whatever way they are demarcated, and there is always an element of arbitrariness in this, over time administrative regions develop common interests, face common problems and are eligible to be appropriate units of representation. And as they are given a representative status, their collective consciousness tends to develop or deepen.

Britain has a highly centralised administrative and political system. Better governance, a greater sensitivity to people's needs and greater citizen engagement with the political process require that more powers and functions should be devolved to the regions, which, though artificial to start with in some cases, gradually acquire a strong sense of administrative, political and even perhaps cultural identity. Even the parliamentary constituencies, which we cherish and whose existing relation to their MP we are anxious to preserve, were once arbitrary and took time to become more or less coherent political units of representation. Regions are no different. They are also favoured by the EU and are likely to acquire greater salience and importance as the building blocks of the new 'people's Europe'. With the devolution of powers to Scotland, Wales and Northern Ireland, England cannot remain a single and homogeneous monolithic unit. The smaller nations feel uncomfortable with, even threatened by, it and tend to generate a pressure towards its greater regionalisation. The English too want greater powers to run their affairs themselves without constant Whitehall interference, and demand a greater regional autonomy.

The House of Lords is the ideal place to give the English regions and the three other nations a collective voice at the central level. Ad hoc regional coalitions of MPs, which currently exist, are no substitute for regionally elected and representative peers, explicitly authorised and expected to speak for their region. The House of Lords can play a most valuable part in uniting the country by helping to build common bonds between the regional and national units, giving the overall British identity a regional basis and depth, and the regional and national identities a much needed wider articulation and framework.

Reform of the House of Lords

The House of Lords, I have argued, performs many functions such as scrutinising and revising domestic legislation, holding the government accountable, representing important but neglected interests, providing a space for calm and non-partisan deliberation, critically examining European legislation, and giving a collective voice to and integrating the regional and national units. All these functions have a bearing on its composition, powers, tenure and so on, though some no doubt have it more than others.

The House currently has around 750 members, making it the largest second chamber in the world. The German Bundesrat, even after the country's unification, has only sixty-nine members. The United States, with five times our population, is happy with 100 members in its Senate; India, with eighteen times our population, sees no need to increase its Rajya Sabha membership of 245; and France, with roughly the same population as Britain, has 331 members in its Sénat. There is no obvious reason for the House of Lords to have such a large membership. It has at present forty domestic, legislative and investigating committees, which between them have just over 400 members. Since some members serve on more than one committee, the total membership of its various committees is a little under 350. This seems to be the optimum size for the House to conduct its business. Such a reduction would also have the further advantages of persuading its members to attend the House more regularly and serve on its committees, reducing public expenditure, and providing each peer with more office space than a small desk in a room of about five and sometimes more.

As for the composition of the House, it would need to comprise two groups: representatives of ethnic minorities, women, experts and people of distinction, and those representing regions and nations. The two groups are representative in related but different senses, and much confusion is created by failing to distinguish them. Regional and national representatives would be formally authorised to speak for their constituents and held accountable for what they say and do. Representatives of ethnic minorities, women and other underrepresented groups do not and should not enjoy such authority. Black peers, for example, carry no authority to speak on behalf of or even in the name of all black Britons. Rather they represent them in the sense that their presence in the Lords is a symbolic recognition that black Britons are accepted and valued by the country as equal citizens, that they would ordinarily be in regular touch with others like them, and that they share broad similarities of experience and interest with black Britons in general and bring to the deliberation some of their important concerns and sensibilities.*

The representatives of ethnic minorities, women and other underrepresented groups would obviously need to be appointed. They could be elected, but it is not easy to see how or by whom. Ethnic minorities have several organisations and none speaks for them all. Like the French we could require them to agree on a single national organisation, but that would amount to an undue interference in their internal affairs, arrest their natural growth, homogenise them and be unlikely to succeed (as the French have discovered). As for experts, persons of distinction, women and other groups, it is obvious that there is not, for each of these groups, a single organisation that can legitimately claim to speak for everyone in that constituency.

As we know from our past and present experiences, a system of appointment can easily become a vehicle of patronage and corruption and forfeit its legitimacy. The best way to guard against this is to build on our experience with the Lords Appointments Commission during the past eight years of its existence. The commission should be a statutory body, draw its membership from within and outside both Houses, and operate within the framework set by Parliament. Since its members are not all peers, and some of them might wish to become one, those serving on it should not be allowed to nominate themselves during their tenure (as is reported

* Hannah Pitkin, *The Concept of Representation*, (Berkeley: University of California Press, 1967) distinguishes four different senses. This is inadequate, and excludes the kind of representation I am talking about here. Ethnic minority or women members are not a 'representative sample' or intended to 'replicate the typical characteristics' of a group. Rather they are 'representative' in a much more complex way.

to have been the case in a couple of instances) or for four or five years after it has ended. The commission should not initiate its own nominations and should only appoint from among those who have applied or been nominated by members of the public or professional organisations. Successful candidates should be expected to sit on the crossbenches unless they choose otherwise after a certain stipulated period. The rationale behind this is to ensure both that no political party has a majority in the Lords and that there is a significant independent and non-partisan presence in it. It may be argued, as I did once in the past, that the commission's nominations should be ratified by both Houses or at least the Lords. While there is something to be said for this, it is best avoided. It runs the risk of politicising appointments, making them unduly contentious and subjecting honourable men and women to a partisan scrutiny protected by parliamentary privilege. As at present, the commission should vet and approve the nominees of the three political parties.

The Lords Appointments Commission needs to ensure that the House is fairly representative in terms of gender, age, ethnicity and so on. Even after eight years in existence, the Lords are only 20 per cent women (though their number appears much higher to casual observers because of their better attendance), 3 per cent ethnic minority members and 4 per cent under the age of fifty. London and south-east England are far more heavily represented than the rest of the country. All this suggests that the commission's procedures and criteria need a careful look.

Like other statutory bodies, the commission should be appointed for a limited and non-renewable period of, say, five years. This is intended to bring in new blood and to prevent its members from developing vested interests or a system of patronage and building up a collective ethos and mind set, as commonly occurs in such bodies. The commission should be required to submit an annual report stating the number and kinds of people who applied, the procedures it followed, its criteria for selection and so on. It is of utmost importance that members of the commission should command widespread cross-party support and enjoy reputation for their integrity. Although it is not the ideal system, its members should continue to be appointed by the Prime Minister, in the absence of a better viable alternative.

As for the representatives of the regional and national units, they are best elected directly by the people. Indirect elections create a self-perpetuating political class and do not engage ordinary citizens. Elections should be held at the same time as those to the Commons, to emphasise that the Lords is as important a part of our constitutional system as the lower House and to ensure greater voter turnout. As with the European elections, those to the Lords should involve proportional representation and reflect the balance of opinion within the regional electorates. This corrects the injustices of the first-past-the-post system on which the House of Commons is currently based and which it is unlikely to change in the foreseeable future.

All members of the House of Lords, be they appointed or elected, should have a once-renewable tenure of five years. Five years is a long enough period to get to know the place and to make one's mark. After five years, their position may be renewed for another five if they have given evidence of their commitment to the place by not only attending it reasonably regularly but also by participating in its debates and/or serving on its committees. Unlike MPs, peers have no constituency duties and can legitimately be expected to do more than make a brief appearance to retain their visibility, vote with the party, or even collect their meagre attendance allowances.* The rationale behind limiting the renewal to one term of five years is to bring in new blood and to prevent a self-perpetuating political class.

I have argued that the House of Lords needs both elected and appointed members. I therefore disagree with those who want an all-elected or an all-appointed House. The fears about a 'hybrid' House are groundless. After all, this is the case with the current House of Lords: many of its members are appointed, but some are elected by the hereditary peers and some, such as the two archbishops, sit ex officio. The only question concerns their

---

* Strictly speaking, the House of Lords has no attendance allowance. It has day subsistence and office cost reimbursement. While most members claim the full amount, which is comparatively small, others only claim what they have actually spent and earn nothing for a whole day's labour. The system of allowances needs to be rationalised and should reward peers properly.

relative proportion. In my view, which goes against that of the royal commission chaired by Lord Wakeham, the elected element should be larger than the appointed. First, it is less prone to the patronage and corruption that bedevil even the best system of appointment that we can think of. Second, regions and nations demand and deserve representation, and will not be satisfied with a token presence. Third, although a greater range of representation and expertise and the discharging of vitally necessary functions are sources of legitimacy, its most important and widely recognised source is election. Any system in which the appointed element is larger than the elected and likely often to outvote it would be widely and rightly perceived to be undemocratic. Somewhere between 60 and 80 per cent elected peers and the rest appointed would therefore seem to strike the right theoretical balance.

The world of politics, however, is never so simple, and naturally, vested interests, differences in judgement and the like lead to differences of opinion. In a vote in March 2007, the Commons approved an 80 per cent elected and 20 per cent appointed Lords by a majority of thirty-eight, though it preferred a fully elected House by a majority of 113. In a similar vote a week later, the Lords rejected both, though it did show some support for the former (114 in favour and 336 against). Although it will not be at all easy, it is thus not impossible to find a common ground between the two Houses.

As an academic used to the stimulating presence of visiting professors from other universities, I have sometimes wondered whether it might not be a good idea to invite each year three or four distinguished international figures as visiting or associate members of the House of Lords for a period of four to eight weeks. They should be widely respected for their experience and judgement and knowledgeable about our political system, but should not be politically active. They would have the right to speak but not to vote, and would be expected to attend the House and interact with its members. They could include such persons as a younger Nelson Mandela, Archbishop Desmond Tutu, a past president of the European Commission, a past secretary general of the United Nations or the Commonwealth, or eminent figures from the developing countries.

The advantages of this are several. Britain is one of the most internationally minded countries in the world, and the appointment of such persons would be an important way to affirm and nurture this sentiment. It might also set an example to other countries and start a healthy trend away from narrow nationalism and the obsession with sovereignty. It would add moral weight to our voice when we press the case for international co-operation and multilateral institutions, and raise our international stature. Above all, it would expose us to different perspectives on global issues, and enrich our parliamentary deliberations and public life in general.*

The reform of the House of Lords must also include other changes. Its members should have a right to resign if they feel that they are not really suited to political life, if they feel that more is demanded of them in terms of time and energy than they had imagined, or if they find that they cannot make the kind of contribution to public life they had hoped for. The title 'Lord' or 'Lady' gives its bearers an exaggerated sense of self-importance, tends to foster vanity among some of them and deference among the rest of their fellow-citizens, and is a source of undeserved privileges in many areas of life such as booking a table at a prestigious restaurant or buying a ticket for the theatre or the opera. The much-favoured term 'senator' is preferable but by no means ideal.

I do not see either why the state opening of Parliament should take place in the Lords, and MPs be summoned to it by Black Rod. The historical rationale for this has long ceased to make sense, and the pre-eminence of the Commons is an established fact. The Queen should open Parliament in Westminster Hall, where members of both Houses have enough space to find comfortable seats. Ideally the state opening of Parliament should be an occasion when MPs and peers mix informally, forget their

---

* I canvassed this idea among some of my fellow peers and senior journalists, and was struck by their enthusiastic support. Two peers were most hostile to it on grounds of national sovereignty, but they were also opposed to British membership of the EU. The idea is not wholly novel and found an embryonic expression at the time of the French Revolution of 1789.

party affiliations, and quietly and each in his or her own way commit themselves to the norms of public life and to the disinterested service of their country. All of them should be expected to attend it rather than barely a fifth, as at present, and even some members of the public could be invited, thereby turning it into a joyous national event. It is time to drop the practice of requiring peers to don their ermine robes, which many find too expensive to buy or hire and which only a few have a chance of obtaining in a ballot. It may not be a bad idea to allow, or even encourage, a diversity of national and ethnic costumes to express and affirm our multicultural society.

As the composition and functions of the House of Lords change, its powers would need to change too. After the 1999 reform, which removed all but ninety-two hereditary peers, a large majority of peers (78 per cent) and a substantial majority of MPs (more than 60 per cent) thought that the House was now 'more legitimate', and could and should become more assertive and do things, including challenge the Salisbury convention, that it had never dreamed of doing throughout the twentieth century.[*] We have no means of knowing what new powers an even more legitimate House than the present one would ask for, and what we would do if the Commons objected to it. This shows how badly we need some kind of written constitution, and why reform of the Lords is not as simple and straightforward a matter as many naively imagine.[†]

---

[*] For a valuable discussion, see Meg Russell and Maria Sciara, 'Legitimacy and Bicameral Strength: A Case Study of the House of Lords', paper presented at the Political Studies Association Parliaments and Legislatures Specialist Group Conference, University of Sheffield, 16 June 2006.

[†] I am grateful to Professor Anant Parekh of the University of Oxford for many long discussions on the subject.

Socio-economic rights and judges

Brice Dickson

Introduction

 n two recent lectures, Jack Straw – secretary of state for justice and Lord Chancellor of the United Kingdom – addressed the issue of whether socio-economic rights should be included in a new British Bill of Rights and Responsibilities. In the first of these lectures, in October 2007, he said:

> If specifically British rights were to be added to those we already enjoy by virtue of the European Convention, we would need to ensure that it would be of benefit to the country as a whole and not restrict the ability of the democratically elected government to decide upon the way in which resources are to be employed in the national interest. For example, some have argued for the incorporation of economic and social rights into British law as they have in South African law. But this would involve a significant shift from Parliament to the judiciary in making decisions that we currently hold to be the preserve of elected representatives, including decisions around public spending and, implicitly, levels of taxation.[*]

On the face of it this is a fairly blunt dismissal of the idea that socio-economic rights should find any place in a British Bill of Rights, and it is consistent with earlier statements made on behalf of the government. However, less than four months later, in his second lecture, Straw seemed to have conceded some ground:

[*] Mackenzie-Stuart Lecture, University of Cambridge, 25 October 2007.

If, for instance, economic and social rights were part of our new Bill, but did not become further justiciable, this would not in any way make the exercise worthless ... The formulation of such a Bill is not a simple binary choice between a fully justiciable text on the one hand, or a purely symbolic text on the other. There is a continuum. And it is entirely consistent that some broad declarative principles can be underpinned by statute. Where we end up on this continuum needs to be the subject of the widest debate.*

Here Straw is suggesting that a British Bill of Rights might declare that socio-economic rights exist in Britain and that legislation will ensure that they are guaranteed, at least to some extent. He may even be adverting to the directives of social policy that are found in the constitutions of countries such as Ireland, India and Namibia. But he still stops short of saying that judges should be empowered to adjudicate upon such rights or directives.

The purpose of this chapter is to contribute to the wide debate which Straw has called for. It aims to convince him that there are three good legal reasons why he should support the argument that little is to be feared from allowing judges to take decisions that impact on public expenditure. The first is that they have already been doing this for years and the sky has not fallen in. The second is that judges know their place and are very unwilling to trespass into areas which most people would agree should be the preserve of elected representatives. The third is that even if judges start flexing their muscles in ways which are unacceptable to Parliament, a Bill of Rights can ensure that Parliament retains the power to alter the law as stated by judges. Overall the chapter seeks to further underpin Charter 88's twenty years of campaigning for rights, freedoms and a written constitution, for a stronger Parliament and more accountable government, and for greater access to power on the part of everyone who lives in the United Kingdom.

* 'Modernising the Magna Carta', lecture at George Washington University, 13 February 2008.

Judges already impact on public expenditure*

The British state, like private individuals and businesses, can in some situations be sued if it breaks the law and causes injuries or financial losses. One of the most basic tenets of the rule of law is that the state is not above the law. Indeed on many occasions it will be expected to meet higher standards than non-state bodies. The most obvious example of this in the United Kingdom is provided by the Human Rights Act 1998, which obliges public authorities to respect certain human rights and leaves them open to being sued by the victims of human rights violations if they do not. Private authorities are not so constrained, although they are obliged to comply with a raft of legislation prohibiting discrimination on a number of grounds. A notable example of a state authority being held liable to pay compensation is *R. (KB)* v. *Mental Health Review Tribunal,* where the High Court awarded between £750 and £4,000 to four patients detained under the Mental Health Act 1983 whose applications for a review of their detentions had been delayed in breach of their right to have the lawfulness of their detention decided speedily by a court.[†]

British courts now also accept that public authorities responsible for the welfare of children can be sued if they do not protect them against abuse, thereby demonstrating clearly that judges already rule on arguments which, if accepted, lead not just to an award of damages to a particular individual but to the expenditure of public money more generally to try to ensure that the injuries or losses suffered will not recur in the future.[‡] In *R. (Amin)* v. *Secretary of State for the Home Department,* for example, the House of Lords ruled that when a death occurs in custody in circumstances where the state is arguably in breach of its obligation to

---

* For a much more detailed case built on this premise, see Ellie Palmer, *Judicial Review, Socio-Economic Rights and the Human Rights Act* (Oxford: Hart, 2006).

[†] [2004] QB 936.

[‡] See *Barrett* v. *Enfield London Borough Council* [2001] 2 AC 550, a position effectively endorsed by the European Court of Human Rights two years later in *Z* v. *UK* (2002) 34 EHRR 3.

protect the right to life, there must be a public investigation before an independent judicial tribunal, with an opportunity for the relatives of the deceased to participate.* The appeal in that case was allowed because the investigation of the death in question had not so far been sufficient. Given the high number of deaths which occur in custody each year,† this decision must have had significant budgetary implications for the government. Another example is *R. (Limbuela)* v. *Secretary of State for the Home Department*,‡ where the Lords unanimously held that the government has a legal duty, founded on Section 55(5)(*a*) of the Nationality, Immigration and Asylum Act 2002, to provide support to an applicant for asylum – even though his or her claim for asylum had not been made as soon as reasonably practicable after his or her arrival in the UK – when it appears on a fair and objective assessment of all relevant facts that the applicant faces an imminent prospect of serious suffering caused by denial of shelter, food or the most basic necessities of life.

There are also innumerable court decisions which did not in the end have significant consequences for public expenditure but which might have done so had the judges felt that the law favoured the losing party. Take *R. (Carson)* v. *Secretary of State for Work and Pensions*,§ a case of conjoined appeals where the two questions were whether pensioners living outside the United Kingdom had a right to receive annual increases to their pensions in the way that pensioners within the UK did, and whether jobseeker's allowance had to be paid to people under twenty-five at the rate paid to people above that age. The Lords gave a negative answer to both questions, although Lord Carswell dissented on the first one. The point here is that during the appeals no-one argued that the questions were beyond the scope of

---

* [2003] UKHL 51, [2004] 1 AC 653.

† There were around 600 deaths in custody in England and Wales during 2007, according to the Forum for Preventing Deaths in Custody. The suicide rate is thirty-three times that for the general population. See David Batty, '600 custody deaths in 2006, study finds', *Guardian*, 21 September 2007.

‡ [2005] UKHL 66, [2006] 1 AC 396.

§ [2005] UKHL 37, [2006] 1 AC 173.

judicial determinations; no-one contended that, because a decision in favour of the claimants would have significant budgetary implications for the Exchequer, the courts should not look at the questions at all. The questions were clearly justiciable.

Moreover, socio-economic matters are already regulated by a wide range of legislation which, from time to time, judges are called upon to interpret. This legislation does not use the language of rights, preferring instead to speak of duties, but it has the effect of creating entitlements which can be enforced through tribunals and courts. Thus, under Section 7(1) of the Education Act 1996, the parent of every child of compulsory school age (five to sixteen) has a duty to cause that child to receive efficient full-time education – suitable to his or her age, ability, aptitude and special educational needs – either by regular attendance at school or otherwise. Section 1 of the National Health Service Act 2006 provides that the government must promote a comprehensive health service designed to secure improvement in people's physical and mental health and in the prevention, diagnosis and treatment of illness; for this purpose the government must secure the provision of services that are free of charge except in so far as charging is expressly provided for by law. Under the Housing Act 1996, Section 193, a local housing authority must provide accommodation where it is satisfied that an applicant is homeless, is eligible for assistance (in other words, is not subject to immigration control), has a priority need (for example, is pregnant, has resident dependent children, is vulnerable because of old age, mental illness or disability, or is homeless because of an emergency such as a flood) and has not become intentionally homeless. Section 21(1) of the National Assistance Act 1948 states that a local authority – with the approval of the secretary of state and to such extent as he or she may direct – must make arrangements for providing residential accommodation for persons aged eighteen or over who, by reason of age, illness, disability or any other circumstances, are in need of care and attention not otherwise available to them. The Chronically Sick and Disabled Persons Act 1970, building upon the 1948 Act, requires local authorities to make arrangements for the provision (among many other things) of practical assistance to sick and disabled people in their homes. By the Health and Safety at Work etc. Act 1974, Section 2(1), it is the duty of every employer to ensure, 'so far as is reasonably practicable', the health, safety and welfare at work of all his or her employees. Section 1(1) of the National Minimum Wage Act 1998 provides that a person who qualifies for the national minimum wage has to be remunerated by his or her employer at a rate which is not less than the stipulated amount, at present £5.73 per hour for employees over the age of twenty-two. The Childcare Act 2006 says in Section 6(1) that an English local authority must secure, so far as is reasonably practicable, that the provision of childcare (whether or not by the authority itself) is sufficient to meet the needs of parents in its area who require such care in order to enable them to take up, or remain in, work, or to undertake education or training which could reasonably be expected to assist them to obtain work.

In each of these examples the legislation effectively creates a right, and tribunals or courts can become involved in deciding whether the legislation has been properly interpreted and applied. The 2006 case brought by a woman who had been refused the breast cancer drug Herceptin is but one high-profile example of such litigation.* Of course, many lawyers and judges never come across these examples because the areas of law in question tend not to be financially rewarding for private legal practitioners; the issues are handled instead by legal advisers in law centres or local advice centres. Many lawyers would not even know where to look for the relevant legal rules governing entitlement to welfare benefits, employment rights, housing or health care. But these rules exist nonetheless and it is already possible to talk about 'rights' in such contexts. Putting these rights into a Bill of Rights would not represent a clear break with the past.

Judges know their place

In recent years there has been no shortage of judicial decisions which have incurred the wrath of government ministers, but it

---

* R. (Rogers) v. Swindon NHS Primary Care Trust [2006] EWCA Civ 392. Mrs Rogers won her judicial review of the trust's refusal to treat her with the drug.

must be remembered that, for every judicial decision that provokes such resentment, there are countless others that go the government's way and excite no publicity at all. This is because the arguments put up by the government are sound ones and are readily accepted by the judges. Both the government and the judges operate within a constitutional setting that has at its centre the doctrine of parliamentary sovereignty and, although one or two senior judges have recently suggested that the time may have come for some exceptions to be made to that doctrine,* it is still unthinkable that a new constitutional dispensation would transfer sovereignty lock, stock and barrel from Parliament to the United Kingdom Supreme Court. The judiciary, I would suggest, are the very last constituency that would want such a transfer to occur. The former senior law lord, Lord Bingham of Cornhill, is certainly of that view, as he has made clear both inside and outside the court room.† The current senior law lord and president-elect of the UK's Supreme Court, Lord Phillips of Worth Matravers, is unlikely to support a different position.

Evidence of judicial restraint is abundant. On several recent occasions individual law lords have expressed a desire to adopt a hands-off approach to issues that are best left to Parliament and the government. In the high-profile case of *R. (Gentle)* v. *Prime Minister*, the law lords were asked to rule that there had not been a proper investigation of the deaths of two British soldiers in Iraq because there had been no full inquiry into whether the invasion of that country by coalition forces in 2003 was legal. The nine law lords agreed that whether such military action was legal was a question a British court could never decide, it being a matter primarily for international law to determine.

In numerous cases where courts have been asked to apply Section 3 of the Human Rights Act 1998 – which requires legislation to be interpreted in a way that is compatible with

---

* See the judgments of Lord Steyn, Lord Hope and Lady Hale in *R. (Jackson)* v. *Attorney General* [2005] UKHL 56, [2006] 1 AC 262.

† See his judgment in *R. (Jackson)* v. *Attorney General* (noted above) and 'The Rule of Law', *Cambridge Law Journal* (2007), vol. 66, pp. 67–85.

European Convention rights 'so far as it is possible to do so' – the judges have resisted interpreting legislation in flat contradiction of the intention of Parliament, to the extent that that intention can ever be clearly identified. Bingham has said that any other approach would be 'judicial vandalism'.[*] In *Ghaidan* v. *Godin-Mendoza*[†] the House of Lords held (with Lord Millett dissenting) that a person in a same-sex relationship was entitled to succeed to his deceased partner's statutory tenancy as his 'spouse', the term used in the Rent Act 1977,[‡] but even this decision can be viewed as judicial obedience to Parliament's clear instruction to adopt a convention-compliant interpretation if at all possible. What is 'possible' in this context means what is consistent with the constitutional role of judges in the British legal system, not what is conceivable by way of judicial activism. Section 3 of the Human Rights Act 1998 has conferred significant power on judges, but it is still a power which is to be exercised within existing constitutional constraints. Thus the word 'spouse' can be interpreted to mean 'male or female sexual partner', but if judges were to interpret it as meaning 'brother', 'sister' or 'friend' they would be stepping outside their constitutional role.

In *Re S (Minors) (Care Order: Implementation of Care Plan)* their Lordships chided members of the Court of Appeal for over-stepping their role as judges.[§] The Lords held that on the wording of the Children Act 1989 a court did not have a supervisory role over how a local authority discharges its responsibilities under a care order. The Court of Appeal's attempt to introduce a 'starring' system could not be justified, even in the eyes of Lord Mackay of Clashfern, who had extra-judicially called for such a system to be introduced. The Court of Appeal was also reversed in *Wilson* v.

[*] In *R. (Anderson)* v. *Secretary of State for the Home Department* [2002] UKHL 46, [2003] 1 AC 837, para. 30. Decisions sailing close to the wind are *R.* v. *A* [2001] UKHL 25, [2002] 1 AC 45 and *Secretary of State for the Home Department* v. *MB* [2007] UKHL 46.

[†] [2004] UKHL 30, [2004] 2 AC 557.

[‡] Sch. 1, paras 2 and 3(1).

[§] [2002] UKHL 10, [2002] 2 AC 291.

First County Trust Ltd,[*] where the Lords held that Parliament could not have intended Section 3 of the Human Rights Act to have the effect of altering the existing rights and obligations of contracting parties under the Consumer Credit Act 1974.

The area of law which perhaps best illustrates judicial awareness of the limits of judicial power is taxation law, another field which is alien to many legal practitioners, although not for the reasons that apply in the case of welfare law. In such cases judges quite often articulate what they can and cannot do without trespassing outside their constitutional role. Thus, in the recent case of *Fleming* v. *HM Revenue and Customs Commissioners,*[†] the Lords ruled that a time limit imposed on taxpayers who wanted to claim repayment of input value added tax was not enforceable by HMRC in relation to claims which had already accrued to taxpayers before the time limit was imposed. But the Lords then refused to say how long this exemption from the time limit should last in light of the principle of effectiveness in EU law and the legitimate expectations of those with accrued rights, because doing so would, in effect, be a legislative or administrative act, not a judicial one. The job should, the judges said, be left to Parliament or to the Revenue and Customs Commissioners.[‡] Likewise, the courts have long walked a very thin line when deciding whether ingenious tax schemes devised by clever lawyers and accountants actually amount to tax avoidance (which is legal) or tax evasion (which is not). The modern approach seems to be to look at the substance of a transaction, disregarding specific steps that have been artificially inserted only in order to obtain a tax advantage.[§] Having said that, courts will not refuse to take decisions which cost the Treasury millions of pounds in lost tax if that indeed is called for by an interpretation of the common law in line with the rule of law. That was the net result of the House's

---

[*] [2003] UKHL 40, [2004] 1 AC 816.

[†] [2008] UKHL 2, [2008] 1 WLR 195.

[‡] Lord Walker of Gestingthorpe dissented on this point.

[§] See *Inland Revenue Commissioners* v. *McGuckian* [1997] 1 WLR 991, where the House of Lords applied the principle it had enunciated in *W. T. Ramsay Ltd* v. *Inland Revenue Commissioners* [1982] AC 300.

decision in *Woolwich Equitable Building Society* v. *Inland Revenue Commissioners*, where the building society was allowed to recover some £76 million which the House said had been illegally demanded from it by the Inland Revenue.*

Judges can be trumped by Parliament

Just as the power of judges to take decisions in favour of certain claimants can be affected by the wording which Parliament chooses for its legislation, so judicial power, once exercised, can be countered by new legislation enacted in response to the decision. Very few campaigners are seriously suggesting that this power of Parliament should be removed by a British Bill of Rights,† although obviously one would not expect it to be exercised in a way that undermines human rights which have already secured widespread recognition internationally and to which the UK government has formally subscribed by ratifying a treaty, nor would one expect a Bill of Rights to be frequently amended (even if it is not formally entrenched).

Two glaring examples of immediate parliamentary reaction to judicial decisions spring to mind, each of them denying rights which the judges had held existed (although it can be argued whether they were human rights or not). The first is the War Damage Act 1965, which was passed expressly to reverse the effect of *Burmah Oil Co. Ltd* v. *Lord Advocate*,‡ in which the law lords decided that an oil company was entitled to compensation for the damage caused to its installations in Burma when British forces were withdrawing from that country during the Second World War. The second is the Northern Ireland Act 1972, which reversed the decision of the High Court of Northern Ireland in

---

* [1990] 1 WLR 1400.

† But see *A New British Bill of Rights: the Case For* (Manchester: Industrial Systems Research).

‡ [1965] AC 75. Viscount Radcliffe said: 'It is for those who fill and empty the public purse to decide when, by whom, on what conditions and within what limitations such compensation is to be made available [at 134E].'

R. (Hume) v. *Londonderry Justices*,[*] where it had been decided that regulations allowing Army officers to order an assembly of persons to disperse were beyond the power of the Parliament of Northern Ireland to make because the Government of Ireland Act 1920 stipulated that that parliament was not to make laws 'in respect of the Army'. The incident at issue in that case occurred before the killings by British Soldiers on Bloody Sunday on 30 January 1972, but the High Court's decision was announced thereafter. The effect was to make some of the Army's actions on that day illegal, but the hastily enacted Northern Ireland Act 1972 retrospectively validated all such actions and said that the Army was to be deemed to have had the power in question since 1920. A starker illustration of the impact of the doctrine of parliamentary sovereignty is hard to imagine.

But the power of Parliament to reverse judicial decisions which are not to its liking cuts both ways. In *Prescott* v. *Birmingham Corporation*[†] the Court of Appeal struck down a decision by the corporation to introduce free travel on its buses for women aged over sixty-five and men aged over seventy. The court said that the scheme breached the fiduciary duty which the city owed to all its ratepayers. Parliament was so appalled at this that it quickly enacted the Public Service Vehicles (Travel Concessions) Act 1955 in order to legitimise such schemes.

The Acts just mentioned are ones which the judges may not have anticipated when they took their decisions (although in the *Burmah Oil* case the government gave advance warning of its legislative intentions during the course of the litigation). But in countless other cases the judges have themselves called for legislation to be introduced to correct an anomaly, or have strongly hinted to that effect. In *R.* v. *Preddy*[‡] the law lords held that people who made dishonest misrepresentations in order to obtain mortgage advances had not 'obtained property by deception' for the purposes of the Theft Act 1968 because, in a situation where one person's bank account was debited and

[*] [1972] NI 91.
[†] [1955] Ch 210.
[‡] [1997] AC 815.

another's credited, no property 'belonging to another' had been obtained by the deceiver. Within six months Parliament had passed the Theft (Amendment) Act 1996 to plug this loophole. In *Bellinger* v. *Bellinger** the House of Lords refused to use its power to interpret the Matrimonial Causes Act 1973 in a way which would extend the rights of post-operative transsexuals to marry, precisely because it knew that legislation on this subject was pending in Parliament. The following year the Gender Recognition Act was passed.

Very few human rights advocates are pressing for social and economic rights to be protected in British law in an absolutist fashion, any more than they have so pressed with regard to civil and political rights. Nearly all European Convention rights – including the right to peaceful enjoyment of one's possessions and the right not to be denied the right to education† – are conferred in a more or less limited way. Either the wording of the relevant convention article is itself guarded or it expressly allows violations of the right if certain conditions are fulfilled. In addition, the European Court has adopted the 'margin of appreciation' doctrine, whereby states are granted considerable freedom to limit rights in a manner which conforms to national traditions.‡ The court is also increasingly willing to interpret convention articles in ways which allow positive and procedural obligations to be implied out of negative substantive obligations, an approach recently advocated with great eloquence by Sandra Fredman.§ A negative substantive obligation is a duty not to interfere with a person's freedom (for example, to enjoy his or her possessions).

---

* [2003] UKHL 21, [2003] 2 AC 467.

† Protected by Articles 1 and 2 of Protocol 1 to the convention, and included within the definition of 'convention rights' in the Human Rights Act 1998.

‡ The doctrine is used to refer not only to the court's willingness to balance individual rights against collective goals, but also to the deference paid to national authorities by an international court. See George Letsas, *A Theory of Interpretation of the European Convention on Human Rights* (Oxford: Oxford University Press, 2007), ch. 4.

§ *Human Rights Transformed: Positive rights and positive duties* (Oxford: Oxford University Press, 2008).

Positive obligations are duties which require a state to actually do something to give substance to a person's rights, such as safeguarding that person's home against neighbouring environmental hazards.* Procedural obligations include duties imposed on states to investigate alleged breaches of rights: what good is a right if proving its breach is beyond the means of the victim of that breach?† But the European Court has been careful, where appropriate, to limit the extent of these positive and procedural obligations by ensuring that they are enforced in a contextual setting, which might take into account, for example, the costs incurred in complying with the right,‡ the threat of international terrorism§ or the cultural background of a people.§§

Even the International Covenant on Economic, Social and Cultural Rights confers rights in a limited way. Article 4 provides that a state may subject the rights it confers in conformity with the covenant to limitations that are determined by law, compatible with the nature of the rights and intended to promote the general welfare of society. The general comments issued in relation to the covenant by the United Nations Committee on Economic, Social and Cultural Rights also make it clear that the rights in question are not absolute. For instance, General Comment 14, on the right to the highest attainable standard of health, stipulates:

* E.g. *Lopez Ostra* v. *Spain* (1995) 20 EHRR 27; *Guerra* v. *Italy* (1996) 26 EHRR 357; *Öneryıldız* v. *Turkey* app. no. 48939/99, decision of 18 June 2002.

† E.g. *Nachova* v. *Bulgaria* app. no. 43577/98, decision of 26 February 2004 (on whether a violent act was racially motivated).

‡ *Poltoratskiy* v. *Ukraine* (2004) 39 EHRR 43, where the European Court held that lack of resources was no justification for prison conditions amounting to a breach of Article 3 of the ECHR (para. 148).

§ *Chraidi* v. *Germany*, app. no. 65655/01, decision of 26 October 2006, where the European Court held that making a suspected international terrorist wait more than five years for his trial was not a breach of his right to be tried within a reasonable time.

§§ *Şahin* v. *Turkey* (2005) 41 EHRR 8, decision of 29 June 2004, where the European Court upheld a ban imposed on the wearing of headscarves by women attending a university in Turkey.

The notion of 'the highest attainable standard of health' in article 12.1 takes into account both the individual's biological and socio-economic preconditions and a State's available resources. There are a number of aspects which cannot be addressed solely within the relationship between States and individuals; in particular, good health cannot be ensured by a State, nor can States provide protection against every possible cause of human ill health. Thus, genetic factors, individual susceptibility to ill health and the adoption of unhealthy or risky lifestyles may play an important role with respect to an individual's health. Consequently, the right to health must be understood as a right to the enjoyment of a variety of facilities, goods, services and conditions necessary for the realization of the highest attainable standard of health.[*]

The South African constitution, often trumpeted as a model to follow in this context, also limits the protection it grants to social and economic rights. The Constitutional Court of that country has rejected the 'minimum core' approach to socio-economic rights and has simply required the legislators to adopt reasonable policies.[†] Even the Hungarian constitution, which on the face of it is quite explicit (in Article 70/D(1), for example, which confers 'the right to the highest possible level of physical and mental health'), is not in practice interpreted in the way that it seems to demand.[‡]

In the United Kingdom, therefore, there would be no difficulty in including social and economic rights in a Bill of Rights – and/or in legislation – while at the same time limiting those rights in a way that accords with Parliament's sovereignty. The govern-

[*] E/C.12/2000/4 (11 August 2000), para. 9.

[†] *Soobramoney* v. *Minister for Health (Kwazulu-Natal)* 1998 (1) SA 765 (CC); *Government of South Africa* v. *Grootboom* 2001 (1) SA 46 (CC); *Minister for Health* v. *Treatment Action Campaign* 2002 (5) SA 703 (CC); *Khosa* v. *Minister of Social Development* 2004 (6) SA 505 (CC).

[‡] See Renata Uitz and András Sajó, 'A Case for Enforceable Constitutional Rights? Welfare Rights in Hungarian Constitutional Jurisprudence', in Fons Coomans (ed.), *Justiciability of Economic and Social Rights: Experiences from Domestic Systems* (Antwerp/Oxford: Intersentia, 2006), pp. 97–127.

ment has already done this vis-à-vis the right to education in Article 2 of Protocol 1 to the European Convention, in respect of which it has registered a 'reservation' with the secretary general of the Council of Europe to the effect that the United Kingdom accepts the principle affirmed in the second sentence of Article 2* 'only so far as it is compatible with the provision of efficient instruction and training, and the avoidance of unreasonable public expenditure'.†

The government should have the courage of its convictions and provide similar legal protection to a range of other socio-economic rights such as the right to health care, the right to shelter and the right to an adequate standard of living. This would be no more than people living in a modern democracy at the beginning of the twenty-first century are entitled to expect from their government. If Jack Straw and his Cabinet colleagues want to send a message to the world that the British government is in favour of a better life for everyone, enshrining justiciable socio-economic rights in Britain's own domestic law would be as good an indicator of the government's bona fides as any other.

---

* 'In the exercise of any functions which it assumes in relation to education and to teaching, the State shall respect the right of parents to ensure such education and training in conformity with their own religious and philosophical convictions.'

† This reservation was first entered on 20 March 1952 and remains in place: see Section 15 of, and Part II of Schedule 3 to, the Human Rights Act 1998.

It's time for a new politics

David Cameron and Nick Herbert

he state of Britain's politics should be a source of concern for all parties. Public faith in politicians and our political institutions is draining away. According to MORI, the proportion of people trusting politicians to put the needs of the country before the needs of their party halved between 1974 and 1999. Trust in Parliament fell from 54 per cent in 1983 to 14 per cent in 2000. The current malaise is not a fashion or a temporary aberration. In many ways, our political system is broken.

The consequences of this estrangement are grim. When people lose faith in politics, they see society differently. They feel powerless to influence the world around them. Civic engagement is affected. Cynicism about politics corrodes public discourse and discourages those who want to make a difference. It undermines effective government and encourages damaging short-termism.

The Conservative Party's ambition is to restore engagement and promote accountability so that we can build trust in the political system. The changes required cannot be effected by political gimmicks or constitutional tinkering. We need to understand the depth of erosion in trust and the sea-change required to rebuild it. Old politics cannot be repaired. A new politics is needed.

New politics requires action on three key fronts: devolving power to the people, strengthening our democratic institutions and changing the behaviour of politicians. We will restore engagement by returning power to people and communities, involving members of the public in decision-making and the delivery of public services to an unprecedented degree. We will apply the principles of responsiveness, accountability and engagement to the big constitutional questions facing the country – reforming our political culture, strengthening Parliament and restoring integrity in the electoral process. And we will do so because we realise that harnessing the power of individuals and communities is the only way to deliver real progress.

If some of our prescriptions are different in important respects, our overall goals are remarkably similar to those of Unlock Democracy. We agree that 'radical change is needed to connect people and politics'. And we want to show that a modern Conservative government will have the radicalism and ambition to drive reform.

Putting our house in order

To mend our broken politics, it is necessary to understand the causes of political breakdown. First, the perception of a Westminster elite looking after itself has caused immense damage, not just to the reputation of MPs, but to politics generally. Greater media scrutiny is a fact of modern life and cannot be blamed for the situation. We must put our house in order. Changes such as MPs no longer voting on their own pay, transparency in allowances and closing the final-salary scheme for MPs' pensions are all essential steps.

Second, money in politics remains a concern. We have proposed a universal cap on donations, to apply to individuals, companies and unions, a step which regrettably the Labour Party does not accept. We should aim to reduce the cost of politics – and we should be deeply suspicious of any attempt under the guise of reform to make the taxpayer pay more, which would only add to disillusionment.

Third, the behaviour of government matters – and no administration has done more to corrode trust than New Labour's. Promises have been broken with a breathtaking lack of shame – not least the manifesto pledge of a referendum on the European Union constitution. Spin has debased proper debate. Repeated reannouncements have attempted to create the illusion of action. Statistics have been manipulated. These are not just partisan criticisms of another party. By common consent, New Labour's style of government has poisoned the political well.

The next government must behave differently. All organisations naturally seek to present matters to their best advantage, but there is an important difference between the legitimate desire to communicate effectively and the manipulation of facts by the government machine for partisan ends. We will put in place mechanisms to prevent government spin, for example statistical independence, new fiscal rules and a statutory limit on the number of special advisers.

The government's constitutional agenda

When Gordon Brown became Prime Minister, his first speech to Parliament was on constitutional reform. Yet the 'work of change' was driven mostly by a desire to distance the new administration from Tony Blair's. It is deeply ironic that the talk about 'trust' and 'renewal' was only a cynical act of political positioning.

Brown's constitutional agenda was notably different in character to the rather more ambitious reforms, such as devolution and Lords reform, begun by his predecessor. Major constitutional issues such as the West Lothian question, the promised referendum on the EU constitution and any real progress on Lords reform were all ducked. Instead, the changes were more modest and largely uncontroversial: topical questions and debate in the House of Commons; increased parliamentary scrutiny of public appointments; and removal of the ability of the Prime Minister to intervene in judicial and ecclesiastical appointments.

Such reforms, though worthy, are inadequate. Lord Norton of Louth described the government's new legislation as a 'Constitutional (Miscellaneous Provisions) Bill'. Lord Falconer of Thoroton went further, describing it as 'constitutional retreat'. Insipid measures will not begin to address the reasons for public dissatisfaction with the political system. They will not remedy the lack of trust that the public has in politics; nor will they satisfy people's demands for a greater say over their own lives and their own communities. Broken politics will not be fixed by citizens' juries or a statement of values.

Indeed, far too many of the proposals border on gimmickry – a new bank holiday to celebrate Britishness; a national motto; citizens' juries – which the government now admits will not be real deliberative decision-making bodies but glorified focus groups. Shallow public relations devices merely discredit constitutional reform and erode trust still further.

Power to the people

In place of gimmickry we need genuinely radical changes to restore public trust in politics, increase public engagement in decisions and ensure better public scrutiny of decision makers. We should begin by recognising that society has changed. We are in the 'post-bureaucratic age'. In a single decade, the internet has revolutionised the way in which people access and share information. People have unprecedented control over their own lives. They demand similar control over the way the state interacts with them. As Jeremy Hunt, the shadow culture secretary, has said, the 'wise state' is being replaced by 'wise citizens' who demand to participate actively and equally in the decisions that affect their lives.

With a natural scepticism about big government and a belief in empowering the individual, Conservatives are not just comfortable in this new world: we relish the potential it brings. So we have promised radical reform in public services, opening up public sector monopolies, enabling companies and third-sector organisations to deliver services, and giving the consumer a real choice over publicly funded services.

But many decisions have to be made collectively. Parents can choose a school for a child, but they can't choose their police force; they can't choose how much to pay in council tax, or whether their country goes to war. The principle for these issues must be that decisions should be taken as closely as possible to the people affected, and that the people who take those decisions should be accountable for them. This means a real transfer of power from central government to communities. And it means trusting communities to take those decisions – even if as a government you don't like the consequences.

We believe that greater use of direct democracy will help make politics more responsive. So a Conservative government will introduce Citizens' Initiatives, forcing politicians to respond to the public. One way of doing this would be to say that if a petition were submitted to Parliament signed by a set number of voters, for example 100,000, there would be a formal debate on the topic. Likewise, local authorities and some organisations are already able to submit Bills to Parliament. We propose that the public, if backed by a petition of one million electors, should also be able to table a Bill for Parliament to vote for, to vote against or to amend.

We have already announced plans to allow residents to veto excessive council tax rises – replacing the bureaucratic instrument of capping with democratic accountability. We also want to see more local referenda. We propose that local people should also be able to call a referendum. For instance, it would improve local democracy enormously if people could initiate the process by submitting a petition signed by 10 per cent of the local electorate. On policing, we have promised radical reforms that would introduce elected police commissioners, accountable to the people they serve, to replace distant and invisible police authorities. And where the public wants it, there is a strong case for elected mayors in our cities and towns, strengthening local accountability and the link between the governors and the governed.

But for empowerment to be meaningful we also need to maximise the amount of reliable, unbiased information on which the people can base their decisions. In the United States they talk about being able to 'google your tax dollars'. So we propose that the UK government should provide detail on every item of spending over £25,000. Parents have become used to using league tables to inform their decisions on where to send their children to school. Home buyers expect to be able to check best-buy tables for mortgage rates. People have a right to similar information on the quality of public service provision. That is why we want to see local councils provide information in formats that allow it not just to be accessed by anyone with internet access, but to be harvested, processed and interpreted in creative and innovative ways by newspapers, think tanks, researchers, pressure groups and interested citizens.

Similarly, we want to see crime mapping at street or ward level so communities can understand local crime patterns and trends and use that information to challenge poor performance and hold senior officials to account. In the age of accountability and the instant exchange of information, the government and the public sector must be equipped to inform and deliver.

Those who believe that constitutional reform is only about great institutions and grand issues, such as the House of Lords or the electoral system, may not see the force of these proposals. In fact, empowering people and communities to take decisions will deliver change on a scale to match any conventional constitutional reform, and it will have enormous consequences on how people judge the political system. People feel locked out of decision-making, and we have to let them back in. Returning power to the people is as much a way to change politics as it is to change public services and deliver a better quality of life to citizens. Reform has a fundamental role to play in giving people a stake and a say, re-engaging them, drawing politics out of Westminster and so rebuilding democracy.

A modern constitution

But we do not intend to ignore the big constitutional questions, not least because we need to repair the damage done by Labour's constitutional vandalism. For instance, Labour have persistently refused to address the consequences of devolution. By treating Scotland and Wales as Labour fiefdoms, and by ignoring this unfairness, they have unleashed the forces of nationalism in Scotland, England and Wales.

By contrast, although we opposed devolution in 1998, we fully accept the settlement and, unlike Labour, we are able to critically assess what needs to be done, free of the baggage and self-interest that has held Labour back. Annabel Goldie, the leader of the Scottish Conservatives, has ensured that they will play a full part in the Calman commission, which will examine the future of the Scottish Parliament for the majority who want to see Scotland remain an equal member of the United Kingdom. In Wales, Lord

Roberts of Conwy is considering the referendum issues raised by the latest Government of Wales Act and Cheryl Gillan, the shadow Welsh secretary, has negotiated protected time in Parliament for discussion of Welsh provisions in general legislation. And in England, Ken Clarke has brought forward persuasive proposals to address the unfairness of the West Lothian question. The common thread running through our approach is that we want to preserve and strengthen the union, improve accountability and ensure fairness. That doesn't mean treating all the UK's constituent parts the same – it means ensuring that we have arrangements which address the different needs of England, Scotland, Wales and Northern Ireland.

On electoral reform, we remain suspicious of any reforms which would destroy the link between a single MP and their constituency and move the vital decision of who governs from the electorate to murky negotiations between parties. We reject electoral experiments, such as weekend voting or electronic ballots, which either are a diversion or undermine secure elections. Our priority must be to restore the integrity of the ballot. We would introduce individual voter registration, as recommended by the Electoral Commission, and address the gross disparities between constituency populations that still persist. And we have continued to seek cross-party consensus for a substantially elected House of Lords.

Strengthening Parliament

But at least as important as restructuring democratic institutions is ensuring that they operate effectively. It is no coincidence that the decline of trust in politics has been matched by an increase in power accruing to the executive and an inability of the legislature to hold the government to account. The trend is not new, but Labour's contempt for parliamentary and Cabinet government has set a new low.

Programme motions in the Commons, intended to ensure that issues receive adequate scrutiny, have been used in such a way that entire sections of important legislation, such as the Criminal Justice and Immigration Act 2008, have received no debate or scrutiny at all. As Tony Wright, chairman of the Public Administration Select Committee, has put it, they are a 'guillotine by another name'. Far from strengthening Parliament, the brutal programming of Bills has served to sideline the House of Commons. The absolute key to restoring power in Parliament is to give the House of Commons the right to determine its own timetable.

Parliament must exercise greater scrutiny of legislation, not least of EU laws. Theresa May, the shadow leader of the Commons, has brought forward proposals to improve scrutiny of European legislation, including strengthening the European Scrutiny Committee by giving it the power to force a debate and a vote on the government's motions, and putting on a statutory basis the convention that UK ministers must gain parliamentary approval before agreeing a decision made in the EU's Council of Ministers.

But Parliament must go further and reclaim its proper role as the place where decisions are announced, discussed and dissected, and ensure that its debates are as topical as the immediacy of the modern media demands. Above all, it should never allow the executive to take the most important decisions without proper debate and approval.

There is now consensus between the parties that in future, decisions over when to go to war must, where time permits, be taken in Parliament. But we have to remember that the decision to go to war in Iraq was the subject of prolonged parliamentary debate and approved by a resolution in Parliament. The EU constitution was in fact the subject of a vote in Parliament. Giving Parliament more votes isn't the issue: the government must respect Parliament. There is a strong case for more free votes and for allowing backbench MPs, not the whips, to choose the members of select committees – through secret ballot if necessary.

As Parliament has failed to hold the government to account, the courts have increasingly been invited to review administrative action, repair defective legislation and even overturn parliamentary decisions. The introduction of the Human Rights Act and the creation of a new Supreme Court dislocated from Parliament increasingly threaten to draw the judiciary into decisions which are in essence political, and so undermine its independence. Strengthening Parliament will be essential to ensure equilibrium between, and separation of, the three powers – the executive, legislature and judiciary. And the Human Rights Act should be replaced with a British Bill of Rights to ensure a proper balance between rights and responsibilities.

Harnessing social responsibility

One of the things that has most damaged trust over the past decade has been the tendency of ministers to make promises that they cannot deliver, and having done so, to demand total control because their reputation depends on it. This problem will not be addressed by structural reform alone. It requires those of us who aspire to govern to behave responsibly.

Politicians should not overclaim about what they can achieve. Conservatives believe in the latent capacity of Britain itself – the talent and energy and compassion of individuals, businesses and communities. Politicians need to stop pretending that they alone can drive change. On the contrary, what we should be doing as politicians is, wherever possible, creating the right structures and environment for individuals and communities to help themselves. The job of government is to get behind people, not to get in their way. That is why we have laid out radical reforms on welfare, schools and prisons, which have in common the principle of creating incentives and drawing in the expertise and experience of charities, community organisations and the private sector.

Our proposals for constitutional reform are not distinct from our policies for public services such as health and education. They reflect our underlying principles of reform: strong communities, localism and accountability to the people.

Of course, there will be those who say that transferring power away from the centre is the sort of promise that is made by oppositions and broken by governments. It is entirely under-standable that people will be suspicious. After all, Labour has consistently broken its promises on constitutional matters. They created the Scottish Parliament, but since losing power in Scotland have treated the Scottish government with barely disguised contempt. They pledged democratic reform of the House of Lords, but only removed the hereditary peers. They beguiled the Liberal Democrats with a manifesto commitment to a referendum on electoral reform, only to break it once in office. They promised the public a referendum on the EU constitution, only to break it as soon as they had got the immediate concern of a general election out of the way.

But if the public is understandably sceptical, and wonders if politicians are serious about giving up some of the power they are seeking, we can remind them that it was a new Conservative government which, back in 1979, introduced select committees – hardly to the narrow advantage of the new administration. And returning power to people and communities will in fact be hugely in the interests of governing effectively at the national level.

We can also point to a clear direction of travel in the modern Conservative Party. Our innovative use of open primaries, in which all registered voters in a constituency, regardless of their political affiliation, may vote in the selection of the Conservative parliamentary candidate, has given us a more diverse and representative range of candidates than ever before. We have taken a lead in requiring our MPs to give details of how they use their expenses and in pressing for meaningful reform of party funding. We have shown that we accept the logic of devolution, and have allowed our parties in Edinburgh and Cardiff to develop their own distinctive policies on devolved issues to reflect the needs of Scotland and Wales.

The constitution belongs to no one political party, and reform should never be driven for narrow party ends. To its great discredit, New Labour's constitutional changes have frequently been partisan, if not in aim – where the need for change was sometimes real – then in practice. Too often ministers pulled blindly at the wires of Britain's delicate constitutional settlement, careless of what they might disconnect.

Constitutional reform should have a higher purpose, and today there can be no greater imperative than to repair our broken politics. The original Charter 88 declared that the freedoms which belong to citizens had been 'rationed' by 'our rulers'. Two decades on, central government has never had so much power.

Britain is rightly proud of the democratic system and values of liberty which it exported worldwide. Today it would be a fine thing if we could show that, in the age of public disaffection and voter disengagement, cynicism about an old and increasingly discredited system can be replaced with the hope of a new politics, where government is more accountable and citizens are truly empowered.

Deaths in custody – truth, justice and democratic accountability?

Deborah Coles and Helen Shaw

t might not be obvious that consideration of the way that the state investigates contentious deaths, particularly those occurring in custody or following contact with the police, belongs in a collection of reflections on democracy. But when citizens die as a consequence of acts or omissions by state agents it is right and proper in a democracy that the circumstances are subjected to the most anxious public and judicial scrutiny. This is recognised in international human rights laws and by Parliament. Here we reflect on how far in practice the state meets its obligations and operates within the framework of its stated beliefs, and what remains problematic.

As the only official public hearing where a death in custody is subjected to public scrutiny in the absence of a criminal prosecution, the inquest is of crucial importance in the search for the truth. The inquest is usually the only opportunity for the family to find out what happened.

INQUEST is a charity that works with the families of those who have died in custody. Through our casework over the last twenty-five years, we at INQUEST have gained a unique overview of the inquest system and deaths in custody. We extract policy issues arising from contentious deaths and their investigation and campaign for changes in practice to prevent deaths. Our casework service informs our research, parliamentary and policy work and we are widely consulted by government ministers and departments, MPs, lawyers, academics, policy makers, the media and the general public. By seeking legal representation to assist them through this long and daunting process, families hope to establish the truth about how their relative died, hold those responsible for the treatment and care of the deceased to account, and prevent future deaths. In contributing to that objective, some meaning and purpose can be given to their loss.

This chapter looks at the investigation of deaths in custody in the context of the numbers who have died and in what circumstances. It addresses the role INQUEST as an independent charity has played in bringing political, policy and judicial attention to the issue: the treatment of bereaved people, the treatment and care of people in the custody of the state and how those charged with their care are held accountable, and the need for reform of the current investigation and inquest systems. It also suggests the setting up of a standing commission on custodial deaths.

Human rights – upholding the right to life

The importance of the proper investigation of such deaths was recognised by the Labour government's incorporation of the European Convention on Human Rights (ECHR) – the most fundamental of which, the right to life, is enshrined in Article 2 – into domestic law by way of the Human Rights Act 1998. This was one of several developments that formed part of the newly elected government's commitment to a new constitutional and democratic settlement. Incorporation of the ECHR was one of the key aims of Charter 88 and reflected the aspiration of one of the main points in the original charter: to 'provide legal remedies for all abuses of power by the state'.

Article 2(1) provides that a person's right to life 'shall be protected by law'[*] and the state is required to take steps to safeguard the lives of those within its jurisdiction. More specifically, this right has also been identified as extending to taking positive steps to prevent self-inflicted deaths in penal custody. Article 2 has been repeatedly

[*] Human Rights Act 1998, Chapter 42.

described as one of the most fundamental provisions in the convention, 'the basic precondition of other rights ... Together with Article 3, the prohibition of torture and inhuman and degrading treatment, Article 2 enshrines the basic values of democratic societies.'* Related human rights case law has established consistent minimum standards for the state's duty to investigate deaths in custody. A key case at the European Court of Human Rights, which determined this, was *Jordan* v. *UK*.† This case set out the five essential requirements of the investigatory obligation: independence; effectiveness; promptness and reasonable expedition; public scrutiny; and accessibility to the family of the deceased.

The human rights legal framework places such importance on the investigation of deaths involving agents of the state because they take place in situations of dependency on and control by the state. When the state denies a citizen's liberty it assumes full responsibility for protecting their human rights and it does so with certain safeguards:

> We do not strip people of their legal rights or their rights as human beings ... rather we believe that those in custody retain many of the rights that they held in civil society, rights which can be and are upheld by the courts. What occurs within custodial settings rightly raises concern, recognised by the courts. Western liberal democracies do not ascribe to the arbitrary misuse of power by the police, prison officers or psychiatric staff. That is why such profound concern arises about deaths in custody and that is why so much emotion and anger is generated by the investigations into these deaths.‡

Deaths within closed custodial environments occur where the only witnesses will be either custodians or other detainees; hence the importance of a robust and independent investigation process

---

* Leslie Thomas, Adam Straw and Danny Friedman, *Inquests: A Practitioner's Guide*, 2nd ed. (London: Legal Action Group, 2008).

† [2001] 37 EHRR 52.

‡ Professor Mick Ryan, opening speech to the Institute for the Study and Treatment of Delinquency (now the Centre for Crime and Justice Studies) conference on deaths in custody, 1997.

that ensures proper public scrutiny of what takes place behind closed doors. In situations where the state has the legal power to use force to control its citizens there is obviously a requirement for the most far-reaching level of scrutiny in cases where the consequence of using that power is a death. Judicial recognition of this was emphasised by Lord Bingham of Cornhill in his judgment in the *Amin* case (brought by the family of Zahid Mubarek, murdered in 2000 by a racist cell mate in Feltham young offender institution in London):

> The purposes of such an investigation are clear: to ensure so far as possible that the full facts are brought to light; that culpable and discreditable conduct is exposed and brought to public notice; that suspicion of deliberate wrongdoing (if unjustified) is allayed; that dangerous practices and procedures are rectified; and that those who have lost their relative may at least have the satisfaction of knowing that lessons learned from his death may save the lives of others.[*]

Parliamentarians have also been concerned recently to comment on the importance of the investigation of these deaths, both during the debates on the Counter-Terrorism Bill in 2008 and in the debates on the Corporate Manslaughter and Corporate Homicide Act 2007:

> Inquests must be, and be seen to be, totally independent, and in public to secure accountability, with involvement of the next of kin to protect their legitimate interests. When someone dies in distressing, high profile circumstances their family need to see and feel that justice is being done, and where state authorities are involved there is a national interest in accountability as well.[†]

One of the best tests of the worth, status and weight of any democracy is the way in which prisoners are treated in state institutions, whether

---

[*] *R. (Amin)* v. *Secretary of State for the Home Department* [2003] UKHL 51, para. 31.

[†] Andrew Dismore MP, press notice, Joint Committee on Human Rights, 6 February 2008.

police cells, state prisons or any of the other catalogue ... How are prisoners treated; what recourse is there if something goes wrong – either recourse later in their hands or in the hands of relatives; and what about the duty of care? I say again that if we do not include this measure in the Bill, what sort of message does that send inside and outside the system? What sort of message does it send inside and outside this country, particularly to those nations that we are trying to impress?*

Indeed, parliamentary interest in the issues raised by deaths in custody has never been greater. Since 2007 debates in Parliament have addressed: the inclusion of such deaths in the Corporate Manslaughter and Corporate Homicide Act 2007; the use of restraint in secure training centres following the deaths of two children; the issues raised by the deaths of women in prison; police use of firearms and the operational guidance surrounding their use; the functioning of the Forum for Preventing Deaths in Custody; and the overall functioning of the inquest system.

Setting the agenda

INQUEST's work with families since the early 1980s has revealed a serious lack of legal and democratic accountability and has led the organisation to develop a critical analysis of custodial deaths. Working alongside bereaved families, INQUEST has been instrumental in drawing national and international attention to the issues arising from deaths in custody and their investigation, and this has made an important contribution to the more recent processes of political and legal reform.

Sustained campaigning by bereaved families and their representatives, and reactions to major disasters such as the *Marchioness*, Hillsborough, Zeebrugge and several rail disasters, to workplace deaths, to the murders of Stephen Lawrence and Zahid Mubarek, and most recently to deaths of military personnel, have focused attention on the inadequacy of existing modes of democratic accountability following contentious deaths. High-profile deaths

---

* Lord Dear, Hansard, HL Deb, 25 Jun 2007, vol. 693, col. 459.

in custody have exposed discrimination, inequality and the unacceptable practices of state agents and institutions. They include the fatal shooting by police of Jean Charles de Menezes in 2005, the restraint-related deaths of fourteen-year-old Adam Rickwood (the youngest child to die in custody) and fifteen-year-old Gareth Myatt in privately run children's prisons in 2004, the disproportionate number of self-inflicted deaths of women in prison[*] and the disproportionate number of people from black and minority ethnic (BME) communities who have died following the use of excessive and unlawful force, including Roger Sylvester, Richard O'Brien, Shiji Lapite, Joy Gardner and Ibrahima Sey.[†] In the last ten years the issues raised have been increasingly addressed by a wide range of authoritative public and voluntary sector bodies whose main focus has not historically been on criminal justice, including the British Medical Association, the Children's Commissioner, the Fawcett Society, the Women's Institute and the National Society for the Prevention of Cruelty to Children.

INQUEST has been at the forefront of ensuring that information about the number of deaths in custody has been made available, analysed and placed in the public domain. Historically these figures were shrouded in secrecy and difficult to obtain. INQUEST's monitoring and casework has shown that between 1997 and 2007, 2,250 men, women and children died in prison and in police custody. Of these, 534 died following contact with the police[‡] and 1,716 died in prison.[§] It is only recently that figures have been made public about the number of deaths in psychiatric and immigration detention.[§§]

---

[*] See Marissa Sandler and Deborah Coles, *Dying on the Inside: Examining Women's Deaths in Prison* (London: INQUEST, 2008).

[†] See Helen Shaw and Deborah Coles, *Unlocking the Truth: Families' Experiences of the Investigation of Deaths in Custody* (London: INQUEST, 2007).

[‡] Excludes deaths involving road traffic incidents.

[§] Includes young offender institutions and secure training centres.

[§§] There was no central collation or publication of figures about deaths of detained psychiatric patients until the Forum for Preventing Deaths in Custody published figures in its 2007 annual report; the same held for deaths in immigration detention until April 2006.

People die in custody in a broad range of circumstances, including: as a result of medical neglect; self-inflicted deaths; following the use of force by police and prison officers, involving firearms, CS spray, long-handled batons, body belts, neck holds and other restraint techniques resulting in the inhibition of the respiratory system (asphyxia); and homicide.*

Many of the deaths raise issues of negligence, systemic failure to care for the vulnerable, institutional violence, racism, sexism and inhumane treatment, abuse of human rights, and lack of state and corporate accountability. Cases often reveal a horrendous catalogue of failings in the treatment and care of vulnerable people in custody or otherwise dependent on others for their care. They raise questions about excessive and inappropriate use of custody for some of the most vulnerable people in society. They also highlight failures to fulfil the state's duty to protect life. Inquests repeatedly identify the failure to implement existing guidelines on the care of at-risk detainees.

Not all deaths in custody arouse wider public concern, lead to complaints or are particularly controversial. But many occur in similar circumstances which raise issues pertinent to broader policy considerations on drug and alcohol use, homelessness, mental health, crime prevention, penal policy, policing and combating racism. Deaths in custody cannot be considered in isolation from issues of poverty and inequality. As well as looking at the individual circumstances of each case, it is necessary to broaden the analysis to take into account the political and social context in which they occur. For example, no discussion of self-inflicted deaths in prison can ignore questions about the propriety of imprisoning people with mental health and/or drug and alcohol misuse problems in institutions ill equipped and ill resourced to deal with their complex needs.

In ensuring that the broader political and social policy context is considered, INQUEST has highlighted the many complex and interrelated issues emerging from deaths in custody. This approach has been endorsed by the parliamentary Joint Committee on Human Rights, which commented:

* See www.inquest.org.uk for further information.

This misplaced over-reliance on the prison system is at the heart of the problem ... Throughout our inquiry we have seen time and time again the links between mental illness, drug and alcohol dependencies, short sentences and potential for self-inflicted death. It must, therefore, be seen that the imprisonment of such vulnerable people is at the root of the problem itself. It is not only that this incarceration is senseless, but that it is in fact the first step on a path that can lead to the self-inflicted death of one person every four days, on average, in our custodial system. Until we change our approach to criminal justice for vulnerable people convicted of petty crime we cannot begin to meet our positive obligations under Article 2 and meet our duty of care to them.[*]

While individual cases often provide the most shocking evidence of systemic and individual failings, a single case is by definition unable to reveal trends or patterns among custody deaths. INQUEST's monitoring and casework has enabled it to take a thematic view of a number of cases which highlight recurring issues. Examples of this include our in-depth work on deaths of children and young people in custody, on the high levels of deaths of women in prison,[†] and on the disproportionate number of deaths following the use and abuse of force involving people from BME communities.

The deaths of six women at Styal prison in Cheshire between 10 August 2002 and 12 August 2003 provide harrowing examples of institutional neglect and systemic failings and demonstrate the failure of the state to fulfil its obligations to protect life under Article 2 of the ECHR. The inquests into the deaths heard evidence that repeated warnings were given to the authorities about the problems faced at Styal but were never acted upon. In 2001 an inquest held into the death of a woman at Styal prison resulted in the coroner's recommendation that a methadone programme be implemented. This did not happen. In 2002 the chief inspector of prisons conducted a full inspection of Styal and

---

[*] Joint Committee on Human Rights, *Deaths in Custody*, third report, Session 2004–05, HL 15-I/HC 137-I, para. 372.

[†] See Sandler and Coles, *Dying on the Inside*.

identified systemic failings, particularly in the treatment and care of women withdrawing from drugs and the detoxification facilities available. Further reports by the prison's independent monitoring board also drew attention to problems of overcrowding, shortages of professional staff and insufficient detoxification facilities. The governor of Styal also gave evidence at the inquests about her unsuccessful bids to secure funding for a dedicated detoxification unit and acute problems with staff sickness, recruitment and shortages. No action was taken as a result of all of these identifiable problems and this led directly to the women's deaths. Had a method existed to penalise gross negligence and systemic failures in the form of a corporate manslaughter offence, some of these deaths could have been prevented.*

Deaths involving the use of force by state agents have been by their nature the most controversial. Historically their impact in particular on police and community relations has been profound, resulting in a lack of public confidence in the investigation system and considerable public anger, particularly among BME communities, at the use of unlawful and excessive force. Misinformation or 'spin' has been a feature of many contentious deaths in custody: there have been concerted attempts by the authorities to tarnish the reputation of the deceased in order to deflect attention away from official incompetence or wrongdoing.† These attempt to demonise the person who has died and create the idea of an 'undeserving' victim. In refusing to acknowledge the systemic features of the circumstances of the death, the state seeks to deny the issue by focusing on 'problem' or 'dysfunctional' families and the deceased's 'criminal' or 'antisocial' behaviour. As a consequence these families have been largely excluded from the debates on victims' rights and

---

* See *Briefing for the Report Stage of the Corporate Manslaughter and Homicide Bill 2006 for the House of Lords* (London: INQUEST, 2007), p. 7.

† See Simon Hattenstone, 'We cannot take them at their word: 'police sources' routinely vilify victims and excuse police actions', *Guardian*, 18 August 2005; INQUEST case briefings at www.inquest.org.uk; 'Fatal shootings by police and the death of Jean Charles de Menezes', INQUEST/INQUEST Lawyers Group/Police Actions Lawyers Group briefing, March 2006.

frequently feel that because their relative has died in custody they are treated as criminals rather than victims.

The use of unacceptable levels of restraint is of particular concern. A young unarmed man, often black,* not suspected of any serious offence and in a reasonable state of health, is confronted by a group of police or prison officers and dies in an ensuing struggle, yet no-one at an individual or corporate level is found to be at fault: such situations have resulted in both bereaved people and communities directing untold anger and mistrust towards the criminal justice system. They have also contributed to high levels of public interest in how the state responds to deaths occurring in its custody.

Ongoing monitoring has shown that a disproportionate number of people from BME communities have died in contentious circumstances. Recent deaths involving the use of restraint and segregation have raised concerns about the overuse of force and isolation of young black men in custody.

Obstacles to justice and democratic accountability

All deaths that occur in detention should be reported to the coroner and an inquest held.† Often the inquest will be the only opportunity for the family to try and hold the state to account for the death. The vast majority of these inquests will be held with a jury.‡ One of the major causes of dissatisfaction with the investigation system has been its lack of independence, impartiality and transparency − it is a process that has until recently been characterised by secrecy. Many investigations were exposed subsequently as inadequate and conclusions about the causes and circumstances of death were

---

* See INQUEST briefings on Brian Douglas, Ibrahima Sey, Roger Sylvester, Wayne Douglas, Rocky Bennett, Richard O'Brien, Kenneth Severin, Denis Stevens and Alton Manning.

† Coroners Act 1988, Section 8 (1).

‡ Coroners Act 1988, Section 8 (3). The Act is silent on deaths in psychiatric detention, immigration detention and secure training centres. We have argued in numerous submissions that the Act should be amended to cover such cases.

dramatically rejected by inquest juries. There have been legal and policy developments that have contributed towards greater openness and accountability in relation to inquests and investigations into contentious deaths either occurring in custody or involving agents of the state. There has been more independence in investigations since 2004 by virtue of the Independent Police Complaints Commission and the Prison and Probation Ombudsman, voluntary protocols to ensure more pre-inquest disclosure of documentary evidence to a bereaved family's lawyers, and limited means-tested public funding for family legal representation. But how much difference has really been made and what are the challenges still faced by bereaved families?

The inquest system is beset with administrative and procedural problems which lead at best to an inconsistent standard of public scrutiny of contentious deaths. Delays of two or three years from death to inquest are not uncommon. This causes difficulty for all involved in the aftermath of the death and damages public confidence in the credibility of the whole system. Bereaved people have described how their lives have been put on hold until they have been through the inquest process. The lack of timely public scrutiny of the circumstances of the death undermines the preventative potential of the coronial process, for it affects the coroner's ability to report matters of concern to the relevant authorities and play a monitoring role in examining standards of custodial care. Delay effectively discourages coroners from using their power under the Coroners Rules to report matters of concern, because where they do so their concerns can be dismissed by the detaining institutions as out of date.

A bereaved family and their lawyers have no automatic entitlement to pre-inquest disclosure of documentary evidence, and practice is inconsistent. Frequently families will attend inquests only to discover that crucial information pertaining to the death has not been disclosed. For example, in two recent cases the 'suicide' note written by the deceased was disclosed more than two years after the death had occurred. The limitations on coroners' jurisdiction means there is a postcode lottery in terms of the experience and approach of individual coroners, and the narrow legal remit of the inquest puts an artificial and invidious limit on its scope and style of conduct, excluding wider policy questions from consideration.

It is clear that understanding why deaths in custody occur requires an examination of their broader social and political contexts. For example, no discussion of self-inflicted deaths in prison could ignore sentencing policy resulting in the overuse of prison, the regimes and conditions operating and the institutional culture of violence and racism that exists.

Sentencing policy and allocation remain outside the remit of most inquests, and yet are crucial in understanding the dramatic increase in incarceration rates in England and Wales. This is clear when we consider the punitive trend which has seen the use of custody for children increase by 90 per cent since 1993. England and Wales have witnessed a greater use of penal custody than most other industrialised democratic countries.* The human costs of penal custody are illustrated by the neglect, emotional damage and physical harm inflicted on children in custody, and the thirty deaths that have occurred since 1990.

Joseph Scholes, a sixteen-year-old boy with known mental health problems, was incarcerated in brutal conditions that after nine days propelled him to acts of self-harm and suicidal behaviour dealt with by placing him in strip conditions, in a canvas suit and isolation. In an ultimate act of despair, he made a noose from a bed sheet and attached it to his cell bars. Gareth Myatt, a fifteen-year-old boy, died in Rainsbrook secure training centre in Warwickshire after three members of staff restrained him. They continued to do so despite him saying that he could not breathe and was going to defecate, and did so. When they released the restraint he was unconscious. Adam Rickwood, at fourteen the youngest child to die in custody, was found hanging hours after being hit on the nose by staff using a painful state-sanctioned 'nose distraction technique'† (which caused his nose to

---

* See Barry Goldson and Deborah Coles, *In the Care of the State? Child Deaths and Penal Custody in England and Wales* (London: INQUEST, 2005).
† This technique involved the application of pressure to a child's nose and was designed to inflict pain on the subject and to distract and confuse them. It was one of the approved physical control and care techniques used on children in secure training centres and was withdrawn in December 2007.

bleed for approximately one hour) in Hassockfield secure training centre in County Durham. Sixteen-year-old Gareth Price was found hanging in Lancaster Farms young offender institution. The coroner at his inquest said he was failed by every agency he encountered, at an individual and managerial level. Also at Lancaster Farms, in November 2007 fifteen-year-old Liam McManus, imprisoned for one month and fourteen days for breach of licence, was found hanging from his window bars.

Officially sanctioned painful restraint methods, strip searching, strip cell isolation and segregation result in unacceptable levels of serious self-harm, suicide and violent death among children and yet there has never been a public inquiry held into any one of the child deaths. Instead, investigation and inquests are held in isolation, and are case specific, limited in remit and subject to appalling delays. What greater abuse of human rights can there be than a child dying in custody? And yet the government continues to deny a public inquiry into the deaths as recommended by the coroner following the death of Joseph Scholes.* Such an inquiry would allow consideration of the wider social, structural and policy issues raised by the deaths and the pressing need to learn from the systemic failings that cost these children their lives while they were in the care and custody of the state.

At present there is no 'equality of arms' in legal funding of inquests. The detaining authorities are always legally represented, which representation is paid for from the public purse. There is no automatic right to non-means-tested public funding for families who are thrown into this process through no choice of their own. This leads to imbalance in legal representation and reduces the chances of an independent, fair and balanced investigation. For families or other interested parties of the deceased to participate effectively in the investigation process they need legal representation.

There are no mechanisms for monitoring, auditing or publishing investigations and inquest findings, and no statutory requirement to act on the findings of these investigations. Unless the findings of

---

* See *A Child's Death in Custody: Call for a Public Inquiry* (London: INQUEST/Nacro, 2003); *Why Are Children Dying in Custody? Call for a Public Inquiry into the Death of Joseph Scholes* (London: INQUEST, 2006).

inquest proceedings are recorded, analysed and acted upon, issues of systemic failure will never be addressed and more unnecessary deaths could occur. In 2006 Harriet Harman, then minister of state at the Department of Constitutional Affairs, said:

> Under the current coroner service, families frequently get overlooked during the inquest process ... The system is fragmented, with no national leadership, and it is not accountable. We have no overview of the system as a whole, or of individual cases. Moreover, the system is not properly accountable to this House, which it should be. Standards are not uniformly good; everything rests too much on the personal qualities and abilities of individuals within the system. The legal framework is downright archaic ... The coroner service must serve the public interest and meet bereaved families' concerns in a way that, frankly, it currently does not.[*]

INQUEST welcomes the government's recognition of the centrality of bereaved people to the investigation and inquest process, but without adequate funding for legal representation they are effectively disempowered from exercising their rights.

Lawyers working with bereaved families, in pushing at the boundaries of the inquest system, have helped to expose problems in systems and practices that have contributed to deaths. If the family have no legal representation, it is unusual for a coroner to conduct the kind of searching questioning that occurs when they are represented. There are custodial deaths that have not been properly scrutinised because families did not have key information or the resources to be legally represented, or because the deceased had no family interested in participating in the inquest or no family at all. A key text on inquests explains:

> While it is true that the adversarial interests of parties appearing before the coroner can sit oddly with the coroner's inquisitorial role, this does not mean that the adversarial forms are always in conflict with the coroner's quest to uncover what happened; rather the competent

[*] Hansard, HC Deb, 6 February 2006, vol. 442, col. 607.

advocate can help the coroner by highlighting shortcomings in the evidence and forcing a reassessment of the evidence.[*]

In contrast, the detaining authorities have traditionally approached the inquest as a damage limitation exercise, attempting to close down questioning and narrowing its remit. Lawyers representing custodial institutions are often instructed to take a defensive approach to the proceedings, trying to shroud what happened in secrecy or to attack the character of the deceased rather than assisting the court in the exercise of an impartial scrutiny of the death. Families' needs are reduced to the lowest priority by institutions concerned to protect their policies, practices and procedures.

In 2007 the government rejected outright a recommendation made in Baroness Corston's report of her review of women with particular vulnerabilities in the criminal justice system. She recommended that families should have access to non-means-tested public funding for legal representation at inquests.[†] This is ironic given that Corston's review was set up in direct response to the disquiet which arose as a result of the diligence of the coroner, assisted by the meticulous approach of the lawyers who represented the bereaved families, in regard to the series of deaths of women in Styal prison.

The obstacles are starkest in the most contentious cases. INQUEST's monitoring has shown how the state uses the inquest rather than criminal prosecution and trial for the public examination of deaths in custody. It is extremely rare for there to be a prosecution after a death in custody even where there has been an inquest verdict of unlawful killing.[‡]

Despite a pattern of cases where inquest juries have rejected the official version of events and found overwhelming evidence of unlawful and excessive use of force, gross neglect or a failure to

---

[*] Hugh Selby (ed.), *The Inquest Handbook* (Annandale, NSW: Federation Press, 1998), p. xxii.

[†] Baroness Corston, *The Corston Report: A Review of Women with Particular Vulnerabilities in the Criminal Justice System* (Home Office, 2007).

[‡] See Shaw and Coles, *Unlocking the Truth*, p. 13.

abide by existing policies and procedures, no-one has been held responsible, either at an individual or senior management level, for institutional and systemic failures to improve training and other policies. Since 1990 verdicts of unlawful killing have been returned in ten death-in-custody cases, none of which has resulted in a successful prosecution. This encourages a culture of impunity and sends a clear message to all involved that when deaths occur as a result of their acts or omissions they will not be brought to account. Through this process the perception is created that state agents are above the law:

> The advanced democratic state, supposedly underpinned by the checks and balances of inter-related, formalised processes of legal, political and professional accountability, claims transparency for its public institutions. [But] inquiries into specific cases and more general allegations of inhuman and degrading treatment have been hindered by powerful staff and management interests.*

This has shaped both community and wider public perceptions of the issues raised by deaths in custody and has contributed to all bereaved families' suspicions and doubts about the system's ability to deliver the truth about the circumstances of their relative's death.

Engaging bereaved families in the political process

People bereaved by a death in custody too often come from poor, working-class and marginalised or discriminated-against communities, and their perception of deaths in custody may well have been shaped by the experience of others in their community and by their experience of contact with the police and state institutions. In circumstances where the relationship between state and individual is already strained, for example in neighbourhoods

---

* Phil Scraton, 'Lost Lives, Hidden Voices: "Truth" and Controversial Deaths', *Race and Class* (2002), vol. 44, no. 1, pp. 107–18.

of poverty or in communities that are already socially excluded, suspicion of the state's motives feeds a sense of further isolation. Individuals in these communities see media reports of a death in custody of someone like themselves and empathise not only with the family's dissatisfaction with the way that the death was investigated, but also with their feelings of anger at their sense of exclusion. The principles of justice that each citizen should be able to place their trust in do not appear to apply to the investigation of the death of a person from their community, whose life experience they share. This increases communities' alienation from the state.

The trust between individual and state is broken down by the perceived lack of accountability, transparency and responsibility following a death in custody. The consequence is a dislocation between the state and some of its most vulnerable citizens, a process that causes cynicism and disillusionment.

The Power Inquiry* was established by the Joseph Rowntree Charitable Trust and the Joseph Rowntree Reform Trust to understand how participation in British politics could be increased and deepened. It identified one of the key reasons for the need to re-engage the British people with formal democracy as the rise of a 'quiet authoritarianism within government'. Our monitoring of deaths in custody, and the context of criminal justice policy and legal and civil liberties in which they occur, leads to a similar conclusion. As Professor Joe Sim has commented, there is a need to 'shift the response of the criminal justice system away from the legalistic authoritarianism that dominates the system at present towards a more empathic understanding of crime and deviance'.†

The inquiry identified that the level of alienation felt towards politicians, the main political parties and the key institutions of the political system is extremely high and widespread. That alienation from politics takes many forms for different groups – women,

---

* *Power to the People: The Report of Power – an Independent Inquiry into Britain's Democracy*, (York: Power Inquiry, 2006).

† Quoted in Richard Garside and Will McMahon (eds), *Does Criminal Justice Work? The 'Right for the Wrong Reasons' Debate* (London: Crime and Society Foundation, 2006).

BME communities, those on low incomes, young people — ranging from a general sense that the system is out of date to a deep disgust at the failure of politics to bring about fundamental improvements in the lives of the most disadvantaged.

The integration of evidence-based casework and policy work has been a powerful tool to effect meaningful policy and culture change. INQUEST has worked alongside families to bring the issues into the public and political arena and challenge official versions of the truth. In this way the collective experiences of bereaved families directly inform the lobbying and policy work INQUEST undertakes. Groundbreaking and important proposals have been made as a result. For example, we have proposed the abolition of penal custody for children and women, the prohibition of particular restraint techniques which have contributed to deaths and serious injuries in custody, and the establishment of a standing commission on custodial deaths.

Conclusion

In many cases it can appear that no matter how disturbing and outrageous the circumstances of some of these deaths, no matter what human rights abuses are vested upon citizens by the state, no-one is ever truly held to account. Deaths in custody and their investigation expose to scrutiny some of the most worrying aspects of the treatment of detainees within the criminal justice system. In uncovering these issues we come face to face with the secrecy and authoritarianism inherent in the system.

The government has consistently resisted calls for a public inquiry into deaths in custody or any individual cases. Most recently it rejected calls for an inquiry into the death of Joseph Scholes to review his treatment and care and issues of sentencing and resources, which were outside the remit of the inquest. This was supported by the coroner, all the major penal reform, child welfare and human rights groups, more than 100 MPs and peers and the Joint Committee on Human Rights. The family of Zahid Mubarek, murdered in Feltham young offender institution, had to go to the House of Lords to secure their public inquiry in 2004.

The level of resistance by the government to greater public scrutiny only underlines how important it is that the families that we work with engage with the democratic process. This provides a counterweight to a tendency towards secrecy and a lack of formal accountability, particularly where people die in closed institutions.

Deaths in state custody are not rare or isolated incidents and they raise important issues of state power and accountability. An open, independent and efficient system of scrutinising them is crucial to maintain public confidence in the care of the state and hold it democratically accountable.

It is essential that the inquest system works, since it is the only public forum in which contentious deaths are subject to public scrutiny and it can play an important preventative role. However the current system is 'not "fit for purpose" in modern society'.[*] The government had promised that a Coroners Bill would be introduced in the Queen's speeches in 2006 and 2007. This did not happen, and while the Bill was included again in the draft legislative programme published in May 2008, it remains uncertain whether the urgently needed reform will happen and the necessary resources made available.

INQUEST's frustration with the failure of the state to learn lessons and the lack of publicly accountable institutions resulted in our recommendation for a standing commission on custodial deaths,[†] which could systematically address the question of deaths in custody. The inquest and the separate investigation and inspection bodies cannot address the issues raised by deaths in custody in the manner necessary to ensure action is taken. A standing commission, on the other hand, would bring together the experiences from the separate investigation and inspection

---

[*] Home Office, *Death Certification and Investigation in England, Wales and Northern Ireland: The Report of a Fundamental Review*, Cm 5831, 2003.

[†] See Greta S. Vogt and John Wadham, *Deaths in Custody: Redress and Remedies* (London: Liberty/Civil Liberties Trust, 2003); Joint Committee on Human Rights, *Deaths in Custody*; Goldson and Coles, *In the Care of the State?*, p. 105; Shaw and Coles, *Unlocking the Truth*, p. 131.

bodies as the most effective way to ensure that the lessons of past custodial deaths are learned in order to prevent or minimise future violations of Article 2 of the ECHR. An overarching body could look beyond individual deaths and identify key issues and problems arising from the investigation and inquest process and monitor the outcomes and progress of inquest findings.

The standing commission would develop policy and research, disseminate findings where appropriate and encourage collaborative working. It could also act as a check and balance on the investigation bodies themselves. It would play a key role in the promotion of an ethos of human rights in regard to the protection of people in custody. It would have an active interventionist role and powers to hold a wider inquiry where it identified a consistent pattern of deaths. Such an inquiry could provide a platform for an examination of broader thematic issues as well as issues of democratic accountability, democratic control and redress after systemic management failings – all of which fall outside the scope of the inquest.

Unlocking the truth about deaths in custody sheds light on the way we treat some of the most vulnerable men, women and children in our society. It is important that we recognise, scrutinise, criticise and argue for reform of the way the state deals with deaths in custody. The closed world of custody means that it is vital that it is open to independent inspection and investigation and held to account when human rights abuses take place. These processes are an indicator of the condition of our democracy.

Why we need to overthrow the quango state

Douglas Carswell MP

Public services in Britain are failing – and conventional public policy solutions no longer work.

Billions continue to be spent on an education system that is not equipping young people with basic skills. The health service keeps soaking up ever greater resources, with fewer and fewer increases in productivity. The criminal justice system is increasingly perceived as failing the law abiding. Britain no longer seems to have effective control over her own borders. Billions continue to be spent on defence projects that seem better suited to maintaining jobs in parliamentary constituencies than equipping our armed forces with the kit they need. Yet more money and a blizzard of central government initiatives do not seem to make things work better.

The longer the list of failure, the easier it might be for Conservatives to simply point at the shortcomings of Labour ministers. Yet it is not only Labour ministers that are at fault. If it were, then a quick change of ministers would be enough to guarantee improvement. Public policy has failed to deliver improvements in public services because the quango state that presides over contemporary Britain, rather than ministers, is the problem.

The rise of the quango state

Real power today rests with officials. Britain is governed by remote mandarins and unaccountable quangos.

New research by the Taxpayers' Alliance reveals the sheer size of the quango state. Alongside conventional Whitehall departments and those bodies overseen by local government, there exists a convoluted hierarchy of some 1,162 different agencies and quangos. They collectively receive more than £64 billion of taxpayers' money each year, and they employ almost 700,000 people.*

It is tempting to blame this process on a decade of Labour. And much of that blame is merited. But the problem runs far deeper than any one administration. During the 1980s, even as they were boasting about 'rolling back the state' – and occasionally even doing so – Tory ministers were rate-capping local authorities, imposing the national curriculum on schools, strengthening the control of the Home Office over police authorities and setting NHS targets.

The aggrandisement of remote elites at the expense of individuals and local communities has been driven by three main factors:

- **Targets, audits and conditions imposed from Whitehall.** It is difficult to think of any area of policy, however arcane, that has not been subjected to dozens of 'plans', 'strategies' and 'public service agreements', each imposing a raft of targets. The scope of such targets has been extended to govern process as well as outcomes. Instead of identifying key goals to guide the work of service providers, targets now serve to impose a prescriptive template directing the day-to-day work of front-line professionals.
- **Centralised funding of public services with strings attached.** Centrally allocated funding is perhaps the ultimate means by which Whitehall ensures compliance with its every demand for how services are run. The degree of that control, across the spectrum of public services and local government, is extraordinary by both historical and international standards.
- **More quangos.** Unprecedented powers are now wielded by bodies which are part of the state machine but outside the democratic process. The Qualifications and Curriculum Authority sets exams. The National Institute for Health and

---

* See *The Unseen Government of the UK* (London: Taxpayers' Alliance, 2008).

Clinical Excellence determines what drugs doctors might give their patients. Crown Prosecution Service guidelines determine whether a local yob might be brought to book. It goes without saying that this is deleterious to democracy. What is less often remarked is that it is bad for civic society. The creation of a ruling caste of state administrators has come at the expense of traditional authority figures. We no longer accord the same respect to the clergyman, the head of a family or the headmaster, because their places have been filled by licensors and clerks and assessors and regulators and inspectors and mediators. It seems positively impolite to draw attention to the most glaring problem of all, namely that, if someone is not directly accountable, he has little incentive to do his job especially well.

An alphabet soup of organisations, from the QCA to NICE, from the FSA to the DPA and the CSA, make the key decisions that affect people's lives. Human rights judges dictate school uniform policies; regional quangos tell us where to build houses; police chiefs decide whether it is a crime to possess cannabis; Eurocrats determine who crosses our frontiers. Elected representatives now have less impact on people's lives than, say, the National Institute for Clinical Excellence, the Highways Agency, the Health and Safety Executive, the Learning and Skills Council or any of a thousand other bodies stretching right up to the European Commission, which, depending on how you measure it, passes between 50 and 80 per cent of our laws. No wonder people don't bother voting.

The ability of elected representatives tangibly to ameliorate their constituents' lives has never been so restricted. Britain has become a post-representative democracy as power has been agglomerated by a class of well-paid and occasionally well-meaning administrators who are immune to the electoral process.

Anti-politics

The last time a Conservative opposition looked as if it was going to form a government, in 1979, more than 75 per cent of voters actually voted. At the last general election a mere 60 per cent took part. Over the intervening two and a half decades, disillusionment with politicians of all parties and indeed with the democratic process has grown – why?

British voters have become habituated to frustration. Their ballots don't determine where their children can go to school, or whether their local hospital stays open, or where the incinerator is sited, or whether the police patrol their street. Decisions which in other countries are made by local councillors are taken in Britain by unaccountable functionaries. The rise of the quango state has diminished the ability of democratically elected MPs and councillors to influence decisions that affect people's lives to the extent that four out of ten voters don't bother voting. Far from being apathetic, non-voters perceptively recognise that those whose names appear on the ballot paper have been rendered increasingly powerless. As our system of representative democracy has given way to a system of post-representative democracy, more and more people have come to realise that there is often little point in voting for a representative at all. As Lord Butler of Brockwell, head of the civil service from 1988 to 1998, has put it: 'All decisions are delegated by politicians, because politicians don't want to take responsibility for them, to quangos, and quangos aren't answerable to anybody. Now what can you really hold politicians responsible for?'

It should hardly surprise us that voters regard politicians as 'all the same', promising the earth but never delivering, when the truth is that politicians have so little discretion to alter policies formulated by health experts, educationalists, human rights lawyers, police authorities and Brussels. The rising public disenchantment with politicians is a measure of the inability to decide on the things in life that matter to the electorate. Politicians promise, but remote elites actually decide.

Many voters no longer see any connection between where they put their cross and anything that will tangibly affect their lives. The complexion of their local council, or of the House of Commons, has less impact on them than that of the Highways Agency, the Child Support Agency, the National Institute of Health and Clinical Excellence, primary care trusts, the Health and Safety

Executive and a thousand other such quangos. Remote elites make decisions, local people take the rap, no-one is accountable, no-one is sacked. This is the way Britain is governed today.

Centralised government equals bad government

Centralised government equals bad government − regardless of which party holds office.

Most of the problems in contemporary Britain − hospitals that infect patients, schools that don't teach, policemen who don't go after criminals and immigration authorities that won't remove illegal immigrants − are caused by a massive centralisation of power around remote and unaccountable institutions.

Why does the centralisation of power automatically lead to public policy failure? There are four main objections to the centralised management of public services:

- **It limits the discretion of front-line professionals.** Centralisation has robbed front-line professionals of the freedom they need to go about their work. It thereby destroys the natural laboratory of autonomous professionals and institutions developing better solutions to common problems.
- **It squanders taxpayers' money on wasteful bureaucracy.** Micromanaging the work of front-line public service providers from Whitehall is an enormous task. It requires the creation of a costly bureaucratic machine devoted to ensuring that front-line staff comply with Whitehall's every demand.
- **It results in unintended consequences.** Central prescriptions for services might be well intentioned, but they rarely result in the intended outcome.
- **It undermines a sense of local belonging.** Centralism has denied people a sense of ownership over locally provided public services and eroded the wider sense of belonging in local political communities. The 'civic gospel' preached by Joseph Chamberlain and other Birmingham politicians in the nineteenth century is the best-known, but by no means the only, illustration of the vitality that used to characterise local politics. In the United States, state and even county

government today is a hotbed of local energy. Yet in the UK, even counties with populations larger than some US states have little freedom to innovate.

Indeed, it is striking that many of the public policy innovations that UK politicians have at one time or another tried to emulate and associate themselves often began life as local, state schemes in the United States: welfare reform from Wisconsin, zero tolerance policing from New York, 24-hour courts from ‚Florida and environmental ideas from California.

The new model Conservatives

Real Conservative modernisers understand that the greatest problem in Britain after Blair is not the Labour Party he left behind, nor his hapless successor, Gordon Brown. Instead, it is the quango state. The new model Conservative agenda is neither reheated Thatcherism nor its repudiation; it is a genuinely post-Thatcher agenda.

Under Margaret Thatcher, the Conservatives' purpose was to decentralise economic control. Privatisation, trade union reform and the 'big bang' in the City: each was about devolving control over the economy. Today's new, revitalised post-Thatcherite Conservatism stands for decentralising control over politics and public services.

The post-Thatcherite Conservative agenda is radical, not managerialist. It is to overthrow the unaccountable elites, not to defend the interests of the quango state. It is a profoundly anti-establishment agenda in the tradition of the Levellers, rather than one of inherited privilege.

New Labour entered government without a plan for government. The Conservative opposition, in order to form the next government, needs to be clear about its vision. As far as the public services go, it should be simple. The government should do less. Where possible, it should empower the individual directly, and where this is impractical, it should prefer local to national action. Let us briefly ponder what this means in practice.

- **The government should do less.** The government shouldn't aspire to run things. It certainly shouldn't try to run schools and hospitals from Whitehall. That means every school should be, effectively, an independent school, run by its head and governors. It means every hospital should be an independent hospital. It means repealing the assumption that just because the state pays for a service – such as health or education – it has to provide that service itself.

  Just as the government shouldn't immerse itself in the detail of running schools and hospitals, neither should it become embroiled in the detail of people's lives. It is a further indictment of the spread of state centralism that two thirds of pensioners have to open up their lives to scrutiny by the state in order to claim means-tested benefits.

- **Give citizens the right to choose.** When the government pays for services it should, wherever possible, fund people to choose, rather than subsidise providers. That's why the right to choose your hospital – from any in the country – is fundamental. Choice drives up standards and stimulates innovation.

  The same is true in education. Schools should be able to govern themselves and parents should be given the purchasing power that the central state currently wields on their behalf.

- **Devolve power to the lowest possible level.** Sometimes you can't give choice to individuals. Policing is a good example, since a police force plainly has to enforce order across a defined territory. It would be wrong to move to a system where consumers could opt between competing police services. But many communities across Britain feel they're not getting the type of policing they want – neighbourhood policing, with officers on the beat.

  It is entirely possible to give communities more of a say over the type of policing they get. We set out in the next section how, by transferring powers from the Home Office, and instead making police forces accountable to local people, it is possible to replace state centralism with greater local accountability.

Within these clear principles, we must set out policies that will reverse the drivers of centralism that inflict damage across the public services. By reversing these drivers, we can transform public services and government, substituting for the vicious circle of centralisation that exists today a virtuous one of greater local control and choice for citizens.

Imagine a system of public services in which there is genuine choice and better quality for everyone; in which there is freedom for practitioners and professionals to get on with their jobs; in which front-line innovation is encouraged and rewarded, not held back by bureaucracy. Imagine communities in which there is flourishing local democracy and a powerful sense of civic pride; where people feel they have a real stake in improving local services; in which voluntary activity is supported rather than suffocated by the hand of state. Realising this vision is the task of our decentralising reforms, encompassing the modernisation of public services and the revitalisation of local government. It has three components: reining back the central state from front-line provision, delivering choice for citizens and delivering choice for communities. Let us now examine in detail how that vision might translate into hard policy.

Radical localism

Power should be pushed from Whitehall to the individual where possible, and to the town hall where necessary.

Set the town halls free
Local councils should be made self-financing, a pre-requisite for genuine local democracy. This could chiefly be achieved by replacing VAT with a local sales tax (LST), to be levied by county or unitary councils.

Local government fiscal autonomy is the starting point for a wholesale transfer of powers and responsibilities to local government. Broadly, areas of policy currently run by the Department for Communities and Local Government could be devolved fully to local government. Those elected to serve in the town halls would set local taxes and be able to make decisions central to their local community, such as the location of mobile phone masts, rather than merely rubber-stamping decisions made on high.

With 75 per cent of the money spent by local councils coming from the Treasury, there is little link between taxation, representation and expenditure at local level. This has the perverse effect of rewarding inefficient councils, eroding accountability, diminishing choice (since political parties cease to be able to offer radically different manifestos) and alienating voters. It is also disagreeable in that it deters good candidates from standing for local government since such candidates must be willing to be micromanaged by a distant bureaucracy.

By happy coincidence, central government happens to raise almost the same amount in VAT (£64 billion) as it hands over to local councils in grants (£66 billion). So devolving the power to tax goods and services to town halls would not be an additional levy; rather it would replace an existing and highly unpopular tax. Unlike VAT, which is complicated and expensive to administer, the LST would be charged just once, at the point of retail. Local councils would be free to vary the rate according to their spending needs. The effect of this would be tax competition, thus keeping rates down and forcing councils to be as efficient as possible in utilising tax pounds to provide services.

Send for the sheriff

While self-financing town halls would have many powers devolved to them, in some cases, such as policing, the aim of local accountability would be better served by having a single directly elected official. Crime is the public's number one concern, and yet people are immune to politicians' promises of 'more police'. The challenge is to explain how a party will reduce crime.

The public itself desires greater local accountability in policing. Appointed and impotent police authorities should be replaced with directly elected sheriffs, with real powers to direct a local police force's priorities. Sheriffs should also have responsibility for supervising public prosecutions in place of the Crown Prosecution Service and punishments in place of the Probation Service. They would appoint and dismiss chief constables, make their own policing plan and control their own budgets, allocated as a block grant. They would answer to local voters for their effectiveness in spending that money in the fight against crime.

Free education

Britain's education system is failing: the value of exam grades is falling and bad pupil behaviour is now endemic. Yet no party has succeeded in convincing voters that things will improve.

The Conservatives should adopt a policy of radical localisation. Schools should become independent, free-standing institutions with full control over their staffing and pupil rolls. New providers should be allowed to enter the market and compete for pupils. Parents should have the automatic right to request and receive the funding for their child's education from their (self-financing) local council, and take this money to a school of their choice.

Parents, rather than here-today, gone-tomorrow politicians, would be the driving force shaping our education system. It would be they, not literally incredible politicians, who would demand, and get, school discipline.

Health

Britain already has one of the most expensive health services in the world, yet it still fails to meet public expectation. The problem with the NHS is not resources, but the fact that it is a state-run monopoly established over half a century ago.

Transferring power over the NHS from national to local politicians would do little to address the NHS's structural flaws. Instead, the aim must be to empower the patient. We should fund patients, either through the tax system or by way of universal insurance, to purchase health care from the provider of their choice. The state would continue to guarantee care for all – yet it would lose its monopoly to provide that care where it could be provided better elsewhere.

Direct democracy

Not all powers can be devolved. Some must necessarily remain with some national authority. Where localism is not possible, those who wield power need to be made more directly democratically accountable.

Democratise the quangos

The executive arm of government is too strong, while the elected legislature is too weak. Tightly whipped MPs have allowed their powers to pass to a series of unelected executive agencies. The heads of each executive agency, along with the permanent secretary of each Whitehall department, should be appointed for a fixed-term contract – but only after a confirmation hearing by the relevant select committee.

It is surely worth standing back for a moment and asking whether it is right for the Prime Minister of the day to exercise the immense powers of patronage at his disposal. Might it not reduce the democratic deficit somewhat if the powers currently exercised under Crown prerogative – the appointment of heads of executive agencies and commissions and also perhaps Foreign Office postings – were transferred to Parliament and carried out before open hearings?

Budgetary controls

At the same time, the Commons – through its select committees – should ratify the budgets of each Whitehall department and its executive agencies annually. Only by giving the elected legislature practical oversight over budgets will it be able to control the quango state's many branches.

Humbling the judiciary

It is the purpose of our elected legislature, not unelected judges, to hold the executive in check. The readiness of judges to take political decisions – that is, to rule on the basis of what they think the law ought to say, rather than what it actually says – is not sustainable, nor is it peculiar to Britain. In almost every democracy the judiciary has sought to expand its powers beyond what the legislature has laid down. The problem with judicial activism is that there is, by definition, no legislative prophylactic against it. MPs can insert whatever safeguards they want, but if a court dislikes a statute it will simply ignore their safeguards. What then can be done? First, the judicial process should be subject to the same principles of decentralisation and democracy that have guided us throughout. This means specifically that the powers currently exercised by the Crown Prosecution Service would be placed at the disposal of the local sheriff, who would, furthermore, have the right to set sentencing guidelines (although not to interfere in individual cases).

Second, there should be a degree of democratic control over judicial appointments. There needs to be a process of transparent parliamentary hearings to confirm senior appointments to the judiciary rather than having senior judges nominated either, as at present, by the Lord Chancellor or, as is now proposed, by a government appointment panel.

Finally, the authority of Parliament should be stated explicitly in a Reserve Powers Act, which would delineate a number of areas where MPs' decisions were supreme. This would be a defence not so much against domestic judicial activism as against the encroachment of foreign jurisdictions. The European Court of Justice has a hunger for power that surpasses even the most activist British judge, and has repeatedly pushed its authority beyond what is written in the treaties.

The European Union

Our approach to European integration flows naturally from our domestic agenda. If we want decisions to be taken as closely as possible to the people they affect, they plainly should not be made in Brussels. If we prefer democracy to unelected quangos, we can hardly subject ourselves to the biggest quango of the lot, namely the European Commission.

If we believe in personal liberty, democratic, accountable and clean government, we cannot remain a member of the EU. Indeed, a number of the policies set out in this chapter – replacing VAT with a local sales tax, a Reserve Powers Act – are incompatible with EU law. If Britain is to be a democratic country, it cannot accept the supremacy of regulations passed by unaccountable functionaries. The Reserve Powers Act should specify that the policies stemming from foreign treaty obligations would come into force only following their specific implementation by Parliament; and Sections 2 and 3 of the European Communities Act should be repealed to the same end.

Politics in the age of YouTube

The internet has revolutionised commerce and business. It has removed barriers to entry, has reduced distribution costs and is a powerful aggregator, bringing like-minded customers or people together. The same forces are beginning to influence politics.

British politics today is dominated by two and a half parties. Each has a hierarchical corporate structure based in London. Either the party machines will have to adapt, or they will be pushed aside. Since the mid-twentieth century, the three mainstream parties have steadily lost market share. Reflecting changes in consumer behaviour, the big corporate brands seem to be giving way to the distinctive and the niche, the local and the particular.

Open source politics is on the horizon, and the days of big hierarchical party politics are coming to an end. Far from fearing this revolution in the making, the new model Conservatives need to embrace this new, deeply Burkean way of doing politics.

- **No more taxpayer-funded politics.** It should be illegal to spend taxpayer money on party politics. Current rules, MPs' allowances and hidden subsidies each favour incumbents and further isolate a rotten and useless legislature from popular accountability. At the same time, the costs of doing politics are nose-diving – if not yet the amounts that party machines spend on politics.
- **Popular initiative.** Citizens should be empowered to trigger debates and votes in Parliament on topics of their choice. Part of the Commons legislation needs to be determined directly by the ordinary citizen, not just MPs and officials. These Bills would be introduced on things that mattered to the people, not merely those that excite politicians. At the beginning of each parliamentary session, having read out her government's proposed legislation, the Queen should then turn to her people's Bills: legislative proposals that have attracted a certain

number of petition signatures and so earned themselves the right to be debated and voted on. There would be no obligations on MPs to pass these proposals, but they would have to take sides and then justify their position to their constituents.

- **Open primaries.** A supine Commons, stuffed with whips' sycophants, is monumentally useless at holding the executive to account. The House of Commons is subservient to the executive because most MPs in it owe their positions to their party. Most MPs face little real prospect of losing their seats since they come from so-called safe seats. Career trajectories once in the Commons are shaped more by the party whips, than by popular opinion outside Westminster. General elections are decided in the hundred or so marginal seats – the rest of the country having little say over who their MP is.

  In order to allow the people to hold their politicians directly to account, we need proper open primaries, so that there is political competition, even in safe seats. If local petitions could be used to trigger council-run primary elections, mainstream parties would soon find that they had to take part in the primary process or lose out to others that had chosen their candidates more democratically.

Conclusion

To some, this new Conservative agenda is deeply unconservative. Some instinctive Tories may prefer managerialism to radicalism. Alas, such 'thinking' – if it can be so described – ignores the profoundly anti-Conservative reality: the default settings of the quango state are left wing. Unless we change them, the centre-right can win election upon election, but still lose. Without radical change, we cannot preserve what is good nor tackle what is bad.

It no longer serves Conservatism to maintain the status quo. On almost every issue of the day, the quango state is to the left even of Gordon Brown and has sought to undermine the elected government from the left. On terrorism, judges invoke the

Human Rights Act to frustrate Labour Home Secretaries. On immigration, tribunals make a mockery of Labour efforts to restrict the mass flow of people into Britain. On education, successive Blairite ministers found their attempted reforms watered down by their own departments. On health, ministers find NICE restricting the availability of precious anti-Alzheimer's drugs and NHS quangos obsessing with 'health inequalities', rather than just providing treatments. On law and order, former Labour Home Secretaries have lamented at how the criminal justice system seems to favour the criminal, rather than the victim.

The quango state is inherently leftist and its default settings always hostile to the centre-right. Why? Because, lacking accountability to the public, the quango state no longer serves the public, but instead the narrow interests of the left-leaning chattering classes. As the Italian thinker Antonio Gramsci foresaw, by capturing civic institutions, the left would be able to successfully impose its views on the world. And so it has come to pass. While there may be a few good judges, probation officers and educationalists prepared to swim against the tide, without accountability the institutions in which they operate are at the mercy of left-leaning orthodoxies.

If the Conservatives want real power, rather than merely seeking to have an ephemeral majority in the House of Commons, we need to marshal the power of direct democracy to hold those who govern us to account. Overthrowing the quango state, not merely having our leader live in Downing Street, should be the purpose of modern Conservatism.

Legal aid laid waste

Geoffrey Bindman

The rule of law is a necessary condition of a democratic society. It is thus a central plank of the Charter 88 project. It is the cement which holds society together. In Britain the rule of law has been embedded in our collective consciousness for nearly 800 years, since Magna Carta. Clause 40 of Magna Carta famously says: 'To no-one will we sell, to no-one deny or delay right or justice.' If we allow an advantage in the legal process to those who can afford to pay for it, we sell justice. Fairness requires equal access to the legal process. Because law has become so complex in modern society, most of those who come before the courts need skilled advice and representation. Without it there is an imbalance which is unjust and which results in unjust outcomes.

That is why legal aid – public funding of legal advice and representation for those who cannot afford to pay for them – is essential. The failure of successive governments to maintain an effective and adequately resourced legal aid scheme is both shameful and short sighted. Unfortunately, the approach of government has always been focused on cost. Instead of seeking to remove the inefficiencies in the legal system which add unnecessarily to the cost of legal services, it has cut costs by squeezing the lawyers. The result has been to drive away from legal aid experienced practitioners without whom the public cannot get the skilled help it needs. Without that skilled help, which is always available to the corporate or institutional party in a dispute, there is no justice, and without justice, democracy is a mockery.

Examples are easy to find. The tenant whose house needs repairs needs to present an effective case in court against his land-lord. A wife may need a court order to keep her violent husband away from her. Both will suffer intolerable hardship without legal representation, which they may not have without legal aid.

The history of legal aid in Britain

Perfectly equal access to justice is of course an ideal that has never been fully achieved, but in Britain the Legal Aid and Advice Act of the 1945 Attlee government was closer to it, in aspiration at least, than any other legislation anywhere else in the world. Its objective was to ensure that those who could not afford legal assistance would receive it at public expense.

When the NHS was created, most doctors went to work full time for it. That method could not be applied to lawyers on the creation of the legal aid scheme, because for many of them the bulk of their work is linked to commercial dealings in property and other forms of business which could not sensibly be financed out of the public purse. Yet, as we need medical help to deal with the health problems which we all face at some time in our lives, so most of us need help when confronting family and employment conflicts, as consumers in disputes with suppliers of goods or services, as tenants in disputes with landlords, and with increasingly intrusive local and governmental authorities, including the police.

For legal aid, the option of a salaried service for publicly funded work, corresponding to the structure of the NHS, has always been available, but from the outset it was more attractive to the government to buy in services from the private profession. Across the country, solicitors' practices could offer the same service to the publicly funded clients as to their privately paying clients. The state would avoid the burden of setting up an alternative structure, and equality of treatment was assured by providing the same service to legal aid clients as to those paying out of their own pockets.

It worked fairly well for some years. In 1963 I started a legal aid practice above a chemist and opposite a Citizens Advice Bureau in a north London high street. Legal aid developed skills in handling the problems of ordinary people, which were often more difficult than those of the rich and powerful. For the young and idealistic it presented a challenge and a source of satisfaction.

How the current crisis in legal aid came about

Many of the firms which had embraced legal aid with more or less enthusiasm at the beginning fell away as the commercial world became more prosperous and legal aid less economically attractive. Law centres, which employed lawyers to provide free legal services, had been established largely by voluntary effort in poorer communities. They depended on local government and charitable funding. They have found it difficult to raise money and over the years several have fallen by the wayside. At the present time several law centres are in crisis and are threatened with closure.

Meanwhile the need for legal advice and representation has grown as governments have increased the volume of new legislation and the crime rate has reached new heights. Businesses are willing to pay more to lawyers to defend their interests with increasing vigour and ingenuity. The cost of legal aid has grown as the workload of legal aid lawyers in the pursuit and defence of claims has increased.

The open-ended nature of legal aid expenditure – impossible to budget for exactly because of the uncertain number and com-plexity of future cases – had been a constant annoyance to the Treasury. Governments realised that they could use their monopoly power to cut fees to the bone. Lawyers were generally unpopular and were assumed (correctly in the case of many commercial lawyers) to be overpaid. Pleas of poverty would not attract public sympathy. And there would always be some lawyers who would feel an ethical obligation to work for little or nothing. So it came to be accepted that legal aid rates could be much lower than those for privately paid work. Rates were slashed year by year in real terms as the government repeatedly refused to raise them in line with inflation.

At the same time the government refused to increase eligibility limits. At its peak some 70 per cent of the population could qualify for legal aid. This percentage steadily declined and today hardly anyone can get legal aid unless they are at the level of poverty which qualifies them for social security benefits. Legal aid has become part of the welfare system, available only to the socially excluded, not a means to provide equal access to justice.

The practice in civil cases by which the losing party pays the winner's legal costs has helped to make this parsimony more tolerable for some legal aid lawyers. The legal aid solicitor can still get paid at private rates if the opposing party, rather than the government, is footing the bill.

Legal aid under New Labour

In 1999, the new Labour government introduced changes in legal aid. The most dramatic was to remove it totally from personal injuries cases (apart from those claiming medical negligence), at the same time withdrawing the longstanding prohibition on 'no win, no fee' arrangements. Thenceforth solicitors could charge up to double costs in winning cases, in order to compensate for the losing cases where they agreed not to be paid at all.

Unlike the US contingent fee system, the lawyer's fee was not to be taken out of the damages but was, as we have seen, to be paid by the losing party. The snag was that an unsuccessful claimant would still be liable to pay the costs of the winning defendant. The claimant had to be insured against this risk. The insurers were paid (and profited) whatever the result.

Permitting conditional fees was seen as an ingenious way to meet the shortfall in the availability of legal aid to those above the means limit. Although legal aid would still not be provided to those above a very low means threshold, solicitors and barristers could agree to take a case on the terms that they would only be paid if it was successful. But it is hard to see why this new freedom for the lawyer to gamble on the result of a case justified the removal of legal aid from those below the means threshold. The government's argument was that solicitors would have their cake and eat it: they would seek legal aid only in the most uncertain cases. So the government would not get the benefit of the clients' contributions in the cases that were bound to be successful. Why go through the bureaucratic processes when the other party was going to pay the lawyers anyway? The effect of removing legal aid from all personal injury cases has been to deny a remedy where there is a legal doubt, even though the case might, were it tested, be resolved in the claimant's favour.

The result has been that solicitors have mostly avoided cases where there is any significant risk of not recovering enhanced fees from the other party. Those whose claims are not straightforward will rarely be offered a conditional fee agreement. Indeed, solicitors who would be willing to take on risky cases are prevented from doing so by their insurers, who demand a high success rate – usually over 95 per cent – as a condition of insuring their clients.

By removing personal injury and other damages claims from the legal aid scheme, the government has weakened the integrity of the scheme and hastened its destruction and replacement by market-based methods of providing access to justice. A large area of legal specialisation has been removed from the legal aid scheme. Because of the enhanced fees in successful cases, which may be the only cases taken, some lawyers have made very large profits, in contrast to their colleagues doing legal aid work in generally more socially important fields such as family and housing law. A study of the income of personal injury and other conditional fee legal practices would undoubtedly demonstrate this. And of course that profit is at public expense, because it is funded largely by insurers, who in turn are ultimately funded by those who pay their premiums. On 25 June 2008, the Ministry of Justice announced an independent review of 'no win, no fee' arrangements by three academic experts. It would be very optimistic to expect it to result in the restoration of legal aid to damages claims, but it is heartening that the problems have been recognised.

Another step, introduced in 1999, was the franchise. Lawyers were to be contracted by government (represented by the Legal Services Commission) to handle a fixed number of cases in areas of work in which they were deemed competent, to be paid for at standard fee rates far lower than those charged to private clients. Franchising has considerable merits. It retains a high degree of independence for legal practices while providing a means of controlling expenditure. The problem has been that the expenditure has been controlled too tightly and bureaucratic intervention into practice management has been excessively petty and burdensome.

Treasury pressure to cut costs has continued and rates of payment have been steadily reduced in real terms. At a time when the profits of commercial law firms have risen exponentially, the polarisation of the profession has never been greater. The pressure to reduce an annual legal aid bill of some £2 billion led the government to look at new methods of cost-cutting. It was hardly surprising that costs grew as the government introduced more and more legislation (including some 3,000 new criminal offences). Nor has the government ever carried out proper research to ascertain the 'cost drivers', the causes of increased costs.

A re-examination: the Carter report

A businessman with no background in the law, Lord Carter of Coles, was appointed to review the system. The title of his report, *Legal Aid: A Market-Based Approach to Reform*, published in July 2006, neatly summarises its fundamental fallacy: that legal services can be equated with the sale of a commodity. That commodity is imagined as a measurable and objective unit of information, independent of the context. This approach assumes that what people need and expect from lawyers is no more than mechanical answers to factual questions, like a 'speak your weight' machine. The crucial personal relationship between lawyer and client, in which the full range of the lawyer's skill and experience is directed at the particular needs of the individual, is ignored.

Carter's analysis (or at any rate the way it has been interpreted by the government and its Legal Services Commission (LSC)) puts the sale of legal services on a par with the sale of soap powder and paper clips. This dictates the recipe for big savings in the legal aid budget. Instead of thousands of small firms of solicitors dotted about the country in the places most convenient to the public, Carter's answer is to concentrate legal aid in a few large factory firms churning out computerised advice in standardised chunks. As he says – and this gives a flavour of his barbarous style – 'Procurement-driven restructuring is likely to see an increase in the average size of firms through growth and mergers.'

Legal fees have for generations been calculated mainly by reference to a combination of factors, including the amount of work required, the level of skill and experience of the lawyer doing the work and the importance of the matter in hand. Naturally, these factors, especially the first of them, cannot be fully assessed in advance. Carter's solution to this dilemma, which so upsets the Treasury, is that 'there should be a wholesale move towards fixed pricing for work'. He continues: 'Fixed pricing should be graduated for more complex work so that cases genuinely requiring more expertise and effort are priced fairly. Exceptionally complex cases should be managed and paid for under individual case contracts with only the most experienced, competitive and competent legal teams providing the service.'

Every case, every occasion for legal advice or representation, is different, so the time, effort and skill are infinitely variable. The paper clip analogy here breaks down. Unless the overall sums paid to the lawyers are sufficient, the only lawyers who can afford to do the work are those who are prepared to cross-subsidise legal aid work from the profits of work done for the private sector. Many legal aid solicitors have cheerfully done this for years but most can no longer call upon surplus profits from private work to balance the books. And of course it is a dubious practice so far as the privately paying clients are concerned. Given a choice, the private clients might prefer to pay less and keep the surplus for themselves.

As a result of the Carter recommendations, the government has opted to open up legal services to market competition. 'Best value tendering' (BVT) will require solicitors to bid for contracts to do legal aid work. In theory those who win the contracts will be those who are able to demonstrate that they can provide an acceptable service at the lowest cost. The problem is that while cost can be easily compared, quality of service cannot. The temptation to cut corners and cut quality will be irresistible, and the experiments so far undertaken to assess quality by 'peer review' have been cumbersome and unreliable, as those who manage the scheme freely acknowledge.

The current crisis

In the current interim period, before BVT comes into effect, the government, through the medium of the LSC, has imposed a series of fixed fees for different categories of cases. The theory is that a solicitor who undertakes a number of cases of similar general character over a certain period will be adequately paid overall on the 'swings and roundabouts' principle. In practice, the rates set are too low, so that the conscientious solicitor will not be paid enough to make his practice viable, and only those willing to skimp on the quality of the work, and use inadequately qualified staff, will survive.

At the root of the government's cost-cutting regime is the statistical anomaly that the Treasury uses to justify its unwillingness to make more money available for legal aid: that in Britain we already spend far more per capita on legal aid than any other country. The minister in charge of legal aid, Lord Hunt of Kings Heath, wrote in the *Guardian* on 27 December 2007 that in England and Wales the cost is £38 per head of the population whereas in Germany it is £4 and in France £3. But our system cannot be compared with other European systems, where the cost of investigation is met not as legal aid but out of another governmental budget. That is because the investigation of the facts is carried out not by the lawyers but by investigating judges. Nor could injustice elsewhere justify it in Britain.

The government has failed to conduct adequate research into the causes of legal aid expenditure and the increase which has taken place in recent years. While it does appear that costs have increased at a higher level than could be accounted for solely by inflation, such evidence as has been found indicates that rises in cost are not due to higher fees paid to solicitors but to the increase in the amount of necessary work.[*] This is the product of increased resources available to privately funded opponents and government-funded prosecutors who have deployed them in an increasingly aggressive

---

[*] See for example Ed Cape and Richard Moorhead, *Demand Induced Supply? Identifying Cost Drivers in Criminal Defence Work* (London: Legal Services Commission, 2005).

and determined way, which imposes matching demands on those who rely on legal aid. Nor has any research been done into the savings to the public purse which good legal advice and representation can achieve. How much expenditure by the NHS and by social welfare agencies is the consequence of unresolved disputes and unredressed wrongdoing?

This brings us back to equality. There is no possibility of justice unless the legally aided litigant, whether in a civil or criminal case, can match the resources deployed by the opposing party. Does this mean that legal aid lawyers have to be paid as much as those in the private sector? They do not expect the inflated earnings which City lawyers succeed in extracting from their commercial clients. Current legal aid rates are a mere fraction of those in the City. Assuming the statistics are accurate, the fact remains that the current budget is insufficient to secure legal aid solicitors a fair wage for their work. That is why there has been a steady drift away from legal aid by experienced members of the profession. This is likely to accelerate as new payment structures are introduced, if the government maintains its present intentions, based on Carter's market-based ideas.

The government's plans are half baked and rushed. The Constitutional Affairs Committee published its report on the government's proposals for 'radical reform' of legal aid in April 2007.* It approved the government's concern with the increase in the legal aid budget in recent years but pointed out that this increase was largely concentrated in two areas of work: crown court defence work and public law children's cases. Other areas of expenditure were stable or declining. It recognised that there had been considerable pressure on legal aid solicitors, many of whom had stopped doing legal aid work.

As the select committee report points out, the government's plan is to change the basis of legal aid by introducing a transitional system of fixed and graduated fees, instead of payment on an hourly basis, as a way of preparing for full competitive tendering for legal aid contracts. There was at the time of the report, and to this day

---

* Constitutional Affairs Committee, *Implementation of the Carter Review of Legal Aid*, third report, Session 2006–07, HC 223.

there remains, a lack of reliable research into the effect of this change. It is clear, however, that the initial stage of fixed fees has already resulted in substantial cuts in earnings, which have driven many legal aid practitioners out of business. The haemorrhage of legal aid lawyers continues apace. Increasingly, legal aid will be delivered by the underqualified, underpaid and inexperienced.

Price competition raises questions about quality. Maintaining standards, in the face of a financial incentive to cut corners and employ underqualified people at reduced salaries to conduct the work, requires rigorous supervision and reviewing. The system of peer review is in operation but so far it has not been possible to recruit reviewers of sufficient skill and experience to perform the task.

The future

The next stage of the reform process, BVT, has not yet taken place. It has already been postponed under pressure from the legal profession. The government has tried to reassure the profession that the competition for legal aid contracts will not lower standards and will result in an adequately funded and efficient legal aid scheme. Experience indicates that this pious hope is not realistic and will not be fulfilled. The opening up of the profession to 'multidisciplinary partnerships' and the legalisation of non-lawyer ownership of and investment in legal practices, with its threat of 'Tesco law' – legal practices managed by commercial corporations – will make equal access to justice an even more remote and impossible dream.

Is there any hope that legal aid can yet be saved? Inadequate resources are at the heart of the problem. The government continues to repeat the mantra that £2 billion annually – barely enough to keep the NHS afloat for a week – is the limit and there is no more money. This is not enough to support adequate legal services as the judicial system is currently structured. The government has been afraid to tackle the structural inadequacies of the system: wasteful court hearings and excessive documentation; the duplication of work resulting from the division of the legal profession into barristers and solicitors; the unnecessary length of trials, prolonged by advocates whose speeches are subject to no time limits. Lord Woolf's reforms of civil procedure, the Civil Procedure Rules 1999, did not go far enough and it is time for a review. A similar review of criminal procedure is urgent. The government cannot hope to keep legal aid alive unless it is prepared to exceed its arbitrary limit on expenditure, at least until cost-saving procedural reforms have been implemented.

Constitutional change and the future of Britain

Gordon Brown MP

This Charter 88 Sovereignty Lecture was given on 9 March 1992.

Foreword to republication

lthough it was delivered more than fifteen years ago, the ideas and principles set out in this 1992 Charter 88 Sovereignty Lecture have continued to shape and guide my approach to constitutional reform over the years. As back then, I believe that constitutional change is at the heart of the debate about the future of Britain. Whether it is deciding whether to go to war, responding to economic change or making our streets safer for our children, we are continually forced to confront how to balance the relationship between the individual, the community and the state.

When I delivered this lecture in 1992, a set of different challenges and events framed thinking on this topic. I was speaking after thirteen years of Conservative rule, much of it under a Prime Minister who believed that there was 'no such thing as society'. The poll tax riots had opened up the wounds of a polarised community. Opposition political parties had established a constitutional convention in Scotland to call for devolution of power. And in 1992, the UK had signed the Maastricht treaty – signalling closer European engagement. Each of these developments challenged old ideas about our institutions and our constitutional settlement. It became a time of profound questioning over the rights of the individual and the role of the nation state.

My address was an attempt to break through the stand-off between those who asserted the inalienable rights of the individual against the monolithic state, and those who saw runaway individualism as responsible for the destruction of social cohesion. The former world-view had been forged in the heat of the Cold War, in support of eastern European citizens as they tore down the Berlin Wall and the dictatorships that had built them. The latter was a response to the spiralling inequality and social breakdown left in the wake of the state's retreat from civil life in the 1980s.

In setting out a new constitutional reform agenda, I wanted to transcend these two world-views by demonstrating the continuing relevance of community and to argue that our central mission must be to unlock the talents of all the people. I said that we needed a new constitutional settlement that recognised that the individual needs the proper and guaranteed protection of a modern constitution so that government is accountable; and that individual potential is best developed in a community, and the community need not be a threat to individual liberty but can assist the fulfilment of it.

So there are two questions that will be asked. The first is: how have we, as a Labour government, so far measured up to the challenge set out in the 1992 Sovereignty Lecture? The second is: what is the task ahead?

I believe the answer to the first question is to be proud but not complacent: that while we have performed well, there is still more to do. Coming into office in 1997, we made bold moves to realise the vision of a modern country, with power rapidly decentralised to individuals, communities and regions. There was devolution for Scotland, Wales and Northern Ireland – allowing the nations that make up the United Kingdom greater power and freedom to determine their own destinies within a British identity. There were reforms to the House of Lords, removing hereditary peers and making progress towards a more democratic system. We introduced a Freedom of Information Act and a Human Rights Act to protect British citizens from abuses of state power. And new duties to promote equality and consult with local communities have also had a positive impact.

But there remained more to do. By June 2007 it was time to go further and pursuing further constitutional change was one of my priorities. So on 3 July I delivered a statement to the House of Commons setting out a constitutional agenda that would build a new relationship between British citizens and their government. Detailed proposals were then set out in a White Paper and draft Constitutional Renewal Bill, published in March 2008.

Some of these ideas were explicitly referenced in my Charter 88 lecture. For instance, the government will consult on the creation of a Bill of Rights and Responsibilities, setting out the entitlements and obligations of citizens, to be respected by the state and the community. We will move forward reform of the House of Lords and seek to enact the will of the House of Commons that a second chamber be either wholly or mostly elected. And we are currently consulting on what day the country should go to the polls and how participation in local democracy can be increased.

In 1992 I emphasised the importance of establishing oversight of the security services and we have now increased the Intelligence and Security Committee's transparency and account-ability to Parliament. We will ensure that it is the House of Commons that makes the ultimate decision on the grave issue of whether to go to war. We are allowing for new parliamentary scrutiny of key public appointments, and reducing the executive's power over judicial appointments. And in order to increase the parliamentary accountability of local and regional decision-making, there will be new regional select committees.

While all of these constitutional reform initiatives are significant in their own right, it is important to recognise that the agenda they represent has a much broader application. As a progressive government, we need to be decentralising power to citizens and communities in all spheres of our activity. So there are four areas in particular where we must do more.

First, we must continue to safeguard and extend the liberties of our citizens. That is why we are giving people new rights to protest outside Parliament, considering a freedom of expression audit for all legislation and re-examining the rules under which historical records are opened to public access only after thirty years. And from

ID cards to pre-charge detention, we will ensure that wherever action is needed by government, it never subjects the citizen to arbitrary treatment, is transparent and proportionate, and at all times requires proper accountability to Parliament and the people.

Second, we need to do more to empower local communities to shape and influence local decision-making. We need to give neighbourhoods and citizens the tools and powers to have a more direct say over issues that affect them. This is why we have published a community empowerment White Paper with proposals to expand participatory budgeting and increase the use of petitioning.

Third, we need to place more power in the hands of citizens as users of public services to shape and influence the way health, education and policing is delivered. It is my firm view that this is the next phase of public service reform. There are a number of mechanisms that can be used. One example is the government's proposal that local neighbourhoods vote to elect representatives to the police board.

Fourth, we need to use the constitutional reform agenda to strengthen our common identity and reinforce the bonds of the union. I am in no doubt that devolution and decentralisation have had a positive impact on the people of Scotland, Wales and Northern Ireland. However, it is time we rediscovered the common values that unite us as the British people, and did more to celebrate the world's most successful multinational state. We don't have to choose between being pro-Scottish or pro-English, and being proud to be British as well. This is why we will consult on a British statement of values to help us define this identity and give the British people an agreed set of principles to rally around.

The Sovereignty Lecture was delivered at a time when we faced a different set of challenges. Nevertheless, I believe much of it is still relevant today. As I said in 1992, the constitution fit for the twenty-first century should be one of the servant state: the state serving the community and the individual, placed beneath a sovereign people and not above it. And by working together to build this new constitutional settlement, we will be better placed to unlock the talents of the British people and move forwards as a nation.

The lecture

Let me state at the outset that this evening I want to put my view that constitutional change – and I mean that in the broadest sense – is at the heart of the debate about the future for our country. Not incidental but integral to our future as a community.

All over Europe, in response to environmental as well as economic and social challenges, there is a growing recognition of the need for a change in the relationship between individuals, community and the state. And I believe that in Britain constitutional change is essential for two quite fundamental reasons. It is vital because it is our responsibility to ensure the individual is protected against what can be called the vested interests of the state. And it is vital too because constitutional change is also a necessary means of advancing the potential of the individual in our community. In other words we have twin responsibilities to individual citizens as democrats: we must never fail to attack the evil wherever the individual is at risk from the encroachment of the state, and we must never lose sight of the good whenever the individual is empowered by the community.

I want to argue that what in truth we require is an entirely new settlement between the individual, community and government. Indeed, in my view a modern view of socialism must retrieve the broad idea of community from the narrow notion of the state and ensure that the community becomes a means by which individuals can realise their potential, not at the expense of individual liberty but in advancing it. In other words I will be making the case this evening for constitutional change from Labour values, for I have always believed it is the historic role of the Labour Party to stand up for individual citizens against all vested interests that frustrate their potential. After thirteen years of a Conservative erosion of liberties we now need guaranteed rights: the right to know, the right to be consulted, the right to participate, the right of communities to run their own affairs.

I will argue not just for Acts of Parliament enshrining in statute the long-held demand for a Bill of Rights, but also that we must now take seriously the case for a European Bill of Rights so that we can protect the citizen from the potential abuse of power by any major public institution that touches our lives. I will argue not just for immediate implementation of a Freedom of Information Act to ensure the flow of information from government to citizen and the right to know – and I believe we could do so in months – but argue also that there should be precise duties guaranteeing the right of individuals to information where it is in the public interest to do so, in the dark and secret corners of the private sector. I will argue not just for reform of the judiciary but for reform of the security services and for a reformed second chamber in place of the anachronism which is the House of Lords. And I will argue the case not just for home rule for Scotland within the United Kingdom and for the importance of the fresh look now taking place into electoral reform, but also for the principle of devolution applied all round throughout the country.

This lecture comes shortly before an election. Originally it was planned to come shortly after an election when calmer seas prevailed. My purpose is not to catch the next day's morning headlines but to reflect on questions that are rather more enduring. I will not list a set of constitutional changes, but will propose what I believe a constitutional agenda must include, not as detailed policy but as parameters for a debate that will continue long after the election.

My main purpose is to set a course for constitutional change. To make it more than just a shopping list of attractive ideas. To place it within a framework of belief about Britain as a community that can reach and touch all our people. To make constitutional change central, to make it popular and thus to make it attainable.

Let me start from Scotland to demonstrate what I mean. Scotland has just seen a unique all–party constitutional convention in which I have had the privilege to play a part: a convention that has included not just one but a number of political parties and also enjoyed broad representation from the churches, local authorities, voluntary organisations, trades unions, and others throughout Scottish society from what might be called civil society. The convention rightly demands a Scottish parliament with entrenched powers. An aspiration first developed in its modern form a century ago, a widely held demand for change which has occasioned twenty Home Rule Bills throughout this century already. An insistent demand for change which has brought administrative devolution as an inadequate substitute for legislative devolution. And now a popular demand that is so pressing and urgent that I believe that in the coming years we shall see the creation of a parliament which will not just be an inspiration to those seeking fundamental democratic change for the constitution in Scotland but throughout the United Kingdom as well.

For against old-fashioned and unacceptable ideas of Crown sovereignty, the convention asserts the sovereignty of the people, with legitimacy and authority flowing upwards and not downwards. It demands, and I believe will secure, the entrenchment of rights including a right to know. It demands more equal representation for women, rightly beginning to tackle the unacceptable underrepresentation of women at all levels of our political system. It demands a reformed electoral system, reflecting the widespread concern about the current system.

In Scotland the status quo is now so discredited that it is no longer an option. And it is because the Scottish parliament is the precursor for one in Wales and regional devolution throughout Britain that the West Lothian question – essentially that different MPs will have differing roles at Westminster – is not a genuine problem in proceeding with change.

Now I understand that the Prime Minister's [John Major's] view of the best solution is that instead of 7,000 civil servants running Scotland immune from Scottish democratic control, we should have 7,000 civil servants running Scotland immune from Scottish democratic control but wearing name tags. But the convention is in fact a response to two deep and widely felt concerns, neither of which I feel he understands. First, that individual rights have been ignored because of the remoteness and the insensitivity of centralised government and, second, that the exercise of power has been separated from the democratic control.

But it is more than that. The demand for change is not just because London is far away but because Scotland is nearer – indeed, home, because the Scottish nation sees itself as a community whose interests cannot be properly advanced by the British state alone without the participation of the Scottish community through its own democratic parliament. Indeed

Scotland is a community that, in recognition of its inter-dependence, has a sense of what must be done by government to ensure individuals can achieve their potential. So there is a demand not just for accountable government but for government used effectively on behalf of the community.

And in transforming the government of Scotland I would argue that instead of retreating towards the old nineteenth-century idea and trappings of an exclusive nation state with army, navy and defence forces and a separate currency – a nation state defined in relation to other nations and mainly in antithesis to its largest neighbour – what Scotland is demanding is a modern national identity, with autonomy on vital social and many economic matters within Britain and Europe. Recognising we are inter-dependent communities, we want to link up across nations, not turn our backs on each other. Achieving, in short, the dream of home rule without the retreat into separation.

But the tumultuous events in Scotland are not the only calls for a new settlement in the United Kingdom. From Clive Ponting[*] to GCHQ, from judicial error to excessive secrecy, we have become more centralised, less sensitive to individual rights and less free than we were. And I have to say that the Citizen's Charters are no compensation for the failure of government and no substitute for the essential reform of government. The problem is much deeper than this. It is about the relationship between individual, community and the state, and I want to put the problem in a historical context.

There have been two attempts at a new settlement of the relationship between individuals, the community and the state in recent years. The boldest was the post-1945 settlement. In 1945 individual freedom was to be guaranteed by social security rather than charity, with the state as provider, ensuring for each citizen welfare, health care, education, social security and work. At the time, and for the time, it was the most ambitious programme of

---

[*] Clive Ponting came to prominence in 1984 after revealing confidential information about the sinking of the Argentinian warship *General Belgrano* during the Falklands War. He was charged under the Official Secrets Act but was acquitted by the jury.

social and economic reform, one utterly necessary for many of the improvements we now take for granted today, not least our National Health Service.

Individual wellbeing was to be advanced by the active state delivering entitlements for the individual. But inevitably, as time passed and aspirations grew, individuals saw themselves less as passive recipients of benefits delivered by government and more as active participants seeking to shape their destiny. And the settlement did not in the end stand the test of time because it often seemed to many that the state and the community were one and the same thing. Nationalised industries acted without the direct involvement of workforce or community. Scotland, Wales and the regions were granted benevolent administration without democratic rights to run their own affairs.

So, despite all the great achievements in health care, social security and education, there was not just an underdeveloped sense of community, but often an assumption that state and community interests were synonymous. Instead of government being an extension of community, it often looked to many like a substitute for it.

The response came in 1979, when Mrs Thatcher encouraged popular resentment against taxation, collectivism, bureaucracy and the local and national state, and attempted a new settlement between individual, community and government. The problem was identified by the new right Thatcherites as too much government and too little individual freedom. Individual wellbeing was to be guaranteed by less government even at the expense of social security. But the new right did not recognise the individual as part of an interdependent community; quite the opposite. The individual was to make his or her own way in the marketplace unaided by government and set apart from any idea of society or community. There was – in Mrs Thatcher's own words – no such thing as society.

The result was that responsibilities conventionally accepted by the community that most of us had assumed would be discharged by government were abandoned or at least substantially eroded and reduced. Not just in social affairs (the responsibilities for public services of reasonable quality and the duty of the community to those in poverty) but also in the responsibility previously accepted by governments of all parties to stabilise the economy. Hence the extremes of boom and bust in the stop-go economics of the 1980s and 1990s. Hence the inability to improve research and innovation and training and education. Hence the now widening training and education gap.

The 1979 settlement abandoned responsibilities for individual wellbeing that government had discharged on behalf of the community, because it was now assumed that these could be left to the individual in the marketplace. The debate was wrongly identified as one between government and no government, when the real issue was better government. The result is that thirteen wasted years for the British constitution have directly contributed to thirteen wasted years for the British economy and for Britain as a community.

Let me say therefore where the heart of the difference in this debate lies. The new right believe individuals fulfil themselves best with no need for society and less need for government. I believe that in a modern interdependent society individual wellbeing is best advanced by a strong community backed up by active and accountable government. And even those who now try to rescue the Conservative Party from the mistakes of crude free-market individualism have a similar problem. Unable to come to terms with a modern view of the constitution or society, their social market economy – dependent on the idea at best of compassion rather than rights – merely heralds a return to nineteenth-century paternalism.

But neither nineteenth-century paternalism nor eighteenth-century free-market liberalism can answer questions of the relationship between individual community and government that now require a modern twentieth-century democratic settlement. A settlement that recognises first that the state may become a vested interest and that the individual needs the proper and guaranteed protection of a modern constitution so that government is accountable. And second, a settlement that recognises that individual potential is best developed in a community and that the community need not be a threat to individual liberty but can assist the fulfilment of it.

It is important for everyone, but particularly important for democratic socialists, that we recognise the need for individuals to be protected against any possible vested interests within the state. Let me explain why democratic socialists more than anyone should be concerned in this way. Conservatives seek few if any additional responsibilities for government, and many suggest much less. They see wellbeing advanced primarily by the individual acting unaided on his or her own; while when I talk of individuals flourishing as part of a community where common needs are met through sharing responsibility, I assume an active role for government. But where I invoke the need for government I have a special responsibility to ensure its accountability. Indeed, those who argue for us to take seriously the responsibilities of government must always be more vigilant in arguing that in the exercise of these responsibilities there must be the maximum openness and accountability.

Holding the state accountable to the citizen is important for another reason. Socialists have long recognised that all societies tend to produce accumulated reservoirs of power. They entrench themselves, threatening to become vested interests – either in the private or public sector – hostile to any kind of reform or change. We have always identified such vested interests as our fundamental target. Nineteenth-century socialism developed as a protest against the power of the main vested interests that then denied opportunity – the power of private capital. Twentieth-century socialists often were slow to realise that vested interests can operate throughout society. Indeed when socialism began as an attack on the vested interests of private wealth it used the state as the instrument of that attack. Yet the state was capable of becoming a vested interest in itself, capable of denying individuals opportunity and frustrating their potential to fulfil themselves.

I see the historic role of the Labour Party as nothing less than to stand up for the individual against any and every concentration of power that denies opportunity to individuals in British society, whether cartels or cliques, whether in the public or private sector. And that is why socialists must demand that individuals have entrenched rights to protect them from the modern state.

But in our concern about the encroachment of the state on the individual we must never forget that community is still necessary as a means for individuals fulfilling themselves. Indeed I believe that the greatest failure of the last decade – and a loss that diminishes us all – has been the denial of the importance of community. Libertarians have been so afraid of the power that society can exercise over the individual they have sought to detach the individual from the very society of which he or she is part. Yet community is vital for the safety, health and development of individuals. Individuals on their own cannot make the streets safe at night. When disease strikes there is no such thing as a one-man health service. And almost all of us here today owe much that we have to the opportunities that have come from the collective provision of education. And take the environment today. Not only is it the case that individuals, no matter how rich, cannot buy themselves out of countryside pollution or urban decay – it is also true that private affluence loses its savour amid public squalor, a recognition that we are dependent each upon one another. So no-one can be in any doubt that there is a public interest in the community not just protecting the individual against pollution but positively acting to demand and ensure the highest standards: a common interest, not only in any one nation but also across the world.

So individuals need community and individuals depend on each other in a community. It is as wrong to see ourselves merely as Robinson Crusoes with no concerns beyond the immediate family, no bonds beyond the front door, no responsibilities beyond the garden gate, as it is to see ourselves as merely the repositories of society's values, somehow subsumed in the social order.

Etzioni has written that individuals stick to each other if they get too close but freeze if they get too far apart. It is time to see the crude dichotomy between community and individuals that has frustrated political discussion in recent years as both unrealistic and damaging. People do not live in isolation. People do not live in markets. People live in communities.

I think of Britain as a community of citizens with common needs, mutual interests, shared objectives, related goals and, most of all, linked destinies. A Britain not of strangers, who only compete, but a Britain of neighbours, who recognise each other and recognise we depend upon each other. A Britain that is not a society of individuals whose interactions are determined by the invisible hand of the free market beloved of right-wing economists, but a society where individuals depend freely and willingly upon what Dr James Stockinger has described as 'the hands of others'. It is, he says, the hands of others who grow the food we eat, sew the clothes we wear and build the homes we inhabit. It is the hands of others who tend us when we are sick and who raise us up when we fall. And it is the hands of others who lift us first into the cradle and lower us finally into the grave.

We must rescue and restore the idea of community – and do more than that, assert how individuals benefit from strong communities, not as a threat to their individual liberties but as an assistance to their fulfilment. Community is not merely the aggregate of individuals joined together temporarily out of convenience – the community, in Bentham's words, as a fictitious body. Nor is it merely the source of authority seeking, in the name of duty, to impose standards of behaviour on warring individuals, because anarchy is seen as a greater danger than authoritarianism.

We must break away from the extreme view of the individual struggling for advantage against a community holding him back and that of the community struggling to hold the anti-social individual down. So I do not support Locke when he says rights are vested in individuals who do nothing more than delegate these rights to a community, and I reject Hobbes when he argues for individuals subordinating all their rights for security. Community arises because we depend on each other.

It is said that the pressure for citizenship in Britain comes from the compassion of the fortunate towards the least fortunate. But modern citizenship is built on the recognition of inter-dependence. It is distinct from individualism, including such paternalism. It recognises the citizen as part of a wider and inter-dependent community. Indeed I believe that democratic socialism was founded on this belief in the value of community and society; that its main inspiration is the ethic of community rather than a theory of economy; and that the idea that individuals realise their potential to the full as part of the society in which they live leads us to embrace the idea that the community should stand up on behalf of individuals against the vested interests that hold them back. It is, let us be clear, community assisting the individual, not the individual subsumed in community or subordinated to it.

But it is partly because the community has succeeded in the past in creating new opportunities that people have become more assertive, with a broader view of what they can achieve, less inclined to be passive recipients of welfare, more inclined to demand the right to realise their diversity of talents, interests and desires to the full. It is significant that all constitutions that have stood the test of time have had an implicit if not explicit view of society and human nature that recognises such aspirations.

The French constitution says that 'the community shall be based on the equality and the solidarity of the peoples composing it'. The Italian constitution 'recognises and guarantees the inviolable rights of man both as an individual and as a member of the social groups in which his personality finds expression'. The American constitution starts with the words 'We the people'. But anyone studying our unwritten British constitution will find implicit in it the idea of leaders and led, the Hobbesian view that the role of government is to empower leaders, unbounded by any limitations, to deal with the threat to security posed by those who must be led.

It is time to escape from that bleak Hobbesian view, a view which, if I may say so, now seems after 300 years and the experience of many other nations to be nasty, poor, British and short. It is now time to think about the liberation of potential and the empowerment of the citizen.

We can see it reflected every day in the permanent influence of the women's movement, demanding genuine liberation in place of what has invariably been second-class citizenship. When women say – for example – that they should not be faced with the unfair choice between the jobs they need and the children they love, they are expressing the legitimate desire to have the right to fulfil their potential. When we think of the rights of children, we think of them growing, through parental support, child care, nursery education, a stimulating environment, the love of friends and neighbours: developing their potential to the full. But the argument for the fulfilment of potential does not apply only to children. Adults too should enjoy the right that we should become the best that we have it in us to become, and not just the best that other people have decided we may be allowed to be.

So the growing demand of individuals is that they should be in a position to realise their potential, to bridge the gap between what they are and what they have it in them to become. And the aspirations of the individual within the community and the means whereby the community responds become a central question to be addressed when we look at how we are to be governed.

Rightly, any programme for a modern society and modern economy and the policies that arise from it must encompass a debate about how markets can work in the public interest, how individuals at work – employees and managers – can co-operate effectively to use capital in the public interest, how we can ensure the highest quality public services that are both accountable and open, and how poverty can be tackled not just in the interests of advancing social and economic opportunities and rights of individuals themselves but in securing social cohesion.

But a modern constitution is essential to protect individuals against the state and to empower them within an interdependent community. In this way the agenda for constitutional change becomes essential to the task of establishing a modern view of society and in my view a modern view of democratic socialism. That agenda will be familiar to supporters of Charter 88 but I want briefly and in conclusion to address certain aspects of it.

First, from the belief that socialism must take on the vested interests of government as well as those of capital and wealth springs the clear need for the rights of the individual to be protected in law in the constitution and to be exercisable against executive power. The method of achieving this can be debated. It could of course be done through an entrenched Bill of Rights, possibly through incorporation of the European Convention on Human Rights. Alternatively, individual rights could be defined through specific items of legislation which are then made subject to a special legislative procedure which in effect entrenches them. On this basis, then, this debate can continue but a Bill of Rights in one form or another there will be.

And this must be accompanied by the affirmative action

essential not just to outlaw sexual, racial and other discrimination – for example by genuinely achieving equal access to the law – but also to positively promote greater equality, ensuring that in a modern society, as I have indicated, civil rights are matched by economic and social opportunities in the workplace and elsewhere. And as the power of European institutions threatens to grow, especially that of the Commission, so does the need for accountability and protection for individual rights. For that reason the European Commission too must be subject to the European Convention on Human Rights. In the longer term I have no doubt we will have to consider a new European Bill of Rights, protecting the rights of European citizens from any abuse of power by European institutions.

We must make freedom of information a priority and in my view there is now an opportunity as well as the demand to act rapidly. It is clear that to make our community more efficient and to protect individual liberty we should have a free flow of information between government and governed. That is why, as Roy Hattersley has outlined, we need a Freedom of Information Act that ensures not only a presumption in favour of disclosure, but also that public interest defence must be available where there is a question mark over the illegitimate disclosure of information by civil servants.

But because of what I say about vested interests as a whole I want to extend this concept in two ways. First, freedom of information should apply not just to the apparatus of the state but to those dark and secret corners of private power. There should be specific obligations on companies to inform employees, shareholders and the public, where it is in the public interest to do so or where it is clearly legitimate for individuals to require such information.

Secondly, freedom of information should be seen not just as a brake upon the natural tendency towards secrecy of powerful institutions. It should be an attempt to actively provide information to the community that needs it. For example, how can we debate seriously the environment, the economy, unemployment, or the state of our public services if we are denied the vital information – the true, not politically doctored, facts and figures – which must necessarily form the basis for such a debate? I believe, for example, that what we call official statistics should come from a central statistical office; not subject to government interference as it is at the moment but independent of government. In this way the constitutional debate is about content as well as about form, about how to make rights effective in practice as well as in theory.

Thus there is a duty in the modern constitution to ensure the best possible consultation throughout our society. Public consultation is a mark of a mature democracy, not only when government seeks to make major legislative changes – for example over local taxation – but also at a smaller scale where new developments are planned. We must also ensure the fullest democratic participation in decisions.

Crucial, obviously, to any debate about the rules governing our society is the method of deciding its government. The debate about electoral reform is now proceeding apace and I welcome it. In Scotland we have already adopted the principles for change in a Scottish parliament, reflecting a growing recognition that the present system is outdated. Indeed I believe there is now a majority in the Labour Party for an open and comprehensive debate on electoral reform.

It should proceed on the basis of fairness, not electoral advantage. It should be because of its intrinsic worth – not as an alternative to winning elections under the present system. Then, in the detail of different systems of voting, the crucial questions arise. Systems are widely varied and have had quite different consequences when they have been tried. The debate, in other words, must concentrate on mechanisms as well as ideals. In particular, I and many others would want to ensure that whatever system is adopted maintains the close link between the constituency as a community and its representative.

We must also widen our notion of what we mean by participation. Throughout the community encouragement should be given to individuals to participate in the major decisions that affect their lives.

There must also be proper accountability for all those who exercise power in the public's name. I favour certain public appointments made subject to the scrutiny of a House of Commons committee, so reducing the prime ministerial power of patronage. But I also favour placing the security services under public scrutiny through Parliament, a reform that is long overdue. We must ensure that those who exercise power, in the executive or judiciary as well as the legislature, are able to reflect the public interest. Measures have been spelled out for increasing the representation of women but it will also be equally important that those who administer the law themselves be more representative. What is fascinating now is that real and profound concern about our legal system can no longer be dismissed as confined to fringe or minority groups. Recent cases have seriously undermined public confidence in our legal system. There must be a thorough reform of judicial appointment.

I believe that there must be a wholesale devolution of power. I have made the case for a Scottish parliament now and for the reform of government in Wales and the regions, pointing towards a written constitution. In replacing the indefensible House of Lords on a democratic basis, consideration should be given to introducing a regional element to the second chamber. But the devolution of power that I favour is far more widespread. I believe that more generally communities should be in a position to take more control over their own decisions.

That is why we must begin a radical discussion of how the community can work to organise its affairs, breaking out of the one-dimensional view of government that has dominated too much of our thinking. Where there is a public interest there need not be a centralised public sector bureaucracy always directly involved in provision. Sometimes the best role for government is merely to enable or encourage, or to act as a catalyst or co-ordinator. At other times government can be partner or simply financier, helping communities to organise themselves. Indeed the constitution fit for the twenty-first century should be one of the servant state, the state serving the community and the individual, placed beneath a sovereign people and not above it.

And finally, part of a new settlement between individual community and government is to reinvigorate the notion of public service. For thirteen years we have heard much about the evils of the public sector, as it has been denigrated. It is time to talk about the value of our public services as a reflection of the shared

concerns of a British society that educates the young, cares for its
sick and disabled, shares responsibilities for the elderly and frail.
Teachers and all those who work in the education service; doctors,
nurses, orderlies, assistants and all those who work in the health
service; the police service; and of course the civil service itself.

With young people it is time to harness idealism and energy in
the meeting of needs by public service. In the 1960s, from
America, there was launched the Peace Corps, an international
commitment to harness the idealism of young people to break out
of the impotence many felt in the face of the threat to world peace.
Now in the 1990s, from Britain, it may be that we should be
considering a new corps, a world environment corps, to harness
the idealism of young people to break out of the impotence many
feel in the face of the threat to the world environment.

We need a British-initiated but world-wide organisation
through which young people can be trained to meet the environmental challenges of our time: whether helping environmental
improvement in Britain, or tackling reclamation or pollution in
other parts of the world. This is one of many proposals that we
could discuss that will over time reinvigorate the idea, central to
the notion of community, that public service is a noble aspiration.

In conclusion, the current movement for constitutional reform
is of historic importance. It signals the demand for a decisive shift
in the balance of power in Britain, a long overdue transfer of
sovereignty from those who govern to those who are governed,
from an ancient and indefensible Crown sovereignty to a modern
popular sovereignty, not just tidying up our constitution but
transforming it.

What I have tried to do is to set the movement for constitutional change within the framework of democratic socialism and
I make no apology for doing that. I have put forward the idea of
a new settlement, based on two requirements: the first, that the
individual is protected against the state, and the second, that the
individual is empowered to develop his or her potential as part of
our community. I believe that the Labour Party is the natural
party of reform in government and that when I argue that the
historic role is to stand up for the individual citizen against vested
interests I also mean that the community should open doors for

the individual, break down barriers that frustrate choice and chances, empower people with new opportunities, using the power of all to advance the good of each.

I have said that central to this is the notion that Britain needs a new view of community, and that this requires in turn a modern constitution to give it effect. I believe that we can break out of the discredited alternatives of old-style state power and new-style individualism. Instead I believe that the challenge of the 1990s is to create, as we move towards a new century, a new settlement between individual and community. One that recognises both our rights and aspirations as individuals and our needs and shared values as a community. Not so much the end of history, as one academic put it, but the opening of a new chapter.

Electoral reform

Helen Margetts

his chapter first considers the various options for electoral reform in the UK, putting forward the main advantages and disadvantages of the various electoral systems on offer as alternatives, including the status quo, first past the post. The second section examines the current state of the UK electoral system, proposing the argument that it is in any case increasingly unstable as the number of parties with substantive support in the electorate increases and that at a certain point reform will be inevitable. In the third section, the chapter considers how the three largest UK parties, Labour, the Liberal Democrats and the Conservatives, have reacted to potential instability, in terms of their approach to electoral reform. The fourth section considers current prospects for reform, in particular a move among some pro-reformers to recommend a majoritarian system, the alternative vote, as an immediate step in that direction.

Options for reform: alternative electoral systems

There is an enormous variety of electoral systems currently in use in countries across the world, but there are four main categories of system that are either currently in operation or have been discussed as candidates for reform in the UK. Two key characteristics of electoral systems generally rise to the forefront of any discussion of electoral reform: whether the system is proportional, in terms of allocating seats in proportion to the votes won by each party competing in the election, and whether the system preserves a link between voters and a single representative of a geographical constituency.

Table 1: Deviation from proportionality in Great Britain, general election 2005

	Seats (number)	Seats (%)	Vote (%)	Deviation
Labour	356	56.7	36.4	20.3
Conservative	197	31.4	33.1	1.8
Liberal Democrat	62	9.9	22.6	12.7
UKIP	0	0.0	2.5	2.3
SNP	6	1.0	1.5	0.6
Greens	0	0.0	1.0	1.1
Plaid Cymru	3	0.5	0.6	0.2
BNP	0	0.0	0.7	0.7
Respect	1	0.2	0.3	0.1
Other	3	0.5	0.1	0.3
Total	**628**	**100**	**100**	**DV = 20.1**

Note: To compute DV calculate the differences (deviations) between percentage vote shares and percentage seat shares for each party in a region (or the country at large). These differences are then added together, counting the minus scores as positive (otherwise the deviations will sum to zero), and then the sum is divided by two. See Rein Taagepera and Matthew Soberg Shugart, *Seats and Votes: The Effects and Determinants of Electoral Systems* (New Haven, CT: Yale University Press, 1989), ch. 10.

Source: Patrick Dunleavy and Helen Margetts, 'The Impact of UK Electoral Systems', *Parliamentary Affairs* (2005), vol. 58, pp. 854–70.

Plurality rule: first past the post (FPTP)

Under plurality rule, representatives are elected in single-member constituencies in which each adult resident has one vote and with the candidate receiving the most votes winning the seat. An oft-cited advantage of plurality rule is the creation of the 'constituency link', so that individual representatives can be held accountable to their constituents. The key criticism is that political parties receive shares of seats in the Commons which are quite different from the shares of the vote that they achieve in elections; the relationship between seat shares and vote shares is continually changing from one election to the next and is strikingly unfair between parties. In short, the British system is not proportional. The first and best-known way to measure this disparity is the deviation from proportionality (DV) score. It shows the proportion of members of a legislature who hold seats which they are not entitled to by virtue of their party's overall vote share in the elections – that is, what percentage of MPs would be replaced by representatives of different parties under a purely proportional system.

Table 1 shows deviations between votes won and seats allocated for 2005, highlighting (in the final column) how the Liberal Democrats were underrepresented by 13 per cent, while Labour were overrepresented by 20 per cent. DV for 2005 was 20, a little lower than the high point of 23 in 2001, when Labour won two thirds of the seats in the Commons on the basis of just over two fifths of the vote, but still far higher than in other countries or in any of the other proportional representation (PR) systems used at other tiers of government. Since 1999, when new systems were introduced in the UK, deviation from proportionality in the European, Scottish, Welsh and London elections has consistently been between 10 and 14 per cent.

Preferential systems: the alternative vote, the supplementary vote and the single transferable vote

With both the alternative vote (AV) and the supplementary vote (SV), MPs would continue to be elected in single-member constituencies, and there would be no need to change boundaries or number. The systems both therefore preserve the constituency link. Under AV, voters are invited to rank the candidates and parties standing for election in order of preference, marking as few or as many preferences as they like. When votes are counted, if a candidate gains 50 per cent of the vote they are elected. But if not, then the lowest-placed candidate is discarded and the second preferences of their votes are allocated across the other candidates. This process continues until one candidate has attained 50 per cent. If voters for rejected candidates have cast second preferences for candidates that have also been rejected, then those voters' third, fourth and subsequent preferences will be considered. SV is a simpler version of AV, in which voters cast only two preferences. Once again, if one candidate attains 50 per cent of the vote then they are elected. If no candidate gains 50 per cent of the first preference vote, then all candidates other than the two with the most first-preference votes are eliminated and their voters' second preferences reallocated between the leading two candidates. Neither AV nor SV are proportional systems: in 1992, for example, AV would have led to a 3 per cent improvement in proportionality as against FPTP, but in 1997 it would have led to a 3 per cent decrease.

The single transferable vote (STV) is also a preferential system, but votes are cast in larger, multi-member constituencies so the single-member constituency link is not preserved and electoral boundaries would have to be redrawn. Here, voters can rank candidates as in AV, but they also have the chance to rank candidates within parties, because parties field candidates in accordance to the number of seats available. Votes are allocated in the same way as AV, but instead of attaining 50 per cent, to win a seat candidates must gain a quota based on the total number of voters and seats. The candidate with most votes above the quota is elected. Any 'surplus' votes of this new MP are redistributed by looking at second preferences. The new totals of votes are examined and the highest candidate above the quota is elected; in turn their surplus votes are redistributed. This process continues until all candidates with votes above the quota level are elected. At this point, when some seats will still be unfilled, the STV system switches over to the AV system, eliminating the bottom candidate and redistributing second preference votes. STV is not a strictly proportional system, but its advocates would argue that it is not designed for proportionality on first preferences. The point is that it is the system offering voters maximum choice, and taking account of second and subsequent preferences is equally important.

List proportional representation

List PR is the system found most widely in Western liberal democracies and has also been used since 1999 for the European Parliament elections. Parties offer a list of candidates to voters in large multi-member constituencies. Voters express a single preference for the party they wish to support and the seats in the constituencies are then allocated to candidates from each party's list in proportion to their level of support. For this reason, list PR is a highly proportional system, although the shape and size of constituencies within which candidates are elected can drive proportionality up. Furthermore, most list PR systems incorporate a threshold of vote share below which parties are ineligible to gain a seat. In practice, proportionality cannot be expected to fall below 5 per cent. The size of the constituency in which seats are allocated and votes cast can vary considerably; in Israel or the Netherlands, for example, the whole country is treated as one constituency.

There are two types of list PR. In an 'open list' system, voters are allowed to express their preferences for candidates within the party list. In a 'closed list' system they are not.

The additional member system

The additional member (AM) system is the one that was most often discussed as the reform option for the UK in the late 1990s. Under AM half or more of MPs are elected locally, using plurality rule elections, and the remainder at a regional level where parties' share of seats would be 'topped up' to bring them into line with their share of votes. A version of AM has been used since 1999 to elect the Greater London Authority, the Welsh Assembly and the Scottish Parliament. Proportionality will depend on the ratio of local to top-up seats; in Germany, where the ratio is 1:1, the system is highly proportional. While, as noted above, under the current system DV is regularly above 20 for UK general elections, in the AM systems used in Scotland, Wales and London it generally falls between 10 and 14 (the practical minimum is 4).

These brief outlines of the various electoral systems under consideration show that there is a tension between the two key distinguishing criteria of electoral systems, the constituency link and proportionality. No system can provide both, because single-member constituencies work against proportionality. In general, those voters in favour of electoral reform argue that pro-portionality is the most important criterion. While supporters of the status quo treasure the constituency link, they also argue that proportionality would have undesirable consequences.

So why is proportionality so important and what are the arguments for and against it? A key argument for proportionality can be made on the grounds of democratic first principles. If democracy means popular control and political equality of that control,* then a highly disproportional system fails the 'equality' criterion. A disproportional system will favour larger parties at the expense of smaller ones. As noted above and shown in Table 1, the FPTP system overrepresents the largest party and under-represents smaller parties. Thus the system has discounted the votes of supporters of the Liberal Democrats and other smaller parties. This characteristic of a disproportional system means that it is more likely to deliver majority (as opposed to coalition) governments, because smaller parties have been filtered out of the legislatures and larger ones have more chance of attaining an absolute majority, something that defenders of the status quo would argue leads to more stable government. However, this stability comes at a cost for those who do not support the largest political parties, working against voter choice. In any case, as the next section shows, the future stability of FPTP in the UK is increasingly in question.

The current electoral system: if it is broken, fix it!

Certainly, for those who argue and campaign for change, the UK electoral system is ripe for reform. During the 2005 general election, the plurality rule voting system itself became an election issue,† with vigorous campaigns to make this the 'last plurality rule election' by the *Independent* and *Guardian* newspapers. Patrick Dunleavy and I have argued elsewhere that the UK is already in a process of prolonged transition to PR,‡ with a marked increase in the number of parties in operation in the UK political system, fuelled by electoral system change at

---

* See Stuart Weir and David Beetham, *Political Power and Democratic Control in Britain: The Democratic Audit of the United Kingdom* (London: Routledge, 1999).
† See Patrick Dunleavy and Helen Margetts, 'The Impact of UK Electoral Systems', *Parliamentary Affairs* (2005), vol. 58, pp. 854–70.
‡ See Patrick Dunleavy and Helen Margetts, 'From Majoritarian to Pluralist Democracy? Electoral Reform in Britain since 1997', *Journal of Theoretical Politics* (2001), vol. 13, pp. 295–319.

other tiers of government: mixed-member systems used in the national assemblies of Scotland and Wales and the London Assembly, list PR for the European elections and, most recently, STV for Scottish local elections. In 2005, the 'two party' share of the vote declined below 70 per cent for the first time and the Labour Party's UK vote share fell to the lowest ever recorded for a majority government. Eight parties, including the UK Independence Party (UKIP), the British National Party and Respect, are all recent additions to the UK party system, with at least seventeen named and registered parties standing in every region of the country.[*]

Table 2: The Effective Number of Parties (ENP) in terms of votes and seats across UK regions, 2005

Region	ENP votes	ENP seats
Wales	3.6	1.6
Scotland	3.6	1.9
North East	2.7	1.2
North West	3.0	1.5
Yorkshire & Humberside	3.1	1.6
Eastern	3.1	1.8
South East	3.1	1.8
West Midlands	3.2	1.9
East Midlands	3.1	2.0
London	3.3	2.2
South West	3.2	2.9
Great Britain	3.4	2.3
United Kingdom	**3.6**	**2.5**

Source: Patrick Dunleavy and Helen Margetts, 'The Impact of UK Electoral Systems', *Parliamentary Affairs* (2005), vol. 58, pp. 854–70.

Another important indicator of the instability of the electoral system is the number of effective parties operating in a political system and the extent to which these parties are represented in the

[*] See Dunleavy and Margetts, 'The Impact of UK Electoral Systems'.

legislature. As noted above, disproportional systems tend to work against the existence and success of smaller parties. The effective number of parties (ENP) can be measured by taking the decimal vote shares of all the parties, squaring them and then adding up the sum of the squared numbers. The ENP score is then given by the reciprocal of the resulting number. The score can be computed not just for the votes allocated by citizens across the parties (ENP votes) but also for the MPs allocated by the electoral system across the parties (ENP seats). Table 2 shows the contrast between these two scores, particularly in Scotland, Wales and the three northern regions of England, demonstrating that in every region more parties are in operation among the electorate than are gaining representation in the legislature.

Josep Colomer has argued that as the ENP in a country's electorate increases, the greater the likelihood that there will be electoral system change towards PR. Crucially, he argues that in majoritarian systems,

> the costs of information transmission, bargaining, and imple-mentation of agreements among previously separate organizations … will waste significant amounts of votes, and voters' dissatisfaction with the real working of the electoral system may increase. Large numbers of losing politicians are also likely to use voters' dis-satisfaction and their own exclusion, defeat or under-representation to develop political pressures in favour of changing to more proportional electoral rules.[*]

Colomer argues that such a shift may occur when the ENP reaches 4. Above this number, 'maintaining a majority rule electoral system would be highly risky for the incumbent largest party'.[†] At this point of course, in the UK at least, a hung parliament also becomes more likely, as the two largest parties' share of votes (and, albeit to a lesser extent in a plurality system, of seats) is eroded by that of the Liberal Democrats and the

---

[*] Josep M. Colomer, 'It's the Parties that Choose Electoral Systems (or, Duverger's Laws Upside Down)', *Political Studies* (2005), vol. 53, pp. 4–5.
[†] Ibid., p. 8.

growing array of smaller parties represented in the electorate. As Table 2 shows, the ENP for the UK has almost reached this point at 3.6, suggesting a high level of instability in its electoral system.

Where do the parties stand?

So how do the largest political parties view reform and react to this instability in the current system? Clearly their approach will be crucial in any move towards reform. Contemporary discussion of electoral reform in the Labour Party originates in the dark days of the 1980s, when it seemed as if the party might never regain power. Discussion at that time focused on Scotland and the work of the Scottish Constitutional Convention (largely consisting of Labour and the Liberal Democrats) on defining devolution proposals in Scotland, later used in a modified form as a model for Wales. In March 1997 Labour and the Liberal Democrats produced a joint concordat on constitutional issues, negotiated by Robin Cook and Robert Maclennan, which among other things promised to hold a referendum on electoral reform for the House of Commons, in which the people would vote on an alternative system to be defined by a commission.

Such a commission, headed by Roy Jenkins, was set up in 1998 to decide on the system, eventually coming up with a mixed electoral system labelled as 'AV+'. This system involved a high share, around four fifths, of MPs being elected locally in single-member constituencies under AV, the remainder to be elected in semi-local top-up areas to provide some measure of proportionality.* The Jenkins proposals ran into strong opposition, as did the pledge to hold a referendum, and in autumn 2000 Labour agreed that a promise to 're-examine'

---

* For details see Patrick Dunleavy and Helen Margetts, *The Performance of the Commissions' Schemes for a New Electoral System: Report to the Independent Commission on the Voting System* (London: Public Policy Group, London School of Economics and Political Science/Public Policy Centre, Birkbeck College, 1998); Patrick Dunleavy and Helen Margetts, *Proportional*

voting reform in 2003 would be included in the 2001 manifesto, leaving the 'PR door ajar'.* In fact, the review never materialised in that parliament but the 2005 Labour Party manifesto again declared: 'Labour remains committed to reviewing the experience of the new electoral systems – introduced for the devolved administrations, the European Parliament and the London Assembly. A referendum remains the right way to agree any change for Westminster.' By July 2007, the plans of the new Prime Minister, Gordon Brown, for the forthcoming years were mainly hinted at in a Green Paper on constitutional reform, which surprisingly omitted all mention of AV, previously debated in Labour circles as the most likely option. In December, Brown gave more indication that he personally was thinking about the issue when he rang to congratulate the newly elected Liberal Democrat leader, Nick Clegg, highlighting constitutional reform as an area where the two men could co-operate.† In 2008, a long-promised 'extensive and intensive review' on the new voting systems introduced in the UK since 1997 was published by the Ministry of Justice, but it was precisely that – a review, which aimed only to 'contribute to the debate on voting systems, which is, and will always be, a political and normative debate'.‡ It made no recommendations, although the authors dismissed many of the arguments commonly made against electoral reform in general and PR in particular.

Meanwhile, signs of overly enthusiastic support for electoral reform in the Labour Party are regarded with suspicion. There has long been a small and dedicated electoral reform movement within the party (the Labour Campaign for Electoral Reform), although its failure to unite around any particular electoral system

Representation for Local Government: An Analysis (York: Joseph Rowntree Foundation, 1999), pp. 1–71; Home Office, The Report of the Independent Commission on the Voting System (Cm 4090, 1998).

* 'Labour leaves PR door ajar', BBC online, 23 March 2001.

† See Nicholas Watt, 'Brown offers to hold talks with Clegg on constitutional reform', Observer, 30 December 2007.

‡ Ministry of Justice: Review of Voting Systems: The Experience of New Voting Systems in the United Kingdom since 1997 (Cm 7304, 2008), p. 17.

has always complicated its ability to make its aims clear, and its support within the party has shown few signs of growing. In September 2006, the MP Clare Short faced possible expulsion from Labour after declaring that she wanted to stand down as an MP to campaign for electoral reform and a parliament in which neither Labour nor the Tories would have an overall majority. Her comments were described as 'completely unacceptable' by the then government chief whip, Jacqui Smith.*

Conservative Party interest in electoral reform peaked in the 1970s, when at the February 1974 election the party won more votes than Labour yet fewer seats, and Harold Wilson became Prime Minister. The pressure group Conservative Action for Electoral Reform (CAER) was formed within the party, and by the late 1970s it had forty-one MPs and sixty peers who supported change,† including Douglas Hurd and Chris Patten. But interest declined and since the 1980s the party has remained resolutely opposed to the question of electoral reform, in spite of its dismal electoral fortunes in elections from 1997 to 2005. CAER continues to exist and has mobilised around STV. One of its members, Tim Bale, wrote an article in *Political Quarterly* in June 2006, arguing that the Conservative leader, David Cameron, should come out in favour of PR, for what for him would be a 'Clause IV moment' – 'a breathtaking act of back-me-or-sack-me symbolic violence against one's own party, the acceptance of which signals transformation'.‡ Pointing out that most centre-right parties in Europe would be pleased with the share of votes won by the British Conservatives in any of the last three elections (31, 32 and 32 per cent respectively) and that many would have no trouble in forming a centre-right government, he argued that the time had come for the Tories to think seriously about electoral reform. At the time of writing, however, there were few signs that the party or its leader had

---

* See George Jones, 'Short faces expulsion for backing a hung parliament', *Daily Telegraph*, 16 September 2006.

† See Hansard, HC Deb, 2 June 1998, vol. 313, col. 187.

‡ Tim Bale, 'PR Man? Cameron's Conservatives and the Symbolic Politics of Electoral Reform', *Political Quarterly* (2006), vol. 77, no. 1, p. 28.

taken his advice. In mid-December 2007, the Conservative leader made an appeal on his 'webcameron' site to the winner of the ongoing election of the Liberal Democrat leader to forge a 'new progressive alliance' (including the Conservatives, the Liberal Democrats and the Green Party) to challenge Brown, but this appeal was rebuffed by the acting leadership of the Liberal Democrats.[*]

The Liberal Democrats (and previously, the Liberal Party) have long been committed to electoral reform in general and the STV electoral system in particular. Their leader from 2005 to 2007, Sir Menzies Campbell, pledged during his leadership election campaign to vote down any Queen's speech 'without a clear and unambiguous commitment for proportional representation' and consistently highlighted the significance of constitutional reform (which, he argues, in the views of many people 'requires' electoral reform) on the Liberal Democrat website. However, he shocked many Liberal Democrat supporters when he failed to include electoral reform as one of the five 'tests' set for a Brown premiership in a keynote speech to party activists at the party conference in 2007. Immediately afterwards, reporters were briefed by an official who indicated that PR would not be a precondition to a coalition deal in the event of a hung parliament. However, the official quit his job and the leader's aides dismissed these comments as unauthorised. In its autumn conference in 2007, the party backed proposals for STV for both the House of Commons and the House of Lords.

In 2007, Campbell stood down, eventually replaced by Nick Clegg, who narrowly beat Chris Huhne in an autumn electoral contest. Some commentators suggested that their approach to PR was the crucial difference between them. While Huhne stated that 'there can be no partnership politics without PR',[†] Clegg would not even discuss terms of partnership deals in a possible hung parliament during his campaign for the leadership.

[*] See Nicholas Watt, 'Cameron offers deal to Liberal Democrats', *Observer*, 16 December 2007.

[†] Polly Toynbee, 'The Lib Dems face a clear choice: get radical or fudge into eternal decline', *Guardian*, 16 November 2007.

However, a letter to the Electoral Reform Society made clear his endorsement of constitutional reform and its place in Liberal Democrat policy:

> A commitment to proportional representation at all levels of government in Britain has been a central plank of the Liberal Democrat policy agenda since the party's foundation. It is absolutely pivotal to any serious attempt to change our country. And I am not willing just to wait for hypothetical coalition negotiations – in a hung parliament that may never happen – to fight for constitutional reform. I want to start that battle now.

In December 2007, Clegg wrote to both Brown and David Cameron proposing the establishment of a new British constitutional convention to examine the country's 'broken' political system, including the electoral system, modelled on the Scottish Constitutional Convention. But in an article on the Liberal Democrat website, he contrasted the warm telephone conversation with Brown shortly after his election as leader and Cameron's less personal and slightly 'pre-emptive' approach (referring no doubt to his 'progressive alliance' proposals noted above), fuelling speculation that 'Labour and the Lib Dems would be more natural bedfellows in the event of a hung parliament' (*The Observer*, 30 December 2007). In general, however, he has been fairly even-handed in his approach, arguing later in 2008 that 'he wasn't about to do deals with a weak Labour Party' in order to achieve reform and that there was 'little merit in playing footsie with either party'.

The alternative vote: a compromise on reform?

By 2008, the prospects of reform did not look particularly hopeful, with 1997 (after the Labour landslide) and 2007 (during Gordon Brown's brief honeymoon period) viewed as the best – and missed – chances for political leaderships to embark on major programmes of constitutional change, including electoral reform for the House of Commons. But by this time, the reform movement seemed to be coalescing around AV as the only remaining possibility, led by (for example) the Labour MPs Peter Hain and Martin Linton (long advocates of AV), the Liberal Democrat Chris Huhne and the general secretary of the Fabian Society, Sunder Katwala. From a pragmatic perspective, AV would have a considerable advantage over more proportional systems in that it might be introduced without a referendum.

So how would AV operate under UK conditions? It is not, as noted above, a proportional system. The best information on how AV would operate comes from two simulations carried out in 1992 and 1997.* In 1992 a full AV simulation showed that election outcomes changed in only twenty-eight constituencies (the Conservatives would have had a net loss of eleven seats, Labour a net loss of one seat and the Liberal Democrats a net gain of ten; this would have deprived John Major of his majority and would have improved proportionality by 3 per cent). In 1997, results would have changed in fifty-seven constituencies, the Conservatives losing fifty-five seats, the Liberal Democrats doubling their representation and Labour gaining seventeen seats; with these results, DV would actually have risen from 21 to 23.5. More recent estimates suggest that if AV had been in operation during the 2005 election, Labour would have attained an even greater majority than it did, estimated at ninety-eight seats rather than sixty-seven, again increasing DV.† In 2008 a poll for the *Telegraph* suggested that 45 per cent of Liberal Democrat supporters would give second preference to Labour and 28 per cent to the Conservatives. While under FPTP the Conservatives' 11-point lead would give them an overall majority of forty-eight, under AV the Conservatives could fail to attain a majority. However, it should be noted that it is not

* See Patrick Dunleavy, Helen Margetts and Stuart Weir, *Replaying the 1992 General Election: How Britain Would Have Voted under Alternative Electoral Systems* (York: Joseph Rowntree Reform Trust, 1992), pp. 1–19; Patrick Dunleavy, Helen Margetts, Brendan O'Duffy and Stuart Weir, *Making Votes Count: Replaying the 1990s General Elections under Alternative Electoral Systems* (Colchester: Democratic Audit, 1997).

† See John Curtice, 'System failure: all votes are equal, but some are more equal than others', *Independent*, 10 May 2005.

straightforward to predict an AV result without the kind of simulations carried out by Patrick Dunleavy and his colleagues, and further such research would be necessary to establish likely results under current UK conditions.

An important indicator of the potential performance of AV comes from data on the second preferences of voters, obtained in opinion surveys when voters are asked to complete an AV (or STV) ballot paper as if they were voting in a general election. Such figures currently favour Labour, but have fluctuated over time and demonstrate that there is nothing inevitable about support from Liberal Democrats for Labour. In 1992, in a large national face-to-face survey, Liberal Democrat voters split more in favour of the Tories than in favour of Labour, in virtually all regions except Greater London and the North.* In 1997, this position was reversed and 49 per cent of all Liberal Democrats gave a second preference to Labour (up from 33 per cent in 1992) while the proportion giving a second preference to the Conservatives declined by more than half from 38 per cent in 1992 to just 18 per cent. The growth of explicit Labour–Liberal Democrat co-operation just before the election noted above may well have contributed to this change. That co-operation has taken several knocks since then, particularly the reluctance to produce a review on electoral reform and the backtracking on a referendum.

However, there are signs from other, less extensive opinion surveys suggesting that the more positive attitude of Liberal Democrat supporters to Labour over the Conservatives has been maintained. After the 2001 general election, in a survey carried out by ICM for Democratic Audit, funded by the Joseph Rowntree Charitable Trust, respondents were given an AV ballot paper with representatives from each party. Of the respondents who claimed to have voted Liberal Democrat in the 2001 general election, 50 per cent gave their first or second preference on the AV ballot paper to Labour, whereas only 12 per cent gave their second preference to the Conservatives (none gave their first preference to the Conservatives). In the 2005 British Election Study (BES), respondents were given a mailback survey which included an AV

* See Dunleavy et al., *Making Votes Count*, p. 14.

ballot paper; the response rate was low but the data gives us some insight into the second preferences of respondents. In England, for those who gave Liberal Democrat as their first preference, more than half (52 per cent) gave their second preference to Labour, while less than a quarter (22 per cent) gave second preferences to the Conservatives. The Greens got 15 per cent and UKIP 10 per cent. Labour supporters too indicated a strong preference towards the Liberal Democrats: 66 per cent of those voting for Labour with their first preference gave their second preference to the Liberal Democrats, with 21 per cent giving them to the Conservatives (unlikely partners) and 7 per cent to the Green Party.

Consideration of any possibility for reform of the electoral system of the House of Commons must take into account the ongoing reform of the House of Lords. Although most of the hereditary peers were removed in 1999 and a royal commission reported in 2000, the second stage of Lords reform has never been completed. But it is generally accepted that the new House of Lords will be largely elected, and if so consideration of the electoral system for the Commons should take place alongside consideration of the system to be used for the Lords. If similarly designed systems are used for the two chambers, they are likely to have similar compositions in terms of parties. In other countries with two chambers, most employ different electoral systems. Australia, for example, uses AV for electing the House of Representatives and STV for electing the Senate.

Conclusion: prospects for reform

This chapter has suggested that the current UK electoral system is unstable and that reform will come eventually, in spite of the success of the UK plurality system in repressing (in terms of seats) the growing number of parties represented in the UK democracy: 'How long can a liberal democracy go on chewing up such huge proportions of the vote and according no representation in return and still remain basically legitimate?'[*] If this instability in the

---

[*] Dunleavy and Margetts, 'From Majoritarian to Pluralist Democracy?', p. 313.

system were to lead to a hung parliament, it seems almost inevitable that it would also lead to electoral reform, as the two main parties, fuelled by pressure from the increasingly large array of smaller parties active in the UK political system and rising voter dissatisfaction, turned to constitutional reform as the only way to achieve a stable government. At this point, the two main parties and their leaders would have to quickly review the evidence and concentrate on electoral reform in a way that neither has done before, suggesting strongly that they would be well placed to place more emphasis on the issue beforehand. The approach of the Liberal Democrats, with their newly elected leader and long-held commitment to STV, will be key to the development of electoral reform proposals. How far they push the issue including the choice of system, their viability as a coalition partner (likely to be high) and their choice of partner (likely to be Labour) could crucially shape the future of electoral reform, appropriately enough given their long-held commitment to the issue.

Meanwhile, with a hung parliament looking unlikely and as the reform movement coalesces around AV as a short-term possibility, it is important to look to the future. AV, another majoritarian system, would preserve the current instability in the electoral system as the UK party system expands, and a further move towards proportionality would remain likely. So, if AV were adopted, what would be the next step? The system most suitable as a modification to AV would be STV, with preferential voting in multi-member constituencies, retaining a similar, if much longer, ballot paper. Reformers who favour STV, therefore, would be more predisposed to back AV in the short term. For those reformers who favour a mixed member system along the lines recommended by the Jenkins commission, SV would be a more viable option. SV would make little difference on AV; indeed in 1997 under the simulation discussed above, the results were exactly the same under the two electoral systems.* SV would also retain some advantages over AV: it prevents the third-placed candidate in a constituency from winning (a key criticism of AV) and it prevents voters' third, fourth, fifth preferences from

* See Dunleavy et al., *Making Votes Count.*

determining the result. Many voters may not want to express more than two preferences (in 1997, 97 per cent gave a first preference and 83 per cent a second, but only 67 per cent gave a third, 31 per cent a fourth, 24 per cent a fifth and 14 per cent a sixth). Most importantly for such reformers, SV would be easier to modify to a top-up system; indeed, it could be argued that the Jenkins AV+ option was unviable precisely because the ballot paper with AV preferential voting as well as an open party list would have been too complex to place before the electorate, and only if a plurality or SV option was used at the constituency level could the system have been implemented. Most reformers agree that choice is vitally important when considering electoral system change, but there is a point where complexity can work against the possibility of voters exercising that choice.

For reformers for whom proportionality is an essential democratic criterion, adoption of either SV or AV could well be considered a step in the wrong direction. Neither is in any sense proportional and there are no precedents of a country making such a change and then going on to shift to a proportional alternative. So any such move must be incorporated into a long-term plan that incorporates concurrent developments in reform of the House of Lords, prospects for further constitutional change and a vision for a democratic future.

The judges, the rule of law and the sovereignty of Parliament

John Jackson

 key feature of a new constitutional settlement – the central demand of Charter 88 in its campaigns – must be the role and authority of the judges. Sometimes overlooked, this is now emerging as one of a number of constitutional matters that need to be addressed with some urgency.

'Be you ever so high the law is above you', a phrase uttered by a mid-seventeenth-century cleric, Thomas Fuller, was famously used by Lord Denning in 1977 when he, wrongly in law, chastised the then attorney general for his misuse of a discretionary power. It might have been used by Chief Justice Sir Edward Coke when challenged in 1616 by King James I to justify his judicial assertion six years earlier that 'when an act of Parliament is against common right or reason, or repugnant, or impossible to perform, the common law will control it, and judge such an act to be void'.

Coke's statement, challenged by the king because he saw it as part of an attack by Coke on his powers, has been interpreted as meaning that the judges could, and should, strike down legislation if it was irrational or contrary to 'natural justice' and as evidencing Coke's belief that 'the law' was a contender with the king and the king in Parliament for ultimate sovereignty.

This interpretation is probably wrong. Although Coke's words are, arguably, ambiguous, it is likely that he meant only that the common law would not admit that which was impossible or repugnant to common sense. Anyway, Coke was an unlikely champion of natural justice: he would have regarded it as an imprecise and dangerous notion. In the event he became prominently involved on the side of Parliament in its struggle with the Stuart kings and nothing more seems to have been heard of the notion that the law itself, represented and defined by the judges, was entitled to the last word and that this was a proper limitation on the sovereignty of the king in Parliament.

Four centuries later Coke's words have had life breathed into them – both by Parliament when it asserted 'the existing constitutional principle of the rule of law' in the Constitutional Reform Act 2005 and by the judges in their reaction to those words. The constitutional position of the judges (and their relationship to Parliament) is becoming so entangled with discussion of the meaning of the rule of law, natural justice – and its derivatives, human rights and liberties and sovereignty, that it is not easy to decide where to start addressing it. The rule of law is as good a starting point as any.

Fuller's words were echoed in 1776 by another Thomas, Thomas Paine, when he stated: 'In America the law is king. For as in absolute governments the king is law, so in free countries the law ought to be king; and there ought to be no other.' But it was not until the late nineteenth century that the expression 'the rule of law' was popularised in England by the constitutional theorist A. V. Dicey.

There have been many attempts to define what the rule of law is. Definition is difficult because, although conceptually a constant, it is prayed in aid, by those wishing to benefit from it, in a wide range of different circumstances. Sometimes it is made more difficult by well-meant but mistaken attempts to include within it the 'rules' of natural justice. In its basic (perhaps only meaningful) form it is a way of stating the desirability of a sovereign body, for example a nation state with control of its territory, having and publishing a set of certain and understandable rules to be adhered to and accepted by those within its area of control and applied by those appointed so to do (who are themselves bound by the rules) in an accessible and public way. There is no need for those rules to be fair or just. There is a need for them to be clear and openly enforceable. Their content will reflect the view of those leading the sovereign body (perhaps claiming divine or astrological authority) of what serves that body's interests 'best'.

In the city states of Sumer (that part of Mesopotamia occupied during – at least – the five millennia BC by people speaking Sumerian), the ruler or king (enthroned by consent or conquest) decided what was 'best' and exercised the power of declaring the law. Only rarely would the king 'invent' new laws. In the main he would be authorising the setting down (occasionally the modifying) of what had been settled as custom and practice over a long period. This setting down illustrates how these ancient city dwellers approached these matters. First were described the facts of a case. Then followed the decision of the judges. And from that followed, as a matter of deduction, the principle or 'rule'. This is consistent with their status as settled, organised and well-integrated communities which did not need 'thou shalt or shalt not' prescription of the kind that was revealed to Moses.

John Sassoon, in his book *Ancient Laws and Modern Problems*, examines how the Sumerian system worked, and worked well, over many centuries in the light of what scholars have deduced from fragments of inscribed clay tablets, engraved steles and the like. The three areas where law was most needed were the family, property and physical injury. Law was needed, not for the purposes of justice or respect for the individual, but because it contributed to social stability – a prime interest of the king (and the community). There was no discernible difference between what we would call criminal and civil matters and it was left to the judges appointed by the king to apply the historic and deduced principles in particular cases in the light of carefully established fact. In Sassoon's view this created the possibility of the judges admitting justice for the individual by deciding what was the 'fair' or 'just' way to apply the relevant principle in the particular circumstances. Although this allows some blurring of the certainty required by the rule of law there is good reason for it to be correct. Social stability would have required broad acceptance by the public of the way matters were dealt with by their 'king' and his agents. Early references to, and condemnations of, 'unjust' judges lend weight to the Sassoon observation.

The recognition of the need for stability came nowhere near the notion of what we call human rights, reflecting what could be expected of or demanded from the state itself (the community and its ruler), other, of course, than the unenforceable right to protection. The boot was on the other foot: the law was there because it was 'bad' for the state, and its ability to perform as protector, if the behaviour of its citizens was not regulated. Sumer did not permit its own versions of Deadwood Gulch.

These ancient legal systems were capable of considerable complexity. They also reflected pragmatism and political sophistication. The laws of Hammurabi (*fl. c.* 1770 BC), the sixth ruler of Babylon, which are preserved on a stone stele now in the Louvre, are a reflection of this. Their most notable feature is that they provide one set of rules which apply to the 'aristocracy' of Babylon and another set which apply to the general citizenry. Broadly speaking, the first reflected the harsh rules of talion, based on retaliation (an eye for an eye and a tooth for a tooth), and therefore also punishment of the innocent, while the second reflected a gentler approach.

The reason for this was that the aristocracy (including Hammurabi) were conquering Amorites, a nomadic desert people who valued the harshness and immediacy of talion as a stabilising factor inhibiting tribal feud. The conquered were urban inhabitants with a long history of stability, no feuding and the practices of just judges. Hammurabi kept his aristocracy in power and feud free in a way that was known to all the citizens of Babylon by this early example of legal pluralism.

The rule of law, in its basic form, clearly ran in these early, technologically advanced, city states. And there was no possibility of tension between the judges and the kings exercising their sovereign right to make and declare the laws. The judges were the servants of the king and their decisions were designed to make his laws acceptable to his subjects as providing certainty and, above all, stability. It was not for the judges to moderate his will by reference to a law 'above' him.

Leaping ahead to England in the early thirteenth century we find a situation remarkably similar to Hammurabi's Babylon. The imposition of land-based military (and tax-gathering) feudalism on the well-established manorial system of the Saxons enabled the Angevin kings to rule England as a single state with some ease. This included the right to make and declare the laws. But the right was not absolute. It was imprudent and impractical to attempt the replacement of customs and practices which had become embedded in the, largely rural and Saxon, population over many centuries. And, in theory at least, the royal pronouncements were made with the approval and consent of the king's most important vassals and the clergy — his council. This reflected the realities of feudal life and the position of the church as a separate estate. The timely provision of soldiers and the efficient collection of moneys depended substantially on the willingness of the great barons to accept their feudal duty to their liege king and of the prelates to co-operate with the civil, albeit royal, authority.

King John overplayed his hand in relation to taxation following costly and territorially disastrous adventures in France. He upset both barons and church. This provoked a crisis, resulting in the negotiation in 1215 of the Great Charter — Magna Carta. Although the opportunity was taken to clip the royal wings by listing a number of things the king could not do to the barons' feudal vassals (for example, no imprisonment without trial — habeas corpus), the more significant provision, in the longer run, was that which placed limits on the royal right to levy taxes without the common consent of the realm.

We have become used to the seductive and romantic notion that Magna Carta was a great 'human rights' document defining the relationship between the common man and the state and setting the yeomen of England free. The truth is that it was a political settlement between great, and potentially despotic, forces competing for power. The yeomen and their womenfolk benefited very little. They were subjects, not citizens. It was not them but their feudal lords who had gained rights under the Great Charter from and against the king.

The limit on the ability to tax without consent, although omitted from later editions of the Great Charter, bore fruit. It fortified the notion of representation, a notion which was alive in Saxon England.

The years that followed the ceremony at Runnymede were turbulent: the tussle between the barons, the church and successive kings continued. But in 1295 King Edward I, seeking to settle his realm, summoned an assembly. This was not the feudal body of eighty years earlier but something different. Professor Frederic William Maitland, in one of his lectures to students of our constitutional history in the late 1880s, included in his description the following: 'The clergy and baronage are summoned to treat, ordain and execute, the representatives of the commons are to bring full powers from those whom they represent to execute what should be ordained by common counsel.' As Maitland observed, 'A body constituted in this manner is a parliament; what the king enacts with the consent of such a body is a statute.' It was the beginning of the concept of sovereign power being vested in the king, not in isolation, but in Parliament and in a parliament reflecting, to some small degree, representative democracy.

As in Babylon and the earlier city states, the judges were appointed by the king to administer his laws, both the laws he decreed and the customary laws he had inherited. They travelled the country (separately from the king after Magna Carta) and it was convenient on occasion for them to serve as tax gatherers also. They were royal servants and their task was to ensure order and stability far more than to deliver justice. A dispute between subjects which was settled by an award between them – as individual subjects – could also result in the imposition of a fine on one of them for having threatened or disturbed the royal peace.

The customary laws tended to be of most relevance to the common people – mainly of Saxon origin – and the king's pronouncements to those of Norman origin, with benefit and obligation under the feudal system. Further echoes of Hammurabi and his Babylon! The tension between the races and their customs had a long-lasting beneficial consequence. As Maitland put it, 'In every direction the force of feudalism is limited and checked by other ideas; the public rights, the public duties of the Englishman are not conceived and cannot be conceived as the mere outcome of feudal compacts between man and lord.' Nonetheless, the rule of law in its basic form ran in England under the Angevins and the succeeding houses of Lancaster and York. The laws were known, respected and enforced, and the king and the judges were 'on the same side'.

By the time of Queen Anne's accession to the throne in 1702 there was a constitutional situation in England recognisably similar to what we know today. The sixteenth century had belonged to the Tudors, Henry Tudor (Henry VII), a shrewd politician and able administrator who had ended the Wars of the Roses by his defeat of Richard in 1485, and his four successors. The century is popularly associated with dramatic events such as the rift with Rome, the dissolution of the monasteries, Henry VIII's political need for a male heir and his marital attempts to procure one, religious persecution of both Protestants and Catholics, the less than cousinly execution of Mary, Queen of Scots by Elizabeth and the defeat of the Spanish Armada. But of equal importance were the increasing significance and affluence of the merchant classes (as a more settled situation made production – particularly of wool – and trade easier and more profitable); the associated growth in the power of the elected Commons, which together with the senior clergy and the peers made up Parliament; and the emergence of professional and political administrators (ministers) drawn from clergy, peers and commonalty and wielding great power as royal servants.

The increasing significance of the Commons stemmed from its tenacious, and potentially blocking, hold on the financing of the king. The king paid for the whole central administration of the realm and its armed forces. The three estates were responsible for the levying and collection of their own taxes; the commonalty was increasingly the largest of them. The tenacity of the Commons was tempered by an understanding that denial of what was asked of it might well jeopardise its right to be asked. The Tudor monarchs had little difficulty in persuading it, and therefore Parliament, to grant them the money they said they needed. This may have reflected an atmosphere created by the activities of the Star Chamber.

The Star Chamber was the common name of a powerful tribunal under immediate royal control (but sanitised by the status and trappings of a 'court') which dealt, particularly but not exclusively, with alleged political dissidence by secret charge and investigation, torture, closed trial and punishment by execution, fine, imprisonment or mutilation. Although the judges and Parliament accepted the Star Chamber, its selective political purpose and secret practices make it difficult to argue that Tudor England was subject to the rule of law. This is despite the increasing prosperity and general wellbeing flowing from the great increase in stability to which the mere existence of the Star Chamber undoubtedly contributed.

The Star Chamber was a part of the inheritance of the Stuarts. Their vigorous use of it in support of their belief in the divine right of monarchs to rule was an important element in fanning the flames of the conflict with those who believed that royal rule could only be exercised lawfully with the consent of the elected representatives of those who paid taxes – the king in Parliament.

A particularly contentious question was whether the writ of habeas corpus could be used to bring before the ordinary courts the cases of those committed to prison by the Star Chamber on suspicion of (political) crime and left to languish untried. Parliament (in fact the Commons, which increasingly was called Parliament) had little doubt what the answer should be: the judges said they were uncertain. Even Chief Justice Coke held that one so committed was not bailable by any court in England – he later recanted after his removal from judicial office and his return to the Commons, saying that he had been misled by a false precedent.

The fact that such a politically sensitive topic could be discussed openly is clear evidence of a shift in power. Members of the Commons, who had succeeded in winning the privilege of immunity from arrest and imprisonment for speaking their minds, and the judges, albeit with timidity, reflecting their position as royal appointees, showed growing independence. By the accession of Charles I the constitutional pot was starting to bubble. As Professor Maitland said, 'Whether a wiser man than Charles could have averted or guided the coming storm, is a question over which we may well think; but everywhere we see that the storm is coming.' That storm and its aftermath dominated the whole of the seventeenth century.

The early gusts carried intoxicating new ideas. A group of

thinkers who came to be called the Levellers pronounced that all men (and they meant men) are born free and equal. Charles might have anticipated George Orwell by saying that his divine right made him freer and more equal than others. The civil war (started and kept alive by Charles, who believed that as a king he was entitled to break all or any of his promises to keep the peace); the military coup which preceded the unlawful trial and execution of Charles; the uneasy relationship which followed between the Commons (which abolished the Star Chamber and purported to abolish both the Crown and the House of Lords), the Lord Protector, Oliver Cromwell, and the army; all these contributed to a situation in which a reduced, impoverished and miserable nation hankered after the 'old days' in which, for the ordinary person, there had been fewer grand ideas and more certainty – even more fun.

The restoration of the Stuart monarchy, celebrated by the stench in Whitehall of the hanged and drawn regicides having their bowels burned under their noses – with the approval of judges and Parliament – resulted, despite the plague and its extinction by the Great Fire of London, in a happier population, more prosperous times and a considerable flourishing of art, architecture, science, music and literature. Politically and con-stitutionally it was less successful. The question of sovereignty had not been settled and, when James II succeeded his older brother, the Stuart taste for absolutism reasserted itself. This resulted in his deposition, legitimised by Parliament as abdication.

Following its recognition of James's daughter Mary as queen, and her consort, William of Orange, as king, Parliament, including a reinstated House of Lords but led by the Commons, negotiated a deal with William. This time round there was no doubt where power lay. The Declaration of Right of 1688, followed a year later by an enacted Bill of Rights, was designed to settle the sole sovereign legitimacy of Parliament in relation to the king – and, importantly in the light of Coke's remarks at the beginning of the century, the judges. The underlying guarantee of the former was that the king would have no money with which to perform his role – or build his palaces – without a grant from Parliament. Politically these were the terms on which William and his Stuart wife Mary, kept carefully short of money, would be permitted to rule.

As in the case of Magna Carta, the Declaration of Right is extolled as an important foundation of our personal freedoms. Again that is a touch romantic. It is much more the settlement of a bruising power struggle, lost by the king again but this time to those (with the money) who claimed to represent the people. Its impact on the ordinary person was small and, probably, unnoticed. Nonetheless, a century in which, at its start, the rule of law in its basic form was under strong challenge, ended with it as an unspoken principle more firmly established in England – which would shortly lose its status as a separate state – than at any time since the days of the Angevins.

In that basic form, the rule of law has run for us during the last three centuries. The features of those centuries – relatively modern history – are well known. The events which contribute particularly to the scenario we now have include:

- the sagacity of Robert Walpole in using the inability of the first two Hanoverian kings (Georges I and II) to speak English to capture executive power for himself and his cabinet of ministers;
- the increasing independence of the judges (now distanced from the monarchy), who, although respecting the dominance of parliamentary statute, took the right to develop the law, by the extension of principles deducible from precedent, so that it reflects social change;
- the development of the franchise, first away from the monopoly of property owners in shire and borough and, finally, to full universal suffrage;
- the wresting of power by the Commons from the Lords, first formally in respect of the grant of money and finally, via the Parliament Acts, potentially in every respect;
- the 'kidnapping' by the political parties of our representative democracy: we vote for party policy, not representation;
- the creation of the United Nations and the European Union;
- the Universal Declaration of Human Rights and its reflection in our Human Rights Act.

All these are part of the background to a new constitutional crisis with which we may be confronted. The certainty which is the essential ingredient of the rule of law has gone.

Our recognition of the monarch in Parliament as our supreme law-making authority is a feature of our affairs which distinguishes us from other sovereign nations which have a written constitution, including the United States and all other members of the European Union. In those countries the constitution, interpreted by the courts – a feature which unavoidably introduces some uncertainty – is the supreme law. Any legislation, even if properly (technically) enacted, which is ruled as inconsistent with the constitution may be declared invalid and be struck down. In our case the notion 'it is a fundamental principle with English lawyers, that Parliament can do everything but make a woman a man, and a man a woman', expressed by A. V. Dicey in words borrowed from an eighteenth-century writer, was subject to no serious challenge until recently. It was believed to be our settled and certain position. What has changed?

In 2005, following a fumbled attempt to change the constitutional position of the Lord Chancellor (only remedied by a private concordat between the Lord Chief Justice and the Lord Chancellor himself), the Constitutional Reform Act became law. The Act provided in its first section that it does not adversely affect 'the existing constitutional position of the rule of law'. In 2005 also, nine members of the House of Lords Appellate Committee delivered their separate judgments in a case brought to challenge the validity of the Parliament Act 1949, on the grounds that the Commons had made a purported use of powers not available to it under the Parliament Act 1911 to impose on the Lords a further reduction in their powers. All nine judges found against the appellants but some of them cast pointed doubt on the absoluteness of parliamentary sovereignty. These two events sparked off considerable judicial and academic debate. Two published lectures by Lord Bingham of Cornhill, the senior law lord, the first in 2006 and the second in 2007, expose and discuss the issues.

In 2006 Bingham remarked that the statutory affirmation of the rule of law as an existing constitutional principle by the

Constitutional Reform Act has an important consequence: the judges would be bound to construe a statute so that it did not infringe an existing constitutional principle, if it were reasonably possible to do so. He remarked further that the Act left the rule of law undefined and went on to propose an indirect definition by a series of sub-rules.

The following year he examined the compatibility of the rule of law with parliamentary sovereignty as we practice and experience it. In his concluding remarks he asked rhetorically:

> [If] we live in a society dedicated to the rule of law; in which Parliament has the power, subject to limited, self-imposed restraints, to legislate as it wishes; in which Parliament may therefore legislate in a way which infringes the rule of law; and in which the judges, consistently with their constitutional duty to administer justice according to the laws and usages of the realm, cannot fail to give effect to such legislation if it is clearly and unambiguously expressed; is there, then, a vice at the heart of our constitutional system?

In answering the question, he dismissed the argument that Parliament could be relied on not to legislate in a way which infringed the rule of law and concluded that, particularly as a consequence of the Parliament Acts, 'our constitutional settlement has become unbalanced, and the power to restrain legislation favoured by a clear majority of the Commons much weakened, even if, exceptionally, such legislation were to infringe the rule of law'. This, he said, seemed to him a serious problem which would not go away if we ignored it and might give rise to a wholly undesirable conflict between Parliament and the judges.

The potential seriousness of what Bingham says emerges from consideration of his eight sub-rules. They are:

1. The need for the law to be accessible, intelligible, clear and predictable.
2. Questions of legal right and liability should ordinarily be resolved by application of the law and not the exercise of discretion.
3. The law should apply equally to all, save to the extent that objective differences justify differentiation.

4. The law must afford adequate protection of fundamental human rights.

5. Means must be provided for resolving without prohibitive cost or inordinate delay bona fide civil disputes which the parties themselves are unable to resolve.

6. Ministers and public officers at all levels must exercise the powers conferred on them reasonably, in good faith, for the purpose for which the powers were conferred and without exceeding the limits of such powers.

7. Adjudicative procedures provided by the state should be fair.

8. The state should comply with its obligations in international law, whether deriving from treaty or international custom and practice.

All of these, except 4 and 8, are consistent with the basic rule of law and would have been recognised in the city states of Sumer. They are, probably, also susceptible to recognition internationally today.

The inclusion of 4 and 8 presents considerable difficulty. Bingham is expanding the rule of law (and thereby the role of the judges as its supposed guardian) into the realms of political legitimacy, the relationship between the individual and the state and international relations – with all their uncertainties. That judge-made expansion, if left hanging in the air, will almost certainly result in the conflict that Bingham fears. It is possible for judges to usurp legislative power by being too inventive in their search for legal principle, validating decisions necessary, as they see it, to protect the rule of law or assuage their moral outrage.

The approach of Professor Joseph Raz, set out in 1979 in his essay 'The Rule of Law and its Virtue' and acknowledged but rejected by Bingham, while less appealing, may be more politic:

A non-democratic legal system based on denial of human rights, on extensive poverty, on racial segregation, sexual inequalities and racial persecution may, in principle, conform to the requirements of the rule of law better than any of the legal systems of the more enlightened Western democracies ... It will be an immeasurably worse legal system, but it will excel in one respect: in its conformity to the rule of law.

The Raz approach, a hymn to uncontrolled sovereignty, avoids the consequences I have identified and, by implication, limits the role of the judges. It would also be a wholly unsatisfactory end to the matter. Not least because our parliament, elected or appointed in a controversial way and substantially controlled by an executive that owes more to political party than people, is not fit to be sovereign to the extent that some, perhaps most, of its members would like.

There is a growing belief that the best way for representative democracy to benefit from a degree of parliamentary sovereignty is to make it work within the more certain confines of a democratically originated (and amendable) written constitution and not at the mercy of the unpredictable views, however honest, of our servants – the politicians and the judges. That is the place where democratic and human rights, the requirement to comply with international law and all the rest of Bingham's carefully considered sub-rules should find their home.

But such a constitution must, in its creation as well as its content, reflect the only ultimately sustainable sovereignty in the modern world, that of 'the people'. It may take time to get there but how to go about this in a practical, fair and open way is one of the most important questions with which we are all confronted. It is also the right background against which to consider the matters discussed in this chapter.

Freedom of information

Katherine Gundersen

'The crucial question', Tony Blair said in 1996, 'is: does the government regard people's involvement in politics as being restricted to periodic elections? Or, does it regard itself as in some sense in a genuine partnership with the people?' Freedom of information (FOI) was 'not some isolated constitutional reform', he added, but 'a change that is absolutely fundamental to how we see politics developing in this country over the next few years'.*

In fact, the public waited considerably more than a few years after Labour came to power in 1997. But the United Kingdom finally has a Freedom of Information Act and early experience suggests it has had a significant impact. However, the Act remains fragile – it has already faced two serious political attacks and further challenges may be on the horizon.

The prospects of FOI ever reaching the statute book at all once seemed remote. The UK was left behind when a number of Commonwealth countries (Australia, Canada and New Zealand) passed FOI legislation in the early 1980s. Although not the first to adopt open-government laws – Sweden did so in 1766 – these countries, with their Westminster-style parliaments, were particularly significant to the UK. Their experience greatly undermined the argument that FOI was incompatible with the concepts of ministerial responsibility and civil service neutrality. By 1997 many other countries, including Ireland, had followed suit and freedom of information was rapidly becoming a global trend.

A decade on almost seventy countries had adopted FOI

---

* Tony Blair, speech at Campaign for Freedom of Information Awards, 1996.

laws.* Most of these share a number of common features. They establish a right of access to information held by government, permitting information to be withheld only where specific exemptions apply. Under some laws, even exempt information may have to be disclosed if the balance of public interest favours openness. Furthermore, applicants who are dissatisfied with the result can complain to an independent body – usually an information commissioner, ombudsman, tribunal or court – with the power to order disclosure.

The rationale for such legislation has a number of separate strands. Left to themselves, governments naturally tend to use their control over information to their own advantage. They disclose that which shows them and their policies in a positive light and withhold information which suggests that mistakes may have been made, policies may have failed or commitments may have been broken, or which supports the arguments put forward by critics and opposition parties.

FOI helps offset this tendency. It promotes honesty in government by making it more difficult for public authorities to say they are doing one thing while doing something else. The knowledge that the public may be able to see documents on which decisions are based helps to deter malpractice and encourages politicians and officials to be more rigorous in their analysis, thereby improving the quality of decision-making. It makes meaningful public participation and informed discussion possible. And it strengthens the hand of individuals in their dealings with the state.

In the UK, FOI attracted widespread public support. A MORI opinion poll commissioned by the Joseph Rowntree Reform Trust in 1991 found that 77 per cent of the public wanted a Freedom of Information Act, which made it the most popular constitutional reform.† FOI was a core demand of the original Charter 88 and the main objective of the Campaign for Freedom of Information (CFOI), which was established in 1984.

---

* See David Banisar, *Freedom of Information around the World 2006: A Global Survey of Access to Government Information Laws* (London: Privacy International, 2006).

† MORI State of the Nation poll, 1991.

It has also been an abiding Labour Party commitment.
Uniquely, FOI featured in every Labour manifesto from 1974 to
1997. However, as successive political scandals – Ponting, Tisdall,
Spycatcher, Matrix Churchill, BSE, cash for questions – highlighted
the dangers of secrecy in the public's mind, the commitment
became more heartfelt and expressed with more urgency. In 1991,
Labour's deputy leader and shadow Home Secretary, Roy
Hattersley, said:

> Anyone who looks at our detailed plans for a Freedom of Information
> Act must know that it is not only suitable for early enactment. It is
> ready for early enactment. If a Labour government was elected on
> Thursday I would be able to send the headings of a Bill to
> parliamentary draughtsman on the following day.*

The 1997 manifesto stated: 'Unnecessary secrecy in government leads to arrogance in government and defective policy
decisions ... We are pledged to a Freedom of Information Act,
leading to more open government.' There was therefore disap-
pointment when FOI was left out of the government's first
legislative programme. Instead a White Paper was promised for
July 1997, but that too was delayed.

Nonetheless, when in December 1997 the government
published its proposals they were a welcome surprise. Contrary to
expectations, the White Paper, *Your Right to Know*,† adopted a
radical approach. Dr David Clark, the chancellor of the duchy of
Lancaster and the Cabinet minister responsible for drawing up the
proposals, described it as an 'all-singing, all-dancing White
Paper'.‡ The respected Canadian Information Commissioner,
John Grace, dedicated two pages of his annual report to the

---

* Roy Hattersley, speech at Campaign for Freedom of Information
Awards, 1991.

† Chancellor of the Duchy of Lancaster, *Your Right to Know: The
Government's Proposals for a Freedom of Information Act* (Cm 3818, 1997).

‡ Public Administration Committee, *Your Right to Know: The Government's
Proposals for a Freedom of Information Act, vol. 1*, third report, Session 1997–98,
HC 398-I, minutes of evidence, Q. 80.

proposals, stating: 'Canada's once brave, state-of-the-art Access to Information Act is being left behind by Britain,' and adding that the UK's White Paper 'represents nothing other than a breathtaking transformation in the relationship between the government and the governed'.*

In many areas the White Paper set the bar high. Its scope was wider than many overseas laws, both in terms of the bodies covered and in terms of the range of information to be made accessible. Most notably, the proposed FOI regime would extend beyond the public sector to the privatised utilities and to private bodies undertaking contracted-out public functions. The grounds for withholding information would be fewer than under the Open Government Code introduced by the Conservative government in 1994† and the test for determining when information should be withheld would be set in 'specific and demanding terms'.‡ Many FOI laws around the world allow information to be withheld if its disclosure would 'prejudice' or 'harm' specified interests such as defence or law enforcement. The White Paper proposed that the normal test should be 'substantial harm'.§ The option of giving ministers a final say over disclosure decisions was specifically rejected. The White Paper stated: 'We have considered this possibility, but decided against it, believing that a government veto would undermine the authority of the Information Commissioner and erode public confidence in the Act.'§§

But the praise that greeted the White Paper proved premature, as the government began to retreat. Clark tried to reassure sceptics that the White Paper was not only his view; it had 'the complete

---

* *Annual Report 1997–1998* (Information Commissioner of Canada, 1998), p. 9.

† Open Government: Code of Practice on Access to Government Information, 1994. This non-statutory code committed government departments to releasing information on request, subject to a number of exemptions, and allowed dissatisfied requesters to complain about refusals to the parliamentary ombudsman.

‡ Cm 3818, para. 3.7.

§ Ibid., para. 3.7.

§§ Ibid., para. 5.18.

and utter endorsement of the government as a whole'.* 'Of course we will listen,' he said. 'But on the other hand we will need a lot of persuading to change it. This isn't something that is going to be watered down as we progress along the way.' Yet press reports suggested that senior ministers and officials were challenging some of the White Paper's fundamental principles. As the struggle continued in a Cabinet committee, Clark lost his job in a reshuffle and responsibility for FOI was moved to the Home Office under Jack Straw.

These developments caused mounting unhappiness among Labour MPs. A parliamentary motion congratulating the government on its White Paper and expressing concern at any delay in bringing forward legislation was signed by 234 MPs, 188 of them Labour. However, their fears were confirmed when the government announced that a draft Bill would not be published until 1999.

The draft Bill itself represented a major weakening of the White Paper's proposals and attracted universal criticism. The *Guardian*'s then political commentator, the late Hugo Young, reflected that:

> Two years in, power has finally suppressed the clearest ideal that Labour formed during its years of impotence. The Freedom of Information Bill marks its definitive transition from a party dedicated to changing the world, into a government determined its own world shall not be changed. The purpose of this reform, as canvassed in opposition, was to alter the balance of power between citizen and state … The Bill now disgorged is a spectacular betrayal of any such idea.[†]

The CFOI pointed out that in many areas the draft Bill was weaker than the non-statutory Open Government Code.[‡]

---

[*] David Clark, speech at a conference on the freedom of information White Paper, 2 February 1998.
[†] Hugo Young, 'The final triumph of all the butchers and whisperers', *Guardian*, 25 May 1999.
[‡] '"Deeply disappointing" information bill "weaker than Conservatives' openness code"', Campaign for Freedom of Information press release, 24 May 1999.

In key areas the White Paper's commitments had been watered down. Its centrepiece – the 'substantial harm' test – was gone, replaced by a simple 'prejudice' test. The draft Bill permitted entire classes of information to be withheld without any test of harm at all. A blanket exemption covered all information relating to the development of government policy, including factual information and scientific advice. Crucial safety information could be kept secret. The binding public interest test promised in the White Paper had been replaced by a discretionary one, with no provision for requesters to challenge decisions about its use. Extraordinarily, public authorities could insist on knowing why the applicant wanted the information – and could restrict what they could do with it. New catch-all exemptions had been devised and a power for the Home Secretary to create new exemptions at short notice inserted.

However, in two areas the draft Bill adopted a more positive approach than the White Paper. Charges for information would be modest and the deliberate destruction or alteration of information would be an offence. But the time allowed for responding to a request was doubled to 40 working days – which would have made the UK's the slowest and most unresponsive FOI regime in the world.

Two parliamentary committees called for sweeping changes to be made. The House of Commons Public Administration Committee reported that the Bill's right of access 'is so hedged about with qualifications and exemptions that it will not cover a large amount of information which the public might want.'* It concluded that 'a failure to make the draft Bill better, as we have proposed, would represent a missed opportunity of historic proportions'.† A special House of Lords committee stated: 'To the extent that the draft Bill represents a move from an enforceable public right of access ... to discretionary disclosure ... it abandons the freedom of information principles expressed in the White Paper.'‡ The government

---

* Public Administration Committee, *Freedom of Information Draft Bill, vol. 1: Report*, third report, Session 1998–99, HC 570-I, para. 29.

† Ibid., para. 160.

‡ *Report from the Select Committee Appointed to Consider the Draft Freedom of Information Bill*, special report, Session 1998–99, HL 97, para. 21.

responded by making some welcome improvements, but serious defects remained when the Bill was later introduced to Parliament. Fortunately, many of these were subsequently corrected.

In the face of political pressure, ministers were forced to 'ease the grip ... at the centre of the Bill'.* The government yielded the power to the Information Commissioner to order the disclosure of exempt information in the public interest, but proposed that ministers and local authorities would be able to veto any such order. However, Parliament obtained a number of important safeguards against the veto's use. First, it would only be available to a Cabinet minister or the attorney general, not junior ministers. Second, ministers promised that collective consultation between Cabinet colleagues would be required before a veto could be issued.† Third, the government agreed to remove the power from local authorities. And finally, a copy of the veto would have to be laid before both Houses of Parliament.

Further amendments included a restructuring of the Bill's public interest test so that to withhold information, authorities had to show that the public interest in doing so outweighed the public interest in disclosure.‡ A statutory duty for authorities to provide advice and assistance to applicants was finally accepted. The power to create additional exemptions by order was removed, plus a relatively minor improvement to the policy formulation exemption prevented 'statistical information' from being withheld once a decision had been taken.

Despite these concessions, the government suffered a series of rebellions. In the Commons, thirty-six Labour MPs voted against allowing the exemption for the formulation of government policy to apply to purely factual information.§ Nevertheless, when the

---

* Mark Fisher MP, Hansard, HC Deb, 5 April 2000, vol. 347, col. 1003.

† This was an undertaking given by ministers during the Bill's report stage in the House of Commons; it is not a statutory requirement. See Hansard, HC Deb, 4 April 2000, vol. 347, col. 922.

‡ Previously the test had been the other way round; that is, the public interest in disclosure had to outweigh the public interest in withholding the information before exempt information could be disclosed.

§ This provision remains in the final Act, though authorities are required to

Freedom of Information Act received royal assent on 30 November 2000, it was a marked improvement on the 1999 draft Bill. The Bill's most obstructive features had been removed, the powers of the Information Commissioner had been strengthened and a binding public interest test gave the Act real potential. However, those who had campaigned for the legislation for so long couldn't help but feel pessimistic about its prospects. We became more so when implementation was delayed.

The government's intention had been to phase in the right of access, starting between twelve and eighteen months after the Act's passage. However, in November 2001, this timetable was abandoned in favour of one which delayed the right of access for more than four years and brought it into force for all authorities at once on 1 January 2005. Press reports suggested that the Prime Minister himself had intervened in the decision.

Once again, the UK found itself bottom of the FOI league. No other country had required anything like four years to implement its legislation – twelve months was the norm. Whatever the official justification that was given, the delay sent a damaging signal about the government's commitment to the reform.

When the Act belatedly took effect in 2005, five new rights to information came into force at the same time. The Freedom of Information (Scotland) Act 2002 provided similar, though slightly stronger, rights to information held by the Scottish public authorities. The Environmental Information Regulations and Environmental Information (Scotland) Regulations, implementing a EU directive,* provided parallel rights of access to environmental information held by public authorities and some private bodies such as utilities. And amendments to the Data Protection Act 1998 strengthened people's rights to see personal information held about them by public authorities.

---

have regard to 'the particular public interest in the disclosure of factual information which has been used, or is intended to be used, to provide an informed background to decision-taking'.

* EC Directive 2003/4/EC of 18 January 2003 on public access to environmental information, *Official Journal of the European Union*, 14 February 2003.

The FOI Act has now been in force for nearly four years and, though there are issues that need to be addressed, its impact has been far greater than anyone anticipated. In 2006, an inquiry by the Constitutional Affairs Committee into the first year's experience of the Act concluded that 'implementation of the FOI Act has already brought about the release of significant new information and that this information is being used in a constructive and positive way by a range of different individuals and organisations ... This is a significant success.'* Lord Falconer of Thoroton, then Lord Chancellor and secretary of state for constitutional affairs, described the Act as the 'single most significant act of any government, in improving transparency, accessibility and accountability. It is the platform for building an improved relationship between the citizen and the state – in which the public can have a greater stake in how they are governed.'†

One reason for this is that the Act has been well used. Although no accurate figure exists for the total number of requests across the public sector, the Information Commissioner has estimated that between 100,000 and 130,000 requests were made in the first year.‡ This represents the top end of expectations, based on overseas experience.§ Ministry of Justice statistics show that after an initial surge in the first quarter of 2005, the volume of requests

---

* Constitutional Affairs Committee, *Freedom of Information – One Year On*, seventh report, Session 2005–06, HC 991.

† Speech at 'Power, Politics and Democratic Renewal: Lessons from the UK and Canada', event organised by Unlock Democracy, Canadian high commission, 6 March 2007.

‡ See Constitutional Affairs Committee, *Freedom of Information – One Year On*, seventh report, Session 2005–06, HC 991, oral evidence, 14 March 2006, Q. 2.

§ Research conducted by the Constitution Unit predicted that there would be 100,000 requests in the first year, rising to 200,000 after a settling-in period. See Robert Hazell, Dick Baxter, Meredith Cook and Lucinda Maer, *Estimating the Likely Volumes, Sensitivity and Complexity of Casework for the Information Commissioner under the Freedom of Information Act 2000 and the Environmental Information Regulations* (London: Constitution Unit, University College London, 2004), para. 5.14.

to central government has settled at around 8,000 a quarter.* By contrast, only a few thousand requests a year were made under the Open Government Code.

The media have been quick to realise the Act's potential. Thousands of media stories based on disclosures under the Act have appeared, many revealing important new information for the first time.† FOI requests have revealed that the government ignored its own scientists when they advised that the methodology of a study estimating 655,000 Iraqi civilians had died in the war was robust and should not be criticised;‡ ministers approved the NHS Connecting for Health computer system despite reports showing that the project's costs exceeded the likely benefits;§ the NHS has saved millions of pounds by cutting the use of agency staff;§§ seventy-four Metropolitan Police officers have kept their jobs despite being convicted of crimes, including twelve who disciplinary panels recommended should be sacked;** the police have been instructed to let offenders off with a caution if they commit one of more than sixty types of crime;†† and De Montfort University changed the exam results of pharmacy students to reduce the failure rate, despite concerns from lecturers and external examiners.‡‡

* See *Third Annual Report on the Operation of the FOI Act in Central Government 2007* (Ministry of Justice, 2008).

† See *1,000 FOI Stories from 2006 and 2007* (London: Campaign for Freedom of Information, 2008).

‡ See Owen Bennett-Jones, 'Iraqi deaths survey "was robust"', BBC News website, 26 March 2007.

§ See Nigel Hawkes, 'Computer costs exceed benefits', *Times*, 25 August 2006.

§§ See 'Hospitals cut agency nurse costs', BBC News website, 30 May 2008. In 2006, FOI requests by the *Daily Mirror* revealed that seventy NHS trusts spent £100 million on agency doctors and nurses; see Matt Roper, 'An NHS little earner', *Daily Mirror*, 27 November 2006.

** See Alistair Foster, '74 Met officers have criminal record', *Evening Standard*, 10 April 2006.

†† See Jack Grimston, 'Police told: let off more offenders with cautions', *Sunday Times*, 2 April 2006.

‡‡ See Tony Haplin, 'The university that cut its pass mark to 21%', *Times*, 20 April 2006.

FOI has claimed its first scalps. The leader of the Scottish Conservative Party, David McLetchie, was forced to resign over improper taxi expense claims after the Scottish Information Commissioner ruled that the Scottish Parliament must disclose full details of travel expenses claimed by MSPs. Since the figures were disclosed, MSPs' expenses claims have fallen substantially after several years of year-on-year growth. FOI requests also played a part in the resignation of Ian Paisley Junior, a minister in the Northern Ireland Executive, revealing his links with and lobbying for a major property developer.[*]

Media use has been crucial in raising public awareness of FOI rights and support for the Act. According to one survey, 60 per cent of the public were made aware of the Act through media exposure.[†] The research also showed that the public is increasingly aware of the benefits of FOI. The percentage of people saying that access to information increased their confidence in public authorities rose from 51 per cent in 2004 to 81 per cent in 2007.[‡] Those who believe that access to information increased their knowledge of what public authorities do reached 86 per cent in 2007, up from 54 per cent in 2004.

Another reason to be positive is the body of case law that has emerged from the Information Commissioner's Office and the Information Tribunal (which hears appeals against the commissioner's decisions). The tribunal, in particular, has adopted a robust approach on the disclosure of government policy advice. In the first appeal on this subject, involving minutes of the Department for Education and Skills' management board, the tribunal set out guiding principles. It ruled that the purpose of the exemption is to protect civil servants, not ministers, stating: 'Despite impressive evidence against this view, we were unable to discern the unfairness in exposing an elected politician, after the

---

[*] See 'Role of FOI legislation in minister's downfall', *Belfast Telegraph*, 19 February 2008.

[†] See *Report on Information Commissioner's Office Annual Track 2007: Individuals* (Hull: SMSR, 2007), para. 4.3. The research involved 1,222 telephone interviews with a representative sample of the public.

[‡] See ibid., para. 7.3.9.

event, to challenge for having rejected a possible policy option in favour of a policy which is alleged to have failed.'*

In other high-profile cases the tribunal has ordered the disclosure of an assessment prepared by the Department of Work and Pensions to help the Home Office develop a business case for the identity cards schemes; ordered the BBC to disclose minutes of the meeting at which its governors discussed their reaction to the Hutton report; required the disclosure of officials' advice to John Prescott, then deputy Prime Minister, on whether to grant planning permission for a controversial tower block in the Vauxhall area of London; ruled that the Office of Government Commerce should release the 'gateway reviews' used in assessing progress in the government's identity card programme;† ordered the release of submissions made by government departments to the Export Credit Guarantee Department in connection with a proposed oil and gas extraction project off the island of Sakhalin, north of Japan; and required the Department for Business, Enterprise and Regulatory Reform to disclose minutes of meetings with the Confederation of British Industry. On the other hand, the tribunal has ruled that the public interest favours withholding submissions to the secretary of state for culture from officials and other ministers on the government's decision on the list of sporting events which should be protected under the Broadcasting Act 1996 from having television rights sold.

However, even in its earliest days, the Act faced two serious political attacks. The first came in October 2006, when the government announced proposals to amend the FOI fees regulations‡ to make it easier for authorities to refuse requests on

---

* *Department for Education and Skills* v. *Information Commissioner and* Evening Standard, EA/2006/0006, 19 February 2007.

† This decision was overturned by the High Court on the grounds that the tribunal breached parliamentary privilege by relying on a select committee's opinion in its findings. However, the court upheld the key elements of the tribunal's approach to policy formulation exemption and the public interest test.

‡ Freedom of Information and Data Protection (Appropriate Limit and Fees) Regulations 2004.

cost grounds. The proposals would have allowed an additional 17,500 FOI requests each year to be refused, about 15 per cent of the total.* The government sought to justify this on the grounds that a small proportion of requests imposed a significant burden. But a report commissioned by the government found that the costs of the Act were comparatively modest – the total cost across the whole public sector was estimated to be £35.5 million annually, including the cost of the Information Commissioner and the Information Tribunal.†

It was clear that the government wanted to introduce the new regulations quickly and without proper consultation. The CFOI highlighted the fact that a Department for Constitutional Affairs minister, Baroness Ashton of Upholland, had promised Parliament that the public would be consulted before any changes were made. This was widely reported in the press and picked up by political journalists and editors questioning the Prime Minister at a press lunch, prompting him to promise a public consultation.

A consultation document with new draft regulations was published in December 2006.‡ There was no assessment of the nature of the requests that would be refused if the regulations were implemented, or the public benefit that would be lost as a result. However, the consultation document acknowledged that the proposals 'would have a greater effect' on journalists, MPs, campaign groups and researchers.§

Fortunately, the government had underestimated the level of opposition the proposals would encounter. Virtually the whole of

---

* See *Independent Review of the Impact of the Freedom of Information Act: A Report Prepared for the Department of Constitutional Affairs* (London: Frontier Economics, 2006). This is the sum of the volume reduction figures for central government and the wider public sector of the first two options shown in Table 3 on page 7 of the report. Page 1 of the report estimates that central government will receive 34,000 FOI requests annually and that the rest of the public sector will receive 87,000 requests, making a total of 121,000.

† Ibid., para. 2.7

‡ *Draft Freedom of Information and Data Protection (Appropriate Limit and Fees) Regulations 2007* (Department of Constitutional Affairs, 2006).

§ Ibid., Partial Regulatory Impact Assessment, para. 41.

the national press published editorials or substantial comment pieces criticising the proposals. The *Daily Mail* declared: 'There is at least one legacy of which Tony Blair could be proud: his government's introduction of the Freedom of Information Act ... How sadly significant that even before he has left office it looks as if that reform is going to be utterly emasculated.'* *Press Gazette* launched a 'Don't kill FOI' campaign which ran for several months, culminating in a petition to Downing Street signed by 1,200 editors and journalists. Many voluntary sector and campaigning groups also voiced their opposition, including Unlock Democracy.

In a parliamentary debate on the issue, the former Labour defence minister Don Touhig said: 'To change the rules that allow public authorities to refuse FOI requests on costs grounds would be mean spirited and certainly unworthy of my party, and of my government, of whom I am immensely proud.'† The Conservative frontbench spokesman Henry Bellingham said:

> A saving of roughly £12 million – just 4 per cent of the cost of the COI [Central Office of Information] – means I do not think we are talking about cost. Are we talking about abuse of the system? Manifestly we are not ... So, if we ask, 'Why change the system?', the answer is simple. Ministers want to curtail the flow of information.‡

The Information Commissioner questioned the practical implications of the proposals. He told the Constitutional Affairs Committee that the existing fees regime was working well and had 'all the advantages of being simple, clear and straightforward and not being a deterrent.'§ Of the government's proposals he later said: 'I fear that they will introduce new layers of procedural

---

* 'Stop this assault on the right to know', *Daily Mail*, 6 March 2007.
† Hansard, 7 February 2007, vol. 456, col 295WH.
‡ Ibid., cols 314WH–315WH.
§ Constitutional Affairs Committee, *Freedom of Information – One Year On*, oral evidence, 14 December 2006, Q. 99.

and, indeed, bureaucratic complexity.'* The committee itself concluded: 'We see no need to change the fees regulations.'†

Extraordinarily, a second attack on the Act was launched at virtually the same time. A private members' Bill, introduced by the Conservative MP David Maclean, sought to remove Parliament from the scope of the FOI Act altogether and create a new exemption for MPs' correspondence with public authorities.‡

The Bill was justified as a measure to protect constituents' privacy, but this was spurious. MPs' correspondence on behalf of individual constituents was already protected under at least two exemptions in the Act, a point acknowledged by Maclean himself. He told MPs: 'Clearly if one writes to a public authority and gives the personal details of a constituent ... that information should be protected. It should quite clearly be protected under the current Act. However, inadvertently someone may release it. This measure would remove that small problem.'§ The real effect of the Bill would have been to prevent disclosure of information about MPs' expenses and allow MPs to lobby public authorities in secret.

The Bill was partly prompted by the disclosure of more detailed information about MPs' expenses under the Act. The Information Tribunal had recently ruled in favour of a request by the Liberal Democrat MP Norman Baker for greater details about MPs' travel claims. The Commons already published the amount paid to each MP for travel, but the tribunal ruled that a breakdown of the figures by mode of transport should also be provided.

This was only one of many requests on the subject of MPs' expenditure. The tribunal has since ordered the Commons to disclose full details of how each MP spends their additional costs allowance (ACA). This is the allowance paid to reimburse MPs for the costs incurred when staying away from their main home

---

* Constitutional Affairs Committee, *Freedom of Information: Government's Proposals for Reform*, fourth report, Session 2006–07, HC 415, oral evidence, 20 March 2007, Q. 31.

† HC 991, para. 104.

‡ Freedom of Information (Amendment) Bill.

§ Freedom of Information (Amendment) Bill Committee, 1st sitting, 7 February 2007, col. 7.

while performing their parliamentary duties. In its decision the tribunal commented:

> The laxity of and lack of clarity in the rules for ACA is redolent of a culture very different from that which exists in the commercial sphere or in most other public sector organisations today ... In our judgment these features, coupled with the very limited nature of the checks, constitute a recipe for confusion, inconsistency and the risk of misuse. Seen in relation to the public interest that public money should be, and be seen to be, properly spent, the ACA system is deeply unsatisfactory, and the shortfall both in transparency and accountability is acute.*

The House of Commons lost an appeal against this decision at the High Court in May 2008. However, the decision has not been universally accepted and some MPs remain unhappy, feeling that the level of scrutiny required by FOI is an unwarranted intrusion into their private lives. But in the wake of the scandal involving Derek Conway MP, suspended from the Commons for misuse of public money in paying his son for work he appeared not to have done, public demands for greater transparency seem unlikely to go away.

The House of Commons approved the Maclean Bill in May 2007, despite efforts by an all-party group of MPs to try and block it. Although officially the government maintained that it was 'neutral' on the Bill, a key part was played by the Parliamentary Labour Party, which wrote to all Labour MPs, urging them to support it. It also had support from Henry Bellingham, who described it as 'a very modest, small Bill'.†

However, the Bill fell when no sponsor was found to take it forward in the House of Lords. A report by the Lords Constitution Committee concluded that the Bill did 'not meet the requirements of caution and proportionality in enacting legislation of

---

* *Corporate Officer of the House of Commons* v. *Information Commissioner* and *Ben Leapman, Heather Brooke and Michael Thomas*, EA/2007/0060, 0061, 0062, 0063, 0122, 0123, 0131 (26 February 2008), para. 33.
† Hansard, HC Deb, 20 April 2007, vol. 459, col. 591.

constitutional importance.'* And *The Governance of Britain*, the Green Paper on constitutional renewal published in July 2007 after Gordon Brown became Prime Minister, finally ended speculation over where the government stood on the matter, stating: 'It is right that Parliament should be covered by the Act.'†

Brown also intervened to stop the fees proposals. In a speech on liberty in October 2007, he announced that the government would drop the proposed changes to the FOI fees regulations. 'We do this because of the risk that such proposals might have placed unacceptable barriers between the people and public information. Public information does not belong to government, it belongs to the people on whose behalf government is conducted,' he said.‡

At the same time, the Prime Minister announced a consultation on extending the scope of the Act to private bodies with public functions and contractors providing some services on behalf of public authorities.§ At the time of writing, the Ministry of Justice has yet to publish a response to the consultation. In addition, Brown announced a review of the thirty-year rule governing the release of records in the National Archives. The review, chaired by Paul Dacre, editor of the *Daily Mail* and editor in chief of Associated Newspapers, will make recommendations to the Prime Minister and the Lord Chancellor late in 2008 or early in 2009.

These initiatives suggest that the immediate future for FOI may be brighter. Brown himself has expressed his commitment to the legislation. In his speech on liberty, he said: 'Freedom of information can be inconvenient, at times frustrating and indeed embarrassing for governments. But freedom of information is the right course because government belongs to the people, not the politicians.'§§ And in the furore following the disclosure under

---

* Constitution Committee, *Freedom of Information (Amendment) Bill*, fifth report, Session 2006–07, HL 127, para. 4.

† Ministry of Justice, *The Governance of Britain* (Cm 7170, 2007), para. 140.

‡ Gordon Brown, speech on liberty, University of Westminster, 25 October 2007.

§ Ministry of Justice, *Freedom of Information Act 2000: Designation of Additional Public Authorities*, CP 27/07.

§§ Speech on liberty, 25 October 2007.

FOI of Treasury officials' advice on the abolition of pensions tax credit, a decision Brown took when he became Chancellor in 1997, he defended both his decision and the FOI Act: 'First, we introduced the Freedom of Information Act 2000. Secondly, I support it. Thirdly, I support the release of the papers.'*

But further challenges to the Act lie ahead. It has been clear for some time that ministers are uncomfortable with the line the Information Tribunal has been taking on access to policy advice. In May 2007, a leaked letter from Alistair Darling to Lord Falconer, then the Cabinet minister responsible for FOI, aired concerns that the FOI Act was putting 'good government' at risk. The letter referred to a 'discernible trend' of cases going against the government at the tribunal and raised the prospect of using the veto to annul adverse decisions in future or amending the Act. Either of these outcomes would represent a massive setback for the legislation.

Since the Darling letter, the government has challenged two tribunal decisions in the High Court.† In both the court has upheld the tribunal's interpretation of the statutory provisions dealing with policy formulation and internal discussions. However, at the time of writing, the tribunal is about to hear the first case involving Cabinet minutes, following the Information Commissioner's ruling that minutes discussing the war in Iraq should be disclosed. This will be the next of what is likely to be a continuing series of critical hurdles for the legislation.

Delays are a more practical problem. In 2006 the Constitutional Affairs Committee reported: 'There is evidence that delays are

---

* Hansard, HC Deb, 17 April 2007, vol. 459, col. 183.

† The first case, *Office of Government Commerce* v. *Information Commissioner & Anor* [2008] EWHC 737 (Admin) (11 April 2008), involved the Section 35 exemption in the Act for the formulation of government policy. The tribunal's decision in this case was quashed on an unrelated point that the tribunal had breached parliamentary privilege. But the court upheld the key elements of the tribunal's approach to Section 35 and the public interest test. The second case, *Export Credits Guarantee Department* v. *Friends of the Earth* [2008] EWHC 638 (Admin) (17 March 2008), involved the exception for internal communications in Regulation 12(4)(e) of the Environmental Information Regulations.

occurring at all stages of the process and there have to date been no penalties for such delays.'* This problem has arisen from the Act's time limits or lack of them. The legislation requires requests to be dealt with 'promptly' and within twenty working days. However, when an authority is considering disclosing exempt information under the Act's public interest test, the time can be extended for a period that is 'reasonable in the circumstances'. Unsurprisingly, this provision is abused and requests are delayed, sometimes repeatedly. In 2007, departments of state extended the twenty-day deadline in almost 10 per cent of requests. Of the extensions, 21 per cent were for forty days or more.†

The problem is confounded by the lack of a statutory time limit for internal reviews. Before applicants can appeal to the Information Commissioner, they must normally ask the authority to review its own decision. If authorities drag their heels at this stage, the commissioner has no power to compel them to do anything. The Information Commissioner has said that he will make greater use of his regulatory powers against recalcitrant public authorities, or where he becomes aware of a pattern of non-compliance. Since 2007, he has issued a number of non-binding practice recommendations, drawing attention to serious shortcomings by authorities. Both the National Offender Management Service and the Department of Health have received such recommendations, largely because of persistent delays in responding to requests. However, these may be of limited effect when the work of the Information Commissioner's Office (ICO) itself involves such serious delays.

At the beginning of June 2008, the ICO had a backlog of 1,363 complaints. Figures obtained by the CFOI under the FOI Act show that for the year to March 2008, the ICO took an average of 514 days to close a case with a formal decision notice. For cases closed without investigation, the figure was 246 days. The consequences of this are obvious.

These problems are partly down to resources. It has been clear

---

* HC 991, para. 15.

† See *Third Annual Report on the Operation of the FOI Act in Central Government 2007* (Ministry of Justice, 2008), Table 9.

for some time that the ICO is significantly underfunded. Its FOI responsibilities are funded by grant–in–aid from the Ministry of Justice. The ICO has been given additional funding from April 2008, but the commissioner has said that while this will allow him to recruit enough staff to meet current demand, it will not be enough to enable him to reduce the backlog in the coming year.[*]

However, if the Act is to be effective, the ICO must provide a more expedient remedy for complainants. As for the legislation itself, the CFOI would like to see several amendments. The time limits need to be tightened to address the problem of requests being delayed. The Scottish Act has fixed time limits for decisions on the public interest test and for internal reviews and the legislation for the rest of the UK should be brought into line. Secondly, the ministerial veto casts a shadow over the legislation and should be removed. The Australian government has just taken such a step, announcing the abolition of conclusive certificates under the Australian FOI Act.[†]

The UK Act has already proved of immense benefit to the public. However, much still needs to be done to ensure it becomes more deeply rooted in our society. The president of the Australian Law Reform Commission, Professor David Weisbrot, said recently: 'It is critical to get the law right, of course – but even more importantly, we need to nurture a strong "pro–disclosure culture".'[‡] This is the task facing us in the next five years.

[*] See Information Commissioner's Office, *Annual Report 2007/08*, HC 670, p. 25.
[†] 'Freedom of Information reform', media release, Senator John Faulkner, 22 July 2008.
[‡] 'ALRC's FOI inquiry deferred pending government reforms', press release, Australian Law Reform Commission, 22 July 2008.

Is it possible to vote for human rights?

Louise Christian

n 10 December 2008 it will be the sixtieth anniversary of the Universal Declaration of Human Rights. Although it was not binding in law, much of it was subsequently adopted in the International Covenant of Civil and Political Rights (ICCPR) of 1966, which assumed the force of law on 23 March 1976. Among the provisions of the Universal Declaration set out verbatim in the ICCPR are those relating to the right of democratic participation.

Article 21 of the Universal Declaration and Article 25 of the ICCPR provides: 'Everyone has the right to take part in the government of his country directly or through freely chosen representatives ... The will of the people shall be the basis of the authority of government. This will shall be expressed in periodic and genuine elections'. Article 28 of the Universal Declaration also states: 'Everyone is entitled to a social and international order in which the rights and freedoms set forth in this Declaration can be fully realised.'

Thus democratic participation in government is a fundamental human right. But how far does our system reflect this in practice? If I want to vote as far as possible in a manner which ensures that those I vote for uphold all the rights in the ICCPR, does our party political system enable me to do so? Should this fundamental human right be one of those protected by a new written constitution, as argued for by Charter 88 and others, which improves on and does not detract from the Human Rights Act? One potential problem with this is that it is crucial that human rights are universal and not restricted to British citizens – as our political parties often seem in danger of suggesting. We already deny votes to non-citizens such as asylum seekers who have been resident here for many years and to anyone who is in prison, and recent citizenship proposals suggested denying voting rights to soldiers. The right of democratic participation – at least in relation to voting – is already in jeopardy as a universal human right.

During the last few years the rights set out in the ICCPR have come under serious attack from government. We have seen foreign nationals detained indefinitely until the House of Lords ruled this unlawful, followed by control orders, which are a form of house arrest without trial or charge. We have seen fair trial rights threatened, including the right to trial by jury, and many new criminal offences and measures brought in which are insufficiently defined to avoid offending rights such as freedom of expression. Others blur the boundaries between civil and criminal law – for example, anti-social behaviour orders. We have seen privacy rights attacked by proposals for data collection and identity cards. But above all the right not to be arbitrarily detained without charge has come under sustained assault.

Nothing has illustrated better the problems of the British party political system in delivering genuinely representative democracy than the extraordinary proceedings in the House of Commons in June 2008 over the government's proposals to extend detention without charge from twenty-eight to forty-two days for people held under the Terrorism Act. It is therefore worth considering what this particular episode says about our system.

That detention without charge under the Terrorism Act affects a fundamental human right is not in doubt. ICCPR Article 9 stipulates: 'Anyone who is arrested ... shall be promptly informed of any charges against him.' Although the European Convention on Human Rights is not as specific, a challenge to the provision in the Terrorism Act as being contrary to Article 5 of the Human Rights Act is being mooted by the new Equalities and Human Rights Commission. As was much discussed during the parliamentary debates, the legal principles forbidding arbitrary detention go back to Magna Carta. The House of Commons passed the proposals against the almost unanimous opposition of the Conservatives and the Liberal Democrats (except for one Tory MP), with the government relying on the votes of the five

Democratic Unionist MPs. It was widely reported that they and Labour backbench MPs had been pressurised or offered incentives and deals to vote with the government. In her speech on the issue Diane Abbott MP said:

> The government machinery has devoted ten days to bone-crunching pressure on potential rebels, again because they do not have the votes ... People whom the Prime Minister has never spoken to in his life have been ushered into his presence twice in forty-eight hours. They should have a shred of sympathy for them.
>
> People have been offered Cuba, and no doubt governorships of Bermuda have been bandied about. Any rebel backbencher with a cause is confident – if they vote the right way of course – that the Prime Minister will make the statement, give the money or make the special visit. That is humorous, but is it right that our civil liberties should be traded in such a bazaar? Is it appropriate or right that we should trade votes at the United Nations on the basis of such political pandering?
>
> The reason why the government have had to put such pressure on people is because they cannot muster the votes.[*]

If our party political system is to deliver representative democracy, the public must have faith in their representatives. Members of Parliament complain that the public are cynical about what they do but recurring revelations about expenses claims, MPs employing their own relatives using public money and the tendency for ex-ministers to find lucrative employment in the private sector all fuel such cynicism. Recently one ex-MP, Neil Hamilton (himself discredited in a financial scandal), told a Sunday newspaper that being an MP is 'money for old rope' and 'you can do as much or as little as you like'.[†] There has to be a suspicion that other MPs (not all of course) act primarily in their own self-interest and are therefore particularly susceptible to the sort of horse-trading (or 'playing ducks and drakes' as Diane Abbott put it) which she says occurred over the vote on forty-two days.

[*] Hansard, HC Deb, 11 June 2008, vol. 477, col. 382.
[†] Quoted in Ali Hussain, 'I haven't a penny to my name', *Sunday Times*, 3 August 2008.

Representative democracy also depends on political parties producing manifestos of what they will do in government, which people can then rely on when deciding how to vote. It is reasonable to expect these manifestos to set out the basic principles and values informing the programme of the political party in question. Of course manifestos are not set in stone and governments do have to respond to events as they happen but voters should be entitled to some idea of what sort of response a government will give.

At the last general election in 2005 the Labour Party manifesto said: 'Police and other law enforcement agencies now have the powers they need ... to hold suspects for extended questioning while charges are brought.' At that time the maximum period of detention without charge was fourteen days and this was an increase from the maximum of seven days allowed under the Prevention of Terrorism (Temporary Provisions) Act, which was renewed annually during the time of threat of Irish nationalist terrorism. The electorate has therefore never had the opportunity to vote on detention without charge for twenty-eight days, brought in by the Labour government in 2006, let alone on the proposal for forty-two days.

The Conservative Party now claims to be the party of liberty (though perhaps not of human rights) and David Davis, previously shadow Home Secretary, resigned his seat in protest at the House of Commons vote for forty-two days. But the Conservative Party manifesto of 2005 makes no mention of any dismay at the erosion of civil liberties, promising only 'robust anti-terror laws' if they were elected. It is also fair to speculate that if the Conservatives win the next general election and Labour become the opposition, their positions on this and other human rights issues may be reversed.

Only the Liberal Democrats complained of the erosion of civil liberties and human rights in their 2005 manifesto, and specifically mentioned detention without charge. But they have never been in government, and their stance might change if they were. Meanwhile it is apparent that the other two parties are adopting positions which are, at the very least, doubted by their own MPs. The oft-expressed view in the Conservative Party that the Human Rights Act should be repealed sits oddly with the stance they have taken on forty-two days, just as the fact that the Labour Party introduced the Act sits oddly with its disregard for the Act's principles and standards.

The overall effect is a severe erosion of the ability of our party political system to deliver participation by the electorate on fundamental human rights questions. This is not to mention the loss of integrity to both politicians and the political system. Democracy is not just about voting – but anyone who was a constituent of one of those Labour MPs who changed their mind on forty-two days at the last minute might well feel let down or confused. It would also be difficult to know whether to vote for a Conservative MP who voted against forty-two days but was opposed to human rights on a whole range of issues and was in favour of the death penalty. Nor are the Liberal Democrats always reliable on human rights issues. Their 2005 manifesto supported control orders placing people not convicted of any criminal offence under house arrest if they are 'time limited and subject to high standards of proof', and recently their new leader, Nick Clegg, made controversial remarks about immigration. Lord Carlile of Berriew, a Liberal Democrat, appointed by the government as an 'independent reviewer' of terrorism legislation, strongly supported the government's position on forty-two days even though there was such strong opposition from other independent experts such as the director of public prosecutions (Sir Ken Macdonald), the previous attorney general (Lord Goldsmith), the previous Lord Chancellor (Lord Falconer of Thoroton) and the previous head of MI5 (Baroness Manningham-Buller).

Thankfully our democratic system does deliver freedom of expression and the organisation Liberty (of which I am chair) has mounted a campaign on forty-two days called 'Charge or Release', which has made up for some of the political confusion in Parliament, increasing awareness of the issues at stake and improving the quality of the debate in public and the media. The campaign showed that neither the United States nor any other country in Europe has such long periods of detention without charge. The issue is of international importance because of the message our government is sending to other governments about the acceptability of arbitrary detention. But ultimately a successful campaign like this only serves to underline the corruption of the formal political process that happens when the political parties distort the will of the electorate.

This raises the question of whether party politics serves democracy well. Should some things be agreed to be above party politics? Commonly issues of morality and religion are so regarded in Parliament, with parties giving MPs free votes on issues such as abortion. But for human rights activists, human rights are equally sacrosanct and something on which we hope we can agree no matter what our views on the economy, the conduct of public services and so on. Among the aims of Charter 88 and now Unlock Democracy is the creation of a 'democratically renewed Parliament', but how in fact is this to be achieved? Some argue for a better Bill of Rights than the Human Rights Act/European Convention. All too often this is an argument for weakening rather than strengthening protections for civil liberties and human rights, and even for rights to be restricted to British citizens rather than being universal for everyone in Britain. Other proposals include introducing proportional representation, although this may not improve democratic accountability if it removes the right to vote for a named representative rather than a political party (as this right may offer more certainty as to how that person is likely to represent the voter in Parliament). If political parties are to continue to have such importance in our system, should there be some rules about the internal democracy of the political parties themselves? And should there be rules to protect the Cabinet system of government and prevent the Prime Minister simply ruling by diktat?

It is ironic that the unelected House of Lords may be the element in our parliamentary system which stops the 42-day proposal. Indeed, it has done so with other proposals attacking fundamental liberties, such as the attempts to remove the right to trial by jury in some cases. While an unelected House of Lords appears to be directly contrary to Article 21 of the Universal Declaration on Human Rights, the words of Article 28 appear to be fulfilled only through its intervention. If reform of the House of Lords were to take the form of making all peers subject to election, the dead hands of the political parties could actually make such intervention less likely. It is of course still possible for the government to override the House of Lords if it strikes down legislation by using the Parliament Act (which can be used once the proposed legislation has been passed twice by the House of Commons and if more than a year has elapsed between the second reading of the Bill and its second passage through the Commons). The government does not always use this mechanism if a measure is strongly opposed but it can.

In the end the only real block to the 42-day legislation may not be any part of the process of democratic government. The end might come instead if it is declared unlawful by the courts, as was the provision in the Anti-Terrorism, Crime and Security Act 2001 which allowed foreign nationals to be detained indefinitely. It is arguably unhealthy if Parliament and the judges are continually coming into conflict, and the provision in the Human Rights Act requiring a declaration of compatibility in all new legislation was meant to prevent this.

It seems to me that the really important factor in all this is that we have a Human Rights Act but not a human rights culture. The drafters of the Act, including Francesca Klug, wanted it to be accompanied by a programme of education and the creation of a Commission for Equalities and Human Rights. Nearly ten years after the passing of the Act, the commission has only just begun work, and there has still been no adequate programme of education. As a result, there is ill-informed hostility to the Act from important sections of the media and political opinion.

Governments do have to deal with terrorism but there is a strong argument that abrogating human rights is counter-productive as well as wrong in principle. If young Muslims see friends and neighbours locked up unjustly without charge for long periods, quite possibly losing their job and reputation in the process, this is more rather than less likely to radicalise them. A government more imbued with a human rights culture than we have ever had would not have attempted to claim, as Tony Blair did, that 'the rules of the game have changed'.

More consensus in government is not necessarily a bad thing and there should by now be a consensus on human rights. If there were, human rights would not be so vulnerable to being traded in for short-term political capital by unpopular governments. Members of Parliament would be ashamed to be seen to change views so radically on issues such as forty-two days. But unless this happens, perhaps we do need to consider whether the system should allow political parties to pressure or offer incentives to MPs when they are voting on fundamental human rights issues. Should these not instead be treated as matters of conscience?

Talking about a revolution

Nick Clegg

Britain's democracy is at a historic turning point. Not in living memory have confidence in politicians, trust in the system, or faith in the government's capacity to change things been as low as they are today. As the quango state proliferates, and local government's position is eroded, it as if Britain has moved into a post-democratic era, where 'expertise' is valued over election and 'independence' trumps accountability.

Yet, as the economy worsens, and globalisation dismantles historic patterns of business, governance and even family life, the need for a politics that works could not be greater. The danger we face is that, if we do not bring politics back to life, and convince people that it has the power to change things for the better, mainstream ideas will lose ground to demagogues, populists and extremists who could tear our country apart. Ten years from now we will look back at this period and see it either as a moment when real, fundamental change began, or as a moment when politics as we know it went into terminal decline.

We need a wholly new way of doing things, a new deal for the governance of Britain. Our political system has got to be taken apart, and power restored to the people. It's only by putting the British people in charge that we will be able to create a nation of real fairness, where there is opportunity for everyone, no matter what their background.

This programme of change that Britain needs is not, and will never be, just about changing the electoral system. A new voting system is a vital but not sufficient step to the rebuilding of the governance of Britain. From health care to education, from family finances to the environment: the power to change things must be given back to ordinary people and families. From top to bottom, the whole way Britain is governed must be rebuilt so people can run their own lives. I am talking about nothing less than a political revolution.

This chapter seeks to set out how that new way of doing things should look. There are six elements to our programme for democratic change: a fair voting system, radical decentralisation, reform of our legislative process and parliamentary procedures, a total overhaul of the way politics is financed, new constitutional protections for individuals, and a step-change in the transparency of our government.

Fair votes and fair elections

In a democracy everyone ought to be confident that their vote counts. But the present electoral system gives huge influence to a tiny number of 'swing voters' in a few marginal seats. Put simply, the system cheats the public, and is no longer fit for purpose. After all, its purpose was never to reflect pluralism – it was designed to maintain a duopoly between two big parties, two big ideologies. Today, our politics are as diverse as our society; in large numbers the public has turned its back on stale two-party politics. In 1955, only 2 per cent of voters supported a party other than Labour or the Conservatives. In 2005, it was 32 per cent. A whole third of the population wanted something different.

The 'other voters', often represented in graphs by a sort of muddy grey colour, actually represent a rainbow of opinions, beliefs and ideas, but for the most part their votes count for nothing. No wonder more and more people simply don't bother to vote at all; so many in fact that in 2001, for the first time in our democratic history, more people didn't vote than cast a ballot for the winning party. It happened again in 2005, and yet with the first-past-the-post system, that winning party can govern as it likes despite a mandate from just 22 per cent of eligible voters.

No tinkering with the way in which elections are run can substitute for radical reform to give voters equality. Holding elections at weekends, internet voting or putting polling stations into supermarkets may be good ideas in and of themselves but they will have little effect if votes – wherever and whenever cast – don't count. If we are to restore hope in, and the capacity of, politics, we must have a system which facilitates choice rather than distorts it; which favours competition, rather than stifles it; and which gives independents and parties a level playing field on which to fight elections. At national and local level, it is imperative for the rebirth of our politics that we move to a more proportional voting system as soon as we can.

Community control

Alone in Europe, and in contrast to the great majority of democracies, our government has become ever more centralised in recent decades, and less and less directly accountable to the public. While the command economies of the Continent – including the former dictatorships – have found ways to devolve responsibility to elected assemblies and officials at regional and local levels, power in Britain has tended to flow in the opposite direction. Ours is the most centralised country in Europe apart from Malta, which is home to fewer people than the London Borough of Croydon. Even the 'devolved assemblies' in Scotland, Wales, Northern Ireland and London have limited roles, while elsewhere in England local authorities have become mere agents for central government. Every major policy being delivered by councils today has 'Made in Whitehall' stamped on the bottom. Fear of the postcode lottery drives an obsession with making things the same, even in wildly different places, which destroys innovation and makes improvement almost impossible.

This fear is wholly misguided. All the evidence I've seen from Europe shows that devolved, locally accountable services are the best way to drive forward improvements that benefit all people, even the most vulnerable. That was the clear conclusion of a pamphlet I wrote in 2002 with Richard Grayson called *Learning from Europe*,* where we studied education systems from across the

---

* Nick Clegg and Richard Grayson, *Learning from Europe: Lessons in Education* (London: Centre for European Reform, 2002).

European Union. It's time for politicians in Britain to wake up to the fact that the problem with 'postcode lotteries' is the lottery element, not the idea of postcode difference. With locally accountable services, we can achieve not a lottery, but postcode choice, where each community can have the services they want, tailored to local circumstances and needs.

The central state must intervene to allocate money on a fair basis, to guarantee equality of access in our schools and hospitals, and to oversee core standards and entitlements. But once those building blocks are in place, the state must back off and allow the genius of grassroots innovation, diversity and experimentation to take off in providing an array of top-class schools and hospitals. This alchemy of clear but circumscribed central direction combined with liberalised bottom-up provision is exactly what underpins the best health and school systems in Europe and the world.

To make this possible, we need to go much further than handing down 'freedoms and flexibilities' on terms decided by national bureaucrats. Power over key public services must be devolved to councils or, where appropriate, to councils working together in agreed regional or sub-regional structures. The National Health Service should be broken down and control over primary care trusts given to locally elected health boards, accountable to local people.

We must also address the fundamental issue of money. Real autonomy for local decision makers will only be possible if communities have control over their own resources. Far too large a proportion of local authority income is controlled and allocated by central government. Across England – from Penzance to Penrith – as much as 80 per cent of local authority spending is paid for by taxes raised in Whitehall. And local councils' ability to raise their own revenue has been severely limited by the council tax. It provides councillors with an impossible choice between cutting local services and pounding the poorest people in their communities with big bills. The system corrodes faith in local politics and blurs accountability, with ministers claiming to have dished out generous settlements while burdening councils with more and more central obligations; at the same time councillors lament the inadequacy of their grant.

This has got to change. The Liberal Democrats would relocalise the business rates, with appropriate equalisation mechanisms and protections for businesses. We would replace council tax with a local income tax, which could then be used to shift the burden of taxation from national to local by reducing the national tax rate and allowing councils to lift their local rate to compensate. While equalisation through a limited grant system will always be necessary, our aim is to move to a system where, broadly, local taxes fund local services.

Financial accountability is the linchpin of local decision-making, and until Labour and the Conservatives accept this and commit to financial decentralisation, their fine words about devolution will continue to ring hollow.

Fixing Parliament

The mother of parliaments has become an anachronism. Its peculiarities are a symbol of a physical, linguistic and emotional remoteness that is corrosive to public engagement. The bulletproof screen that shields the visitors' gallery, the high fences and the signs that remind you at every turn that trespassers will be prosecuted: these are potent and constant reminders of the total separateness of our parliament from the people it serves.

Parliament must be overhauled completely, to become more representative, more transparent and better able to hold the government to account. That means transforming the way the House of Commons works, reconnecting MPs with the electorate, restoring trust in legislators, reforming the House of Lords and making ministers genuinely accountable to Parliament. Both Houses of Parliament must be strengthened to perform their core responsibility of scrutinising the work of the government of the day, both in terms of new laws and in terms of executive action.

There are countless ways in which Parliament could be improved. I want business to be agreed, as in every other decent parliament in the world, by an all-party business committee instead of by the government. A joint programme committee of both Houses would ensure better co-ordination of the introduction and progress of business, together with a reconciliation procedure between the two Houses to prevent sterile 'ping-pong' at the end of a session. I would like to ban ministers from giving press briefings before giving information to the House, and I'd have a weekly short debate on a matter of topical interest. We should have a quarterly question time for each of the regions of England to allow for cross-cutting questions on matters relating to the region.

Fiscal and spending scrutiny should be massively increased. We should have a three-day debate on the spending programme following the comprehensive spending review, with provision for amending proposals. We should ensure that estimates days provide for better continuing scrutiny of government expenditure, providing specialist support to MPs to strengthen fiscal examination, and allow the committee on the Finance Bill to take evidence on the impact of fiscal measures.

To strengthen Parliament's control of the executive, ministerial appointments should be subject to confirmation hearings in Parliament. A two-thirds majority should be able to vote ministers out of office. A parliamentary vote should be required to send troops to war and approve all foreign treaties. We should have parliamentary scrutiny of proposals for changes to the machinery of government, and double the frequency of appearances of the Prime Minister before the Liaison Committee. Key civil service and quango appointments should be subject to confirmation hearings, too.

The role of backbenchers should be strengthened. Early day motions that attract support from a third of the House should be considered and voted on in debate. We should also enhance private members' Bills with deferred voting, extra time on Wednesdays after 7.00 p.m.* and time guaranteed for a second reading of any private members' Bills passed in the House of Lords.

Parliamentary committees should be strengthened. They should be allowed to subpoena witnesses. We should require ministers to appear before a relevant committee to outline

---

* This is the only appropriate time, as the House rises late on Mondays and Tuesdays and MPs generally return to their constituencies on Thursday afternoons.

government positions before attending any meetings of the EU Council of Ministers. All government quangos should face annual parliamentary committee scrutiny. And appointments should be made by secret ballot, not by party whips.

To reduce the amount of bad legislation that is passed by our parliament, we should introduce sunset clauses for all legislation so that laws fall unless explicitly renewed every few years. We must allow opposition days to be used at the discretion of the party to which they are allotted to make progress on parliamentary Bills – so the government cannot avoid scrutiny. We should increase the opportunities for post-legislative scrutiny to assess the effectiveness of legislation. We should substantially increase the resourcing of parliamentary draftspeople to speed up and improve the drafting of legislation, and make available the assistance of parliamentary counsel to all parties at committee and report stage.

And finally, reform of the illegitimate House of Lords cannot be postponed yet again. It is unacceptable that, nearly 100 years since the creation of a second chamber with a popular mandate was promised, part of the national legislature is still dependent on patronage, from centuries past and more recently. MPs have voted decisively for direct elections to a new House (we would call it the Senate to detach it permanently from the peerage) and since the primacy of the Commons must prevail we would introduce the necessary legislation immediately.

Money in politics

The relationship between money and politics is rotten, and it is hollowing out our whole political system. Both of the Big Two parties are in hock to millionaire businessmen, trade unions or both, and that's bad news for us all. When cash determines the rules, they will always be weighted in favour of people with the largest wallets.

We need to get money out of politics – now. Tinkering is not enough, though we may need to take small steps initially. We need a universal system where no donation over £25,000 is allowed. Even this seems a lot to most people, who can't even dream of circumstances in which they'd have £25,000 spare to give to a political party. But it would be a huge shift in our politics, which remains bought and sold by million-pound donations from the unions and tycoons. By cutting out the big-money donors, we can shift influence back where it belongs: to the people.

All parties have vested interests to defend, and all parties must surrender them. Unions, on top of their £25,000 limit, should be able to channel money from their members to the political parties. But they shouldn't only be channelling money to the Labour Party. The old labour-versus-capital divide is over. It is nonsense to imagine that every member of a union is a Labour supporter, and I believe it undermines the unions' brand – their endeavour to represent every worker equally – if they are so rigidly affiliated.

On the other side of the fence, the Conservatives have a different set of interests. Their last general election campaign, and their plan for the next one, is built on the premise of massive central spending to prop up local campaigns. Lord Ashcroft, a Conservative peer, is pouring millions of pounds into marginal seats. Their inbuilt cash advantage means the Conservatives are very reluctant to see spending limits reduced or a real cap on donations. But spending has to be slashed too: no party should spend more than £10 million a year, not just in an election year, but every year.

There have been many calls for state funding for our political parties. My concern is that it will seem like a discredited establishment propping itself up with taxpayers' money. I would rather put control directly into the hands of people. So I want us to seriously consider following the proposals of the Power Inquiry, which suggested allowing every voter to donate £3 to a party of their choice via the ballot paper in a general election. The money would come from public funds but only if people wanted to donate it – there would be an extra box on the ballot paper for them to choose.

However we support political parties, we shouldn't put up taxes or cut vital investment to pay for it. Schools and hospitals come first. The money must come from cutting the cost of politics in other ways. We must use the opportunity of a shift to fair votes to reduce the number of MPs and peers. I'd like to see 150 fewer MPs, which would save us about £30 million a year, and we could also cut the government's £200 million advertising budget. Some government advertising is important, public health campaigns for example, but there is plenty that serves no useful purpose except to promote incumbency by telling everyone how marvellous the government is. In the months before the last general election, the government spend on advertising suspiciously doubled – and then doubled again. This isn't legitimate marketing, it's self-promotion, and it must stop.

The surveillance state

The government is seeking to intrude on our lives in more areas than ever before. Labour uses the spectre of terrorism as a blank cheque to advance the surveillance state. There are more than four million CCTV cameras in Britain, one for every fourteen people. The national DNA database is the largest in the world, and contains profiles of more than one million people who have never been convicted of any offence. Meanwhile, our children are being added to biometric databases by stealth, as their fingerprints are routinely taken in school. Privacy International says surveillance is 'endemic' in British society. Only Russia, China and Malaysia spy more comprehensively on their citizens and our constitutional protections against undue surveillance are worse even than theirs.

The government's proposed National Identity Register (NIR) is simply the latest step in a growing trend. Despite recent events that have shown government to be incapable of holding important personal data securely, the NIR will eventually contain biometric data on every one of us, stored along with our signature, our date of birth, our nationality, our National Insurance number, our passport number and more.

Meanwhile, Labour refuses to fight terrorism with justice. It has instead eroded civil liberties in a futile attempt to gain security by ceding liberty. The government's measures on control orders and on pre-charge detention show neither respect for the principle that people are considered innocent until proven guilty, nor any aspiration towards proper prosecutions of those who threaten our safety. It is true that the nature of modern terrorism poses huge challenges to our criminal justice system. But our response should be to reform, streamline and strengthen our system to bring terror suspects before court, rather than circumvent due process altogether.

Two decades of illiberal government have, in summary, undermined the delicate balance between the powers of the individual and the state. British freedoms both ancient and modern have been abandoned and should be reinstated. So a vital part of the new settlement for Britain would be a Freedom Bill to roll back the state and protect the citizen from its overweening power. Such a Bill would bring an end to identity cards and the storing of innocent people's DNA, and would remove some police powers which can be misused, such as the power to break up 'public assemblies' of just two people. We would put in place new safeguards to force government departments and large companies to inform people when their data is lost or misused, and to compensate them as a result. And we would strengthen the Data Protection Act to ensure citizens had access to all data held on them.

Freedom of information and transparency

When government is remote from the people, it fails to engage its citizens and risks fatally undermining democracy. In Britain, these systemic failures are powerfully augmented by what seems to be an impenetrable government machine, considered the province of lobbyists, politicians and officials: what the journalist Peter Oborne terms 'the political class'. Liberal Democrats would open it up, by shining a floodlight of public scrutiny on the operations of Whitehall and of all public authorities. We would start by publishing a list of ministerial meetings each month, to make clear who has had access.

The Liberal Democrats welcomed and supported the Freedom of Information Act 2000. Its implementation since 2005 has presented the public, the media and opposition politicians with an immense opportunity to expose problems in the machinery of government. The Act has moved British governance out of its opaque cul-de-sac, but there is much more to do before our government is truly transparent. Too many exemptions to the present Act mean officials and ministers can all too easily fob applicants off. Though we welcome the recent government retreat on weakening the Freedom of Information Act still further, we recommend several measures to strengthen the existing regime.

First, we would strengthen the role of the information commissioner to ensure that he and his office are funded by, and directly accountable to, Parliament, which in turn would ensure that citizens' private information is kept private and that public information to which citizens are entitled is disclosed.

Second, we would limit the time available to public authorities deciding on a request where consideration of the public interest test is relevant.

Third, and perhaps most importantly of all, we would radically broaden the scope of the Act to ensure that all authorities providing a public service are covered. At present the British Potato Council is covered by the Act, for example, while Network Rail and the public utility companies are not. The water industry, as a result, remains an unaccountable monopoly. We subscribe to the basic principle that where there is no choice but to pay for a service, the way in which it is operated and the way in which citizens' money is spent ought to be open to public scrutiny.

Large private contractors which carry out work on behalf of the state ought also to be subject to the provisions of freedom of information legislation. Capita, which among other things administers the London congestion charge and is in the process of renewing Birmingham City Council's IT system, handles many millions of pounds of taxpayers' money each year, and should therefore be subject to the same rigorous scrutiny as a public authority. Similarly, the new 'academy' schools, which are built and funded from the public purse, are at present outside the terms of the Freedom of Information Act. This is a clear anomaly since the total capital costs of building 200 academies will be around £5 billion.

Liberal Democrats have a clear presumption in favour of disclosure in public affairs. Transparency should be the rule, opacity the exception. The Freedom of Information Act leaves British governance in a translucent limbo; we would bring it out of the shadows.

A popular constitution for a liberal Britain

My proposals – and those of my party – would transform British politics and transform Britain. They are the cornerstone of my simple ambition: to make Britain the liberal country its people want it to be.

Our approach has at its heart the desire to promote individuals and their rights, to cement communities and respond to their priorities, to roll back the centralised state and to make its remaining functions subject to the sharp spotlight of public scrutiny. We would embody this radical shift towards a liberal Britain in a popular constitution drafted for the people, by the people.

Traditionalists take pride in Britain's 'unwritten constitution'. In fact, it is already partially written. There are piecemeal laws to regulate the way parts of the country are run, and the Human Rights Act attempts to protect the citizen. We must subject these existing arrangements to a real public trial in a constitutional convention where randomly chosen members of the public would outnumber political nominees.

Together that convention would elucidate a clear statement of the contract between the British citizen and the state. In my view that statement should not, as the government proposes, make rights contingent on duties. It should make power contingent on accountability. I would make the people the ultimate arbiter of that test by asking them to endorse their new constitution in a UK-wide referendum.

Twenty years ago, Charter 88 called for a new constitutional settlement. Some of its goals have been half realised. But in 2008, we need more than half measures and halfway houses. Britain needs and deserves an agreed, comprehensive constitutional settlement embodied in a single source to which we can all refer. In short, Britain needs a liberal constitution, drafted, endorsed and owned by its overwhelmingly liberal population.

Privacy

Simon Davies

rivacy has become one of the hot topics of the twenty-first century. At a moment in history when people are increasingly aware of the need for constitutional reform to preserve freedom, the state of this fragile and ancient right has become a matter of general concern.

Hardly a day passes without a department or corporation being accused of violating privacy. Intrusive and invasive proposals for collecting and processing personal information are widespread, witnessed most dramatically in the current mania for building massive centralised databases.

People in Britain are now accustomed to surveillance and scrutiny. Mass CCTV, airport security, credit checks, constant demands for identity documents, intrusion by TV licensing inspectors, mandatory DNA collection, workplace surveillance, drug tests and criminal record checks are commonplace. And those are just the most obvious and visible intrusions.

It might at first be tempting to imagine that the collection and processing of so much information has become merely a fact of modern life. And, after all, the honest citizen should have nothing to fear. However, for many people, the loss in 2007 of the child benefit records of every family in Britain served as a wake-up call for such issues. Personal information that has real value to the individual and to the state is increasingly at risk of disclosure to criminal interests, and this threat has fundamentally changed the significance of the privacy issue.

People are told, with some justification, that Britain is now one of the world's foremost surveillance societies, an assessment that succeeds in occupying millions of column inches a year in the popular press. Yet behind the fact of such surveillance are pernicious dynamics and drivers that go to the heart of our democracy. From its inception, Charter 88 was keenly aware of this trend and sought privacy protection long before the issue had become popular. Nearly two decades were to pass before the mainstream press took up the cudgel.

What is privacy?

Historically, this complex mechanism sets the boundary between the intrusion of state and society, and the right of an individual to say 'go away'. It is not a 'selfish' right. Rather, it is a means of determining the autonomy of the individual, set against the values of society.

In recent years this perhaps arcane concept has found political traction. The Tory flagship newspaper, the *Daily Telegraph*, saw the writing on the wall in the mid-1990s, using its 'Free Country' campaign to mutate almost overnight into a paper espousing individual liberty and freedom from surveillance. Ten years later, the Conservative Party itself surprisingly took the same path, opposing the government on such issues as identity cards.

However, despite this remarkable controversy, few people agree on the precise meaning of privacy. In its early ambition to establish a Bill of Rights, the Labour administration of Gordon Brown asked people to consider what it means to be British. Few people could agree on an answer to that question. Similarly, privacy means different things to different people. It is perhaps the most unruly and controversial of all human rights. Theoretically, the term equates to the right of people to decide for themselves how their personal information should be used. In reality, everyone makes value choices about which forms of privacy invasion to accept or reject. Most do so by way of gut instinct rather than careful analysis.

Moreover, the definition of privacy varies widely according to context and environment to the extent that even after decades of academic interest in the subject, the world's leading experts have been unable to agree on a single definition. One pioneer in the field, Alan Westin, described privacy as 'part philosophy, some semantics, and much pure passion'.* On that last point, at least, everyone agrees.

Even before the terrorist attacks of 11 September 2001, the privacy issue had never been simple. The protection of individual privacy has always been one of the great polemics of public policy. At its heart is an ancient struggle for power. This struggle is played out each day in countless forms. With each security initiative – be it CCTV, national security, email surveillance or workplace monitoring – society struggles daily to assess competing claims for the right either to maintain privacy or to pursue surveillance.

Privacy and culture

Privacy is neither a modern nor a Western concept. While the idea of privacy as a fundamental human right still raises eyebrows in many developing countries, the concept is familiar at an intimate level to the citizens of those cultures. For example, limits to intrusion into private and bodily space are respected and understood in many Asian and Middle Eastern cultures while some governments that deny privacy as a human right are willing to practise it in the face of calls for transparency of official information.

At societal and governmental levels, privacy may be viewed with some suspicion, and yet at a personal level, each person draws a curtain around certain aspects of family and private life. In Thailand, privacy invasion by the state often goes unchallenged, and yet the boundaries of personal space in family and religious life are universally acknowledged and respected.

In some respects, privacy is a little like freedom: the less you have of it, the easier it is to recognise. And, like the concept of freedom, privacy means different things to different cultures. In France, it equates most closely to liberty. In America, it is an inseparable component of individual freedoms – particularly freedom from intrusion by federal government. Many European countries interpret privacy as the protection of personal data. Since the days of the huge campaign against their government's

* Alan F. Westin. *Privacy and Freedom* (New York: Atheneum, 1967), p. x.

proposed identity card in 1987, most Australians have viewed privacy as a measure of state power, while the government views it as a set of strictly defined legal rights.

Privacy under threat

Yet while the issue is more complex than ever, it has never been more pressing. There has probably never been a time in history when so much information has been amassed on the population at large.

Details of the average economically active adult in the developed world are located in around a thousand major databases – enough processed data to compile a formidable reference book for each person. Electronic visual surveillance in urban centres is almost ubiquitous. Nearly all forms of electronic communication are now routinely scanned and profiled. Companies too are making vast investments in surveillance products and services. Sales are booming in geographical tracking by mobile phone, workplace drug-testing equipment and monitoring systems, and spying equipment for domestic use, available from high street stores.

These activities have spawned a burgeoning economic sector. In Britain, the surveillance industry in all its forms – private investigators, police, credit agencies, security services and others – employs more than a million people. This population of professional snoopers is explained in part by the emergence of mass surveillance. In the past, surveillance was based on the targeting of specific individuals or groups. Now, systematic surveillance in a growing number of fields proactively profiles millions of people at a time. It is now common knowledge that the power, capacity and speed of information technology are increasing rapidly, while the cost and size of components are falling. The extent of privacy invasion – or certainly the potential for it – grows correspondingly. But it is not merely the increased capacity and decreasing cost of IT that creates threats to privacy. Global systems such as the internet remove geographical limitations (and legal protections) to the flow of data.

The joining together of systems and the development of com-mon technical standards are leading to the elimination of technological barriers between systems. The computing power once only found in vast mainframes is now available in a laptop – or a memory stick.

Public response to threats to privacy

Traditionally, public reaction to privacy invasion has been contradictory and unpredictable. While opinion polls consistently indicate that people care about privacy, public opposition even to the most blatant privacy invasion is sporadic. Everyone, no matter what their personal circumstances, is concerned about intrusion. For a single parent the threat may arise from constant intrusion by benefits authorities. For an employee of a company the threat may be subtler, yet no less significant. Intrusion takes many forms, from covert monitoring to outright harassment.

Whether through cause or effect, privacy now occupies an unenviable place in the catalogue of human rights. Throughout the past quarter-century, no other fundamental right in the arena of public policy has generated such turbulence and controversy. And yet, as the British academic James Michael has observed, 'privacy is the right from which all other rights derive'. It is central to the freedom and autonomy of people, and it is perhaps the key factor that limits the power of the state.

To those with a strong interest in the protection of their rights, privacy protection is one way of drawing the line at how far society can intrude into a person's affairs. In that context, privacy is a question of power – yours, the government's, your family's, your employer's, your neighbour's.

At its most dramatic level, privacy reins in the zeal of government. At a more profound level, it creates a bedrock of decency in human relations.

The threat to privacy from states

Nevertheless, in recent years, parliaments throughout the world have enacted legislation intended to comprehensively increase governmental reach into the private life of nearly all citizens and residents. Competing 'public interest' claims on the grounds of security, law enforcement, the fight against terrorism and illegal immigration, administrative efficiency and welfare fraud have rendered the fundamental right of privacy fragile and exposed. The extent of surveillance over the lives of many people has now reached an unprecedented level. Conversely, laws that ostensibly protect privacy and freedoms are frequently flawed – riddled with exceptions and exemptions that can allow government a free hand to intrude on private life.

At the same time, technological advances, technology standards, interoperability between information systems and the globalisation of information have placed extraordinary pressure on the few remaining privacy safeguards. The effect of these developments has been to create surveillance societies that nurture hostile environments for privacy.

Governments have created hundreds of key policy initiatives that, combined, may fundamentally destabilise core elements of personal privacy. Among these are proposals for the creation across society of 'perfect' identity using fingerprint- and iris-scanning biometrics; the linkage of public sector computer systems; the development of real-time tracking and monitoring throughout the communications spectrum, including mobile phones and, via GPS, vehicles; national DNA databases; the creation of global information sharing agreements; and the elimination of anonymity in cyberspace.

Public engagement with these developments is marginal. Increasingly, people feel unsettled about surveillance and are anxious to protect their privacy, but seem powerless to take direct action. The problem for civil society – or indeed anyone wishing to challenge surveillance – is not simply the sheer magnitude of the threat, but also its complexity and diversity.

It is important for each country to decide rationally and openly which elements of personal privacy should be lost, but it is also important for each country to understand how far down the path of mass surveillance it has already travelled. Most governments recognise the value of individual privacy, even if they privately despise it. However, the past ten years have witnessed an assault on privacy by the UK government that is almost without precedent in the democratic world. The government has largely abandoned any responsibility for protection of privacy – or, at least, abandoned any responsibility to keep surveillance in check. While it is true that many government departments are obsessed with their own data protection compliance, they are less interested in controlling surveillance.

There are dozens of examples of recent laws that have encroached substantially on privacy. The Communications Data Bill (2008) would require communications providers to hand over all traffic records (such as who calls who, who emails who, and mobile phone location information) so it can be archived by government. This proposed measure would create a surveillance infrastructure far more intrusive than anything yet seen in almost any democratic country. The Health and Social Care Act 2001 removes the traditional right of patients to control their own health information, transferring the ownership of this data to the secretary of state. The Identity Cards Act will place all key personal information under the control of the Home Secretary, imposing substantial requirements on individuals to comply with demands by the state to furnish information, attend meetings or report changes of personal circumstances. Legislation since 1995 has permitted a range of public authorities the right to share information on every UK resident. The Police and Criminal Evidence Act 1984 and the Serious Organised Crime and Police Act 2005 between them create a far-reaching web of invasions, including compulsory acquisition and permanent retention of DNA for even the most trivial offences or even for mere arrest. Each of these laws progressively undermines the provisions of the Data Protection Act 1998, a law designed (albeit to a minimum standard of protection) to preserve citizens' rights over personal information. It is little wonder that when the government proposed the most intrusive and far-reaching identity card system in the world, involving a register of unprecedented scale, there was little that any existing law would do to interfere with the scheme.

Conclusion

This systematic erosion of citizens' rights might to one extent be intellectually sustainable were it not for the sheer hypocrisy of its many perpetrators. MPs who cheerfully support laws intended to force citizens to yield personal information have opposed demands for disclosure of their own expenses. Police, most of whom support the idea of mandatory DNA testing, refused en masse to be tested because of fears of paternity checks of their own ranks. Senior civil servants are often happy to see the Data Protection Act eroded, but are frequently not prepared to ensure that the Freedom of Information Act is properly enforced. Commentators decry privacy while ensuring that their own telephone numbers remain ex-directory, and prominent politicians lobby for a secure data system for VIPs in the national identity card scheme. The double standards continue endlessly.

At a time when trust in government is plummeting, officials and MPs must learn that privacy is a public interest in its own right. They must understand that a society without privacy loses its stability.

Even the most zealous privacy advocate understands that there is a need to negotiate an equation between the desire for full autonomy and the demands of an information-hungry government. It is time for our elected representatives to adopt a similar view and learn to respect our privacy in the manner that they would like the world to respect their own rights. If this sea-change does not occur, citizens should consider taking matters into their own hands. With the exception of those cases where the law compels accurate information, a few innocent mistakes in the data you place onto paper forms and computer systems can easily be justified. Plausible deniability is a game that should not be reserved for the elite.

Democrats and optimists please come this way

Simon Hughes

'm a born optimist, and I consider being optimistic about democracy, with all its inherent weaknesses, to be a good and justified thing. Just think back to the wonderful experience of the first post-apartheid election in South Africa, or the excitement generated over the years by so many of the by-elections and general elections in this country and elsewhere.

The recent publication *2008: State of the Future* is a report backed by organisations including the Rockefeller Foundation, UNESCO and the World Bank, and has contributions from 2,500 experts around the world. Among many subjects considered, the report shows that fewer than half of the world's population live in a country with a democratic government, and more than a third live under authoritarian regimes. Of those living under a democratic government, participation in the democratic process was at 60 per cent in 1985 but is now at only 42 per cent, and is projected to fall to 35 per cent by 2017. Clearly, the percentage of people voting in elections worldwide is falling. But even though global trends are towards less political participation, there can be no inevitability about this.

So, rather than repeat the many criticisms of the current system as it exists, I have a 'Hughes plan' – actions which I think could and should be taken to increase democratic engagement and involvement the length and breadth of Britain.

I am clear that there are many people out there who have never thought of elected office and who have never been asked, but who would be just as good at it as the rest of us. So, to encourage greater involvement in politics, we ought to try new things. Now is the time. We ought, for example, to start regular adverts in newspapers, magazines and on websites aimed at recruiting those who might be interested in standing for public office. These adverts should be run in every part of Britain, in all our communities and in all major community languages. I want to persuade the radio, television and internet media to run competitions too. I want to persuade TV companies as soon as possible to run shows such as *Who Wants to Be a Member of Parliament?*, *Who Wants to Be an MEP?* and *Couldn't You Do a Better Job of Running Your Council?*. In Scotland, Wales and Northern Ireland I hope that we can have programmes for their devolved assemblies and governments: *Who Wants to Be an MSP?* and so on. And in London, I'm sure there would be lots of interest in an elimination series of *Who Wants to Be the London Mayor?*. Each serious applicant would be given the core details of each party's philosophy and policies, be publicly assessed by party representatives, and then be referred on to the party of their choice for career planning. Political parties could also make clear if they were looking for particular people with particular characteristics or qualities – young people, women, trade unionists, candidates from black and minority ethnic communities and so on. (I know that this raises politically sensitive issues and so there would have to be careful handling to make sure the balance was right between short-term positive discrimination on the one hand and the general need to avoid discrimination on the other.)

The next task is to get the rest of the community more engaged in political choices, even if they are not standing for election themselves. When youngsters reach sixteen and before they move on from compulsory schooling, it would be good to have a sort of graduation ceremony for each of them – with electoral registration as one part of it. Every February there should be a well-publicised countdown to a national registration and census day on the last day of that month. This should be not just to register every voter, but to register everybody lawfully living in the UK. There could be a worthwhile reduction in council tax or the equivalent in another tax for all those who register by the annual census and registration date. Once annual registration has gone through, each registered adult would receive in return a confirmation of their rights, including voting, as well as details of their representatives at each level of government together with a summary of what the representatives are responsible for.

We should renegotiate our national voting times and cycle. The objective would be to give maximum certainty and the ability to plan and avoid times when voting is less convenient for many people. The regular and traditional spring elections, when there are voting days for one or more groups of local councils across the UK, London government and the devolved governments in Scotland, Wales and Northern Ireland, should be on the second weekend of May every year (to avoid all bank holiday weekends), and over two days, either Saturday and Sunday, or Sunday and Monday. Any local referenda or national consultation votes could happen at the same time. Postal votes for these elections or referenda would be sent out on 30 April so people would vote as near to polling day as possible. This pattern would mean that, apart from Westminster general elections, the only different regular election cycle would be the five-yearly June elections for the European Parliament – and they could also be held over two days, and moved from their current Thursday to the Friday and Saturday of the agreed EU-wide voting weekend in June.

I hear more and more complaints that people know little or nothing of candidates they are asked to vote for. It would help then for all registered voters to be given before voting a minimum of basic information, independently produced, about all the candidates. These should include core personal information – full name, date of birth, occupation, previous elected political experience and, I believe, their main address over the previous twelve months. It would be possible to require one or two other personal details that were thought to be relevant. A little objective information like this might help people feel more able to choose the sort of elected representative they want – as well as ensuring that previously elected representatives were held to account better. (It would also reduce the chance of people claiming long-time local residence, when they had at most only recently lived locally or never really lived there at all!)

Every candidate should also have to provide, within a limited maximum number of words, a plan for how they intend to use the powers of the authority to which they want to be elected. In addition, before each annual round of elections, the main official audits published during the previous year for the council, assembly or parliament up for election should be republished in summary form, with comparisons with earlier years – so everybody can see how those who have been in office have been performing. At every level of government, a cross-section of randomly selected residents should be invited to carry out annually a citizens' audit of all those elected to principal councils or higher office. The citizens' audit would also be published in good time for the annual elections.

Voting in all elections should be preferential, with voters marking all candidates in every election in their order of choice. On polling days there should be voting stations at all the main places where the public go – railway stations, bus stations, bus stops, colleges, supermarkets and so on (including outside places like sports grounds during the season and well-attended places of worship on worship days). Everybody should be able to vote at any polling station within the boundaries of the council area they live in.

After the results are declared, the council, assembly or parliament should have until 1 June for a handover period. Those elected would use this time to form their administration, for confirmation that the new cabinet or executive members have the confidence of their legislature, and for a vote of confidence in the new administration by the new council, assembly or parliament. This would be a prerequisite before the new administration took over. The extra weeks for the new central or local representatives to get their political houses in order could reduce the nonsensical media pressure to have governments formed, ministers announced and local administrations agreed within hours of the polls closing.

We could easily make councils' executives, directly elected mayors and devolved and national governments more accountable. All powers held by executives, governments and elected mayors to arrange their own business and timetable could be taken away and given to the councils, assemblies and parliaments. In the Westminster parliament this would mean a business committee, representative of Parliament, fixing the agenda instead of ministers.

Consultations carried out by local and central government often have very feeble responses. This could be drastically improved by having quarterly consultation dates by which all major consultation responses had to be submitted. If everybody knew that all major local or national consultations ended on dates as regular and easy to remember as 1 February, 1 May, 1 August and 1 November every year, then there would be a much better chance that people would remember these, and be able to respond. Central and local publicity could regularly remind people which consultations were ongoing in each quarter.

Much less frequently, once every ten years for example, there ought to be an official democracy audit and an automatic independent review of the structure of government – backed up by a cross-party agreement not to tamper in between. As someone whose whole political life has been committed to devolution of power from the centre, I believe that high on this agenda should be efforts to improve those parts of UK local government which full democracy has not yet reached – where in practice devolution has not effectively happened yet! Those parts of the community which still don't have a parish or community council should be asked if they want one, and should be encouraged and incentivised to take more local power and responsibility. Unitary local government has now arrived in Scotland, Wales and Northern Ireland; at the next ten-yearly review we ought to offer unitary local government across all of England too. This must be done much more sensitively than has been the tradition of local government reorganisation over the last forty years; traditional county allegiances in England are very important to people generally, and not just to cricket fans! But I am also clear that in areas still with two tiers of local government, the division of responsibilities between district and county councils often reduces accountability, with neither level of council seeming to have enough power for people to think that it's worth voting for them. Nonetheless, until there is a broad local consensus in any area as to how to move to unitary local government, then two-tier local government should obviously continue. As a further step of devolution to local government, lower-tier and unitary councils ought to be able to fix their own business rates, but with businesses which pay rates having a bigger influence by participating in a second (advisory) chamber of the local council.

At the regional level in England, recent plans are emerging whereby regional government agencies or quangos become accountable to new select committees of MPs. Provided these select committees are properly representative, this is a good start towards accountability in the English regions. But fixing the political balance of regional select committees to reflect the political balance not of the region but of the whole of the House of Commons is absolutely the wrong way to proceed. Only locally representative regional select committees can command regional and national public confidence. There is also still a lot of unhappiness about how appropriate the shape and size of the English regions are. It really is time for a big debate in England about where we should have our regional boundaries, as well as whether and how we could now move to an English tier of government or regional government in England (or both or neither).

At UK level, I have long had a very clear personal outline view about the best constitutional model for the United Kingdom. Unlike some others in my party, and going further than my party's policy, I strongly believe in a properly federal United Kingdom with four national assemblies and four small national governments, and then with a United Kingdom parliament and government 'on top'. Addressing this issue – increasingly now called the 'English question' – will also require a reconsideration of the formula (the 'Barnett formula') for redistributing money around the UK. It seems to me quite reasonable to formally review the UK constitutional and financial settlement from time to time, and when we have the UK funding debate is the logical time also to have the 'big constitutional debate' about powers and levels of government across the UK. A constitutional convention would allow a regular, managed but not too frequent debate about national and UK powers and levels of government. And just to make it clear: at local level, businesses which pay rates could be represented in a second (advisory) chamber of the local council. In return, local councils ought to be able to fix their own business rates. A decision by any one UK country to support significant power (even up to independence) moving down from the UK government to a national government must gain public approval in the country concerned and ideally from a majority of voters across the UK, as well as a majority in the UK parliament.

It won't surprise you to know that I believe that we would also be better served by fixed terms for the House of Commons (which could be four or six years), and fixed terms for the devolved assemblies and the second UK chamber ending at fixed dates in between. The UK parliament itself also still needs significant change. The unelected, historical Lords must give way to an elected, modern Senate. (It is a small point, but it seems fair to me that those British overseas territories which we still administer could be represented here too). The Commons should have fewer members, the exact figure worked out after we reach the best consensus about the appropriate number of people whom we should ask MPs to represent. The number of MPs thereafter should be linked to population growth, but the number of senators could be fixed. Implementing the proposal from the late Roy Jenkins of a change of voting system for the House of Commons to the alternative vote plus would keep the basis of a personal constituency link between MPs and those they represent, and also deliver a proportional outcome by adding some non-constituency MPs to achieve an accurate UK-wide political balance. It is my strong view that this is the best way in the foreseeable future to achieve a representative House of Commons, not least because it is the only decent arrangement on offer which is likely to gain enough political agreement. (If we wanted in one go to tackle the gender problem then we could put two constituencies together and require that each pair of seats elect one man and one woman. Yes – seriously!)

I gather that we may soon have to do some major maintenance work on those parts of the buildings of the Palace of Westminster which include the House of Commons itself. This would be a great opportunity physically to reconfigure the Commons chamber so that we could sit, debate and vote in a more appropriate semicircle, rather than stay confrontationally facing each other in two blocs as we have up till now.

Election campaigns should of course have limits on candidate spend as well as total party campaign spend. We could also ask the

Advertising Standards Authority (ASA) to take responsibility for policing national political advertising – reviewing formal complaints that national party or national or regional candidate advertising was not 'decent, honest or truthful'. The ASA should be given the power to recommend to the Electoral Commission financial penalties on parties or individuals who are judged to have broken the rules.

During four years travelling around Britain as federal president of the Liberal Democrats, I have become more aware than ever that there are many talented people who would be great in politics, and who have not yet become involved but who haven't ruled it out. Where real power and responsibility is given to a council, assembly or parliament, or to an executive locally or nationally, then there are more important decisions to take, and more real choices to put to the electorate. It has always been very difficult to persuade central government to let go of any power. But we must never give up in this struggle, because the more devolution of power there is, the more interested people will be in using it and in voting to influence it. There is no need to feel depressed about national or local democracy. Elections where every vote counts and every candidate has something relevant to say, and where lots of bright new people are regularly challenging those already in office, could unlock our democracy, even more than we could imagine. Who knows? There might even be contests as exciting as the Wimbledon 2008 men's singles final and politics as exciting as the 2008 US Democratic and presidential campaigns. And all with very good prizes to play for!

Democracy meets diversity: an equality and human rights perspective

Trevor Phillips

t seems incredible that it is twenty years since Charter 88 was born. We owe much to the way it identified and drew to public attention the need for democratic and constitutional reform, redefining the relationship between citizens and the state.

It is arguable whether human rights legislation would have been put on the British statute books as early as 1998 or whether the Equality and Human Rights Commission itself would hold the remit for both equality and human rights, had not Charter 88 blazed this trail. It is widely credited for creating the political mood that lead directly to major constitutional reforms – devolution to London, Scotland and Wales, the Freedom of Information Act and the Human Rights Act – almost as soon as Labour took up office in 1997.

We have come a long way since 1988, and the landscape has changed dramatically. Britain is now more diverse than ever before and old–style government – at all levels – is failing to engage much of society, particularly those on the margins whose voices need to be heard. One necessary characteristic of Charter 88 was that it concentrated on change in our constitutional structures, devolution and the voting system. Some of this has been achieved but much change has been piecemeal.

Arguments are now being made for a comprehensive joining up of the various pieces of legislation passed since 1997. The Commission welcomes the opportunity this presents for a debate about changing our political culture – leading to a new constitutional settlement for the twenty-first century, with equality and human rights at its heart.

We are, I think, moving in the right direction. The *Governance of Britain* Green and White Papers and the publication of Lord Goldsmith's citizenship review[*] provide a platform for a long overdue debate about the relationship between the citizen and the state. There is much to be unpacked and potential minefields abound, but we will only make progress through engaging with these issues in an accessible way.

The Equality Bill that will shortly be put before Parliament provides an opportunity for Britain to adopt a new approach to equality law, one that links the legal framework to a competitive economy and the fulfilment of individuals' potential. For the Commission, launched in 2007, our starting point is that real equality has to mean more than just the absence of discrimination, and it can't be about treating everybody the same.

Our focus is on each of the freedoms that people need in order to achieve their potential – including participation, personal autonomy, dignity and self-respect – and the theme of our first year's work is 'bringing people together'. We want to close the gaps in society, not just regarding poverty, social mobility and opportunity but also in power, inclusion and integration – giving everyone in society a voice and the opportunity to be heard.

Recognising our differences has to be balanced with what binds society together. For some, the key challenge facing the world today is how we live with the planet. For the Commission, it is about how we live with each other. That is why we are already referring to ourselves as the 'Commission for Equality, Human Rights and Good Relations'. If equality and human rights are the central pillars of our remit, then good relations are our foundations. They are fundamental to living together harmoniously in all our diversity, in a society built on fairness and respect in which people are confident in all aspects of this diversity.

Living well together requires some basic mutual understanding

[*] Lord Goldsmith QC, *Citizenship: Our Common Bond* (Ministry of Justice, 2008).

about what is and what is not acceptable in our society. Human rights get a bad press in Britain. They are mostly seen as belonging to the undeserving while access to decent housing, health care and employment is denied to law-abiding citizens. However, we believe that our current Human Rights Inquiry will show that the articles and values contained in the Human Rights Act can provide a framework for how we live together, giving ground rules for a fairer society.

This is where a Bill of Rights for Britain, as Charter argued, could have an important role to play, if framed in the right way. There has been much debate about whether it should replace the Human Rights Act, but a Bill of Rights will be stronger if it builds upon these basic universal principles. Eight hundred years on from Magna Carta, Britain, unlike other countries, has no written constitution and as such lacks a statement of fundamental values which could help steady the country in times of rapid change.

Equality has to be recognised as the bedrock of a society built on fairness and respect, and it is also a key principle of human rights law. So, while the devil will be in the detail, the Commission broadly welcomes the introduction of a Bill of Rights as an opportunity to articulate Britain's commitment to equality and carve it in tablets of stone. The Bill of Rights should include a constitutional guarantee of equality – a provision which will make it impossible for this or future governments to pass laws that exacerbate inequality. Alongside a forthcoming Equality Act, this package of historic legislation could form the basis of a more equal and fairer society.

Of course legislation alone is not enough. Charter did much to push for structural change but we also need to change the political culture to one which lets diversity flourish. We must do more to stem the growth of the power gap in society that affects rich and poor, mainstream society and underrepresented groups. Our politics needs to be accessible to all, to give a platform to all groups within society, allowing those who have not been heard to speak for themselves. That means having more representative democratic assemblies which mirror our society.

But the heart of our democracy, demographically speaking, is shockingly unrepresentative. In 2005, women made up 20 per cent of the House of Commons (the highest ever proportion of female MPs), but less than 2.3 per cent of MPs were from ethnic minorities. And more than half of respondents to a Stonewall survey thought that people in politics were likely to conceal their sexual orientation – although almost 90 per cent would be comfortable if their own MP was gay.* Among lesbian, gay, bisexual and transgendered respondents to another Stonewall survey, there was a widespread belief that they would face prejudice from political parties if they wanted to be selected to run for Parliament or as local councillors.†

On present trends, even when the great-great-grandchildren of today's legislators at Westminster cast their votes, they will not enjoy the sight of a Parliament with equal numbers of men and women, or substantial numbers of ethnic minority MPs. In contrast, the Scottish Parliament (40 per cent women) and the National Assembly for Wales (50 per cent women) have achieved more equal gender representation through positive action by some political parties. At a local level, in 2006 only 30 per cent of councillors were women and 0.9 per cent were ethnic minority women. There are more councillors aged over seventy than under forty-five. The membership of local strategic partnerships (LSPs) is 60 per cent female – that is, at lower levels. Only a quarter of LSP chairs are women.

All this matters, if for no other reason than because what our leaders do is strongly influenced by who they are. Given the lack of diversity within our political leadership, there is little wonder that things change so slowly. These shortcomings undermine the legitimacy of our democratic system and weaken our ability to pass and implement socially just laws and policies.

The new government taskforce aimed at recruiting and retaining more ethnic minority women councillors is long overdue and will be important for the long term. So will the National Equality Taskforce, which is looking more broadly at the bigger picture of

---

* See Katherine Cowan, *Living Together: British Attitudes to Lesbian and Gay People* (London: Stonewall, 2007).
† See Ruth Hunt and Sam Dick, *Serves You Right: Lesbian and Gay People's Expectations of Discrimination* (London: Stonewall, 2008).

inequalities – including the impact of income and social class. Both taskforces should be linked together. Elected assemblies and LSPs need to radically overhaul their membership to boost diversity at the level where strategic priorities for local, regional and national areas are decided. Only when they start to reflect the diversity of the communities that they serve will they begin to hear those other voices and effectively deal with the issues as they affect us all.

The Catch-22 of underrepresentation is that the less diversity there is, the harder it is to engage others, not just to participate in voting but to encourage them to follow in their representatives' footsteps. However difficult it may be for parties with dwindling memberships and volunteers to engage new blood, a failure to do so creates a vacuum which the far right will happily fill, and the cost to good relations will be great.

In order to build a fairer society, we need to ensure that everyone has a stake and the opportunity to influence decisions which affect their lives – regardless of gender, race, disability, age, sexual orientation, religion, belief, caring responsibilities or socio-economic status. The vote is a symbol of our equality and we need to recognise how important those changes that Charter espoused are.

Happy Birthday to Charter 88, and congratulations to Unlock Democracy for this opportunity to reflect on the influence it has had in pushing the door towards a fairer and more democratic Britain. I hope that in 2028 people will look back and see that the Commission has influenced our society towards incorporating equality and human rights into the mainstream as successfully as Charter 88 has put democracy at the top of all of our agendas.

I'll end with a word or two from John Stuart Mill, who knew a little bit about the virtues of civic engagement and representative government:

There is no difficulty in showing that the ideally best form of government is that in which the sovereignty, or supreme controlling power in the last resort, is vested in the entire aggregate of the community; every citizen not only having a voice in the exercise of that ultimate sovereignty, but being, at least occasionally, called on to take an actual part in the government, by the personal discharge of some public function, local or general ... From these accumulated considerations it is evident that the only government which can fully satisfy all the exigencies of the social state is one in which the whole people participate; that any participation, even in the smallest public function, is useful; that the participation should everywhere be as great as the general degree of improvement of the community will allow; and that nothing less can be ultimately desirable than the admission of all to a share in the sovereign power of the state.

Let the people decide

Zac Goldsmith

ritish politics is in a dangerous state. More and more people feel they have less and less control over the political process. Consequently they have less and less interest in being involved in it. Trust in that political process is at an all-time low. A Mori poll in 2005 found that only one in five people trust politicians and even fewer trust the word of government ministers. In the same year, only 37 per cent of people aged between eighteen and twenty-four bothered to vote in the general election and allegiance to political parties, meanwhile, has dropped from 44 per cent to 14 per cent. The last two elections had the second and third worst turnouts since 1900. Only 1918 was worse – and that was amid the chaos of demobilisation after the First World War.

Twenty years after Charter 88 kick-started the debate about decentralising power in the UK, we have reached a tipping point. The Commission on Parliament in the Public Eye warns that the UK is now very close to the point where a government could not claim democratic legitimacy. Politicians know this and are concerned. In the run up to the next election, all politicians will tell us that they're trying to encourage more popular involvement. They will bemoan their own failure to engage the public and talk of the 'apathy' of the electorate. They will commission expensive campaigns to persuade people of the importance of voting, and come up with gimmicky ideas to 'engage' young people such as voting online or by text message, as if democracy were a series of *Big Brother*.

But all of this will miss the point entirely. For the underlying assumption – that people aren't interested or are apathetic – is false. A million people marched in London against the war in Iraq. Half a million people took to the streets in opposition to the ban on hunting. Millions of people are involved in community and charity work and in 'single-issue' pressure groups. We are, in fact, a highly politicised nation. The reason that fewer and fewer of us turn out to vote is not that we aren't interested in politics. It's because the way politicians 'do' democracy in Britain leaves people with a feeling of disempowerment. People feel a lack of control over their lives and the decisions that affect them directly. There is a perception that, no matter which party you vote for, little changes.

At national level, politics is increasingly seen as a power game restricted to remote elites. For the 1,500 or so days in between general elections – when people can choose between two political parties with whose views they almost certainly do not agree in their entirety, and which are in any case increasingly similar in outlook – we are denied any access at all to the decision-making process. After that, we have no choice but to accept one, often bad, decision after another.

At local level, our democracy has been denuded of its powers by governments of both main parties over the last two decades. And the centralised nature of our politics means that local elections are not seen as important in their own right but more often as a reflection of the national standing of the parties. It is widely felt that these polls matter little in any case because power resides elsewhere: in Westminster, Whitehall and Brussels.

This is something I've directly experienced. Shortly after being selected as a parliamentary candidate for Richmond Park, where I grew up, I was contacted by a local campaign group that was trying to prevent the opening of a new Sainsbury's. In 2007, the company had applied to build a new store in a much-loved shopping area of Barnes, a district in the constituency. The local council was bombarded with letters of protest from residents who were concerned about increased traffic and the effect on the local independent shops they had grown to love. The council rejected the company's application but was swiftly overruled by the National Planning Inspectorate in Bristol – more than 100 miles away from Barnes.

In protest, a local resident, David Rossiter, formed the White Hart Action Group and at a packed public meeting it was decided that the residents would commission a professional, independent referendum on the future of the site. On their behalf, I contacted Electoral Reform Services and we set a date. Sainsbury's was invited to review the question and to include in the referendum package a letter to residents. A month later, the referendum was held and the turnout was greater than in the previous general election. Some 85 per cent of people voted against the new store. The referendum has no teeth in law, and the company has so far chosen to ignore it. But as an expression of people power, the point was made.

At supra-national level, meanwhile, political decisions made by the European Commission or the World Trade Organization are seen to undermine national government in any case. The overall result is a feeling of helplessness: a sense that power is not in the hands of the people, but in the hands of unconcerned and unrepresentative elites. If the government decrees that genetically modified foods are safe and consequently removes what little protection exists for the British consumer – well, we have no choice but to accept it, even if science and public opinion say we shouldn't. If a supermarket is granted permission to build a large out-of-town store, there is absolutely nothing that local citizens can do about it. From motorway construction to 'faith schools', the removal of civil liberties to the banning of popular pastimes – if the people don't like it, there is very little they can do about it.

A new approach

Clearly we need to rethink the relationship between people and power, and to develop a model of political citizenship that is appropriate for our times. We need to undertake a radical and urgent reform of our political system – none of the limp suggestions we have so far seen from mainstream parties are anywhere near enough. We need the equivalent of a new Great Reform Act, to galvanise the people and rejuvenate democracy.

The principle on which this new wave of reform should be based is a simple one: localism. Power needs to be diffused throughout the community. The wider and more genuine the levels of decision-making, the more people become involved and the healthier the society. There are some things which, by their nature, we can do effectively only together with our international partners. Nothing, however, should be done internationally that could be done better in Westminster. And nothing should be done nationally that can be done locally.

At a time when Britain has been described as suffering from a 'social recession', where trust in politics and engagement in the decision-making process is at an all-time low, a more localised, direct system of democracy would bring obvious benefits.

We need direct democracy in Britain

It is time to place less faith in the power of Big Government and to recognise that a sustained change in values can only be built from the bottom up, underpinned by a broader consensus in society than exists today. What this means, very simply, is that ordinary people are given significantly more real power to intervene on any political issue, at any time of their choosing. With sufficient popular support, existing laws can be challenged, new laws can be proposed and the direction of political activity, at local and national level, can be determined by people rather than elites.

Direct democracy would radically transform politics. Not only would we be able to stop many unpopular things from happening; we would also be able to kick-start positive changes. The whole process of calling a referendum would ensure more widespread and much better-informed debate.

This isn't a new idea. Direct democracy is used widely in other, more responsive democracies around the world, including, notably, at state and local level in the USA. Under Californian law, voters are able to initiate a process where politicians can be 'recalled' from office. If enough signatures are collected, voters are presented with a ballot asking them first if they believe the politician should be recalled, and in the event that a majority answer 'yes', they are asked who they want as a replacement. The process has been tried on a number of occasions. California governors Pat Brown, Jerry Brown, Pete Wilson and even Ronald Reagan all faced unsuccessful recall attempts. However,

in 2003, voters successfully recalled the sitting governor, Gray
Davis.

The campaign spanned the summer of 2003. After several legal
moves failed to stop it, California's first-ever gubernatorial recall
election was held on 7 October and Davis became the first
governor recalled in the history of California. He was replaced by
the action movie hero Arnold Schwarzenegger.

The practice of direct democracy is even more common in
Switzerland, which frequently uses referenda in major decisions
taken by the twenty-six cantons that comprise the country's
federal structure. In Switzerland, if 100,000 signatures can be
collected within an eighteen-month period, then a proposal can
be proactively put on the ballot paper and voted on by the public.
If it is passed, then it becomes law.

One example of this in practice is the so-called 'Alpine
initiative'. In 1987, the canton of Uri was badly damaged by
violent storms. As a result, the huge transit roads that run through
the region had to be closed. Noticing the beneficial effect this had
on air quality, the people of Uri decided that they wanted the
roads to remain closed. So they began organising a referendum to
demand that all heavy goods should be carried by rail (with the
exception of goods loaded or unloaded in Switzerland), and that
there should be no further expansion of the Alpine transit roads in
their region. Despite heavy pressure from the federal parliament,
the united people of Uri won their battle and the motion was
approved in 1994.

Wellbeing
There is a growing body of evidence pointing to the crucial
importance of citizens having adequate means to express democratic freedoms and, in particular, the opportunity to influence the
decision-making that affects their everyday lives. Countries which
offer strong political freedoms and civil liberties tend to report
higher levels of wellbeing.

When comparing life satisfaction between cantons in
Switzerland, researchers have shown that differences in the
structure of direct democracy have a stronger effect on wellbeing
than income. Direct democracy has benefits for people who

participate in referenda as well as for the Swiss public generally. A survey comparing budget decisions in more than 130 Swiss towns found that public expenditure and debt are lower in cities that require their citizens to approve a budget deficit. An example would be if a municipality wants to finance a capital project, say a new swimming pool, and then repay the loan out of surplus tax revenue over the next ten years. Cantons with direct democracy also report higher overall productivity and lower corruption, and their citizens are better informed about the issue concerned.

Making it work in Britain
In Britain today we have a well-informed and educated population with the ability to make decisions relating to aspects of governance. It is time to place more confidence in them – in us – to act responsibly by giving them a greater sense of control over decisions that influence the quality of everyday community life.

Direct democracy would help strengthen dialogue between the governed and governors, empowering those sections of the community who feel their voice is not heard. Concerns that those with financial backing could skew the agenda can be addressed by placing a limit on expenditure, just as applies for general election campaigns.

It is vital that any new mechanism for giving local people greater ownership of decisions that affect their communities is genuine, and seen to be so. The tendency of politicians to concede the principle of power-sharing while attempting to retain control of decisions in practice has done much to deepen cynicism and disengagement from the political process. Politicians must face up to the reality that the popular view of them is 'they'll say anything to get elected but do exactly what they want once they win'. We should be wary that any reform is real rather than cosmetic, substantive rather than a gimmick.

Direct democracy is a principle that resonates throughout a nation's political life. The key principle, however, is that decisions are always taken at the lowest possible level. As an example: if there is a proposal to build an incinerator in a particular borough, people living in that borough would be able to 'earn' the right to hold a referendum if they manage to collect a specified number of signatures. If the issue is still more local – a proposed road, say, or a supermarket – then the referendum would be held at the level of the ward. The same process would apply, only at a more local level still.

Referenda could happen nationally too, if enough people demanded it. In Switzerland, this has long been the case. That country's population is approximately 7,500,000; it takes 1.3 per cent of the population to initiate a referendum there. If the UK adopted the same methodology, it would require roughly 900,000 signatures to trigger a referendum. We would, of course, need debate about the kind of issues that could be influenced, made or reversed via referendum. Issues relating to war, for instance, would need to be exempt, as an elected government would need to be able to make speedy decisions. Constitutional issues, like the transfer of powers to the EU, though, would justify use of a national ballot initiative.

Trusting people to use the political power that is rightfully theirs would help transform attitudes to politics, bring home a sense of responsibility and opportunity and help to make the UK a more hopeful and functioning society.

Conclusion: where do we go from here?

Peter Facey

emocracy is a big subject. The contributors to this book have covered a spectrum of issues ranging from devolution and localism through to inquests and the right to life, yet we could fill another book with things that have not been mentioned. For one thing, talk of electoral systems is meaningless to a person in a care home whose voting card is torn up by well-meaning but paternalistic carers. We have discussed the courts and the right to privacy but haven't touched on the UK's libel laws. We could dedicate whole chapters to the rights of children or immigrants in a democratic society. Europe has not been discussed in detail, and neither have the challenges which globalisation and climate change represent.

Democracy, to an extent, is also in the eye of the beholder. I have to admit to baulking, for instance, at Douglas Carswell's proposal to put the Crown Prosecution Service's role in the hands of elected local sheriffs, and at Bhikhu Parekh's suggestion of appointed 'representatives of ethnic minorities, women and other underrepresented groups' in a reformed House of Lords. Happily, though, in each of these contributions I would say there is more that I agree than disagree with. The gap between what Alexandra Runswick calls the 'democratic populists' and the 'democratic constitutionalists' is not as great as I suspect many on opposite sides of that debate imagine. There is room for passionate disagreement, but the sincerity of both sides is clear to see and needs to be recognised.

No political philosophy has a monopoly on democracy. Stuart Weir and Democratic Audit were denouncing the 'quango state' years before Labour got into power. It is deeply ironic that in the United States the Republicans are stalwart defenders of the written constitution, while in Canada the Conservative Party is moving forward with Senate reform. Looking at our own history, the early-twentieth-century Liberals failed to honour John Stuart Mill's legacy and introduce electoral reform, much to the dismay of the founding Labour Party leader, James Keir Hardie. Power corrupts the powerful regardless of their political hue. In case this book occasionally reads like a polemic against the current government, it is only because after eleven years in power it is they who are most up for scrutiny. The siren calls for governments to ignore pleas for democratic reform can be all too tempting. If David Cameron and Nick Clegg truly believe they can do a better job than Gordon Brown in this area, they would do well to remember that.

A final point on the themes of this book: the problem with any collection such as this, written months before publication, is that there is a danger it will be out of date before it is even printed. Several of our contributors have alluded to the government's attempts to extend pre-charge detention to forty-two days for terrorist suspects. At the time of writing it looks highly likely that the House of Lords will block this legislation. The Lords' Constitution Committee has been highly critical of these proposals and the former MI5 chief Baroness Manningham-Buller used her maiden speech to denounce the legislation from the floor of the Lords.[*] It is even possible that the government will see sense and drop the plans altogether.

But what goes around comes around. On my desk is a copy of the front page of the *Guardian*, dated 30 November 1988. This is the edition which featured Charter 88's first advert. The main story focuses on conflict between the European Court of Human Rights and the Thatcher government over whether extending pre-charge detention to *seven* days conflicted with the European Convention on Human Rights.[†] And as Anthony Barnett and Stuart Weir relate in these pages, the same indifference, cynicism

[*] See Hansard, HL Deb, 8 July 2008, vol. 703, col. 647.
[†] 'Ministers may alter terror bill', *Guardian*, 30 November 1988.

and clichés that greeted them at Charter's inauguration back in 1988 were recycled by the political class for the benefit of David Davis and his decision to take the campaign against pre-charge detention to the streets of his constituency in the form of a by-election. Despite Benjamin Franklin's best efforts, the powerful will always be tempted by the Faustian trade of a little liberty for a little security.

Where will we go from here? Predicting the future is a mug's game, but if there is consensus on anything in politics at the moment it is that we need to reform our political system. If Labour wins the next election, we are likely to see more progress on House of Lords reform, while if the Conservatives win, we are likely to see more experiments with direct democracy. Both parties are currently talking up decentralisation and 'localism', but even though the Conservatives are a little fuller throated in this respect, neither party is willing to contemplate giving local authorities greater tax-raising powers. With nationalists in power in Scotland, Wales and Northern Ireland, we are likely to see further devolution. The question of how England, with 85 per cent of the UK's population, is governed is set to become increasingly central. But it is one thing to get Westminster to give up power in what for many is seen as the Celtic fringe; it is another entirely to get it to give up a controlling interest over what happens in the cities and counties of England. This can be seen in the fact that even though London has regained its city government, it has far fewer powers than Scotland, Wales or Northern Ireland and collectively central government has far more influence over the day-to-day affairs of London than the mayor and assembly.

Parliament is likely to have its powers strengthened, but will continue to be dominated by the whipping system. Both major parties are committed to a Bill of Rights, but whether this will be a step forwards or backwards remains a very open question. The Conservatives are committed to scrapping the national identity card scheme, but despite the efforts of David Davis, they appear wedded to the culture of surveillance that Labour has accelerated over the past decade. By contrast, with party finance reform and parliamentary expenses it looks as if we are set for yet more procrastination – all three parties know what they must do but lack the political will to do it. Without such reforms, 'sleaze' will continue to alienate the public from politics for some time to come.

But there remain two areas of democratic reform that have always been central to Charter 88 and which we cannot rely on the political class itself to progress: electoral reform and a written constitution.

The need for electoral reform

If you believe in representative democracy, then it follows that you believe that parliaments should be representative. Yet it is remarkable how efficient our political system has been in placing individuals in key positions of power who simply do not accept that argument, or who come up with convoluted arguments for how, by some alchemical process, first past the post (FPTP) somehow delivers representative democracy. The facts speak for themselves: in 2005, six voters in ten supported a party other than Labour, yet Labour won six in ten of the seats in the House of Commons. In fact, they won fewer votes than the Conservatives got in 1997, at the 'height' of the Tories' unpopularity. If ever there was a British political scandal, it is this.

What is worse, this system means that while swing voters in marginal constituencies are granted a pre-eminent position, the rest of us are left out in the political wilderness. Parties pile on top of each other to reach the centre ground and come up with ever more creative ways to emphasise their remarkably similar policies on the issues their pollsters tell them the 'average' voter puts on the top of their list – such as crime, health and education. Meanwhile, difficult issues which the swing voter is deemed not to care sufficiently about are simply ignored.

Labour at least seems to tacitly acknowledge the indefensibility of FPTP. No elected institution created since 1997 has used FPTP: even elections for executive mayors use a system called the supplementary vote, where people are given a first and second choice. The European Parliament elections were changed to a proportional system in 1999 while local elections in Scotland have used the single transferable vote since 2007. And we may well see progress continue in this area in the foreseeable future. Electoral reform for local government in Wales enjoys broad cross-party support, including inside the Conservative Assembly Group, making this a good bet for future progress. It is even possible that we will see progress regarding electoral reform for English local government. The Councillors Commission, set up by the Department for Communities and Local Government, proposed allowing local authorities to experiment in this area.*

MPs are less willing to reconsider the electoral system when it affects them directly, and the prospect of introducing a system of fair votes in the House of Commons remains as distant as ever. The government's review of electoral systems published in 2008 is remarkably positive about the experience of electoral reform in the UK but it insists that changing the system for the Commons should not even be considered until the one used to elect the second chamber has been decided. With the distinct possibility that the reformed second chamber will use a proportional system of some kind, discussion within Labour circles has moved towards the UK adopting an Australian-style system in which the lower house would be elected using the alternative vote system (a preferential voting system for single-member constituencies – see Helen Margetts's article in this collection for more details) and the upper house would be elected by a proportional system.

While a move to such a bicameral system would remove the worst aspects of FPTP and would be a neat compromise, it would not lead to the transformation of our political culture that many supporters of electoral reform view as crucial. The campaign for proportional representation (PR) in the House of Commons will continue.

Historically, there have been four main objections to the move towards a proportional system: it is too complicated; it leads to weak and unstable government; it gives political parties too much

* See Councillors Commission, *Representing the Future: The Report of the Councillors Commission* (Department for Communities and Local Government, 2007).

power; and it would destroy the 'constituency link'. With our trials of electoral systems in the UK over the past decade, it has been demonstrated that the first two objections are simply wrong, the third only applies to certain systems and the fourth is much more complicated than it first appears.

The assertion that PR is too complicated has been proven to be wrong. Even where there have been large incidents of spoiled ballots in an election in the UK using proportional voting methods, it has invariably been a result of the design of the ballot papers rather than confusion over the voting system itself. With a change in ballot paper design, the number of spoiled ballots cast in the London Assembly elections fell from 119,000 in 2004 to 48,000 in 2008.*

The second objection – that PR leads to weak and unstable governments – is particularly interesting. A decade ago, this was a particular obsession with opponents of electoral reform but this objection is rarely made in public these days. Stable government has proven to be entirely consistent with electoral reform, with successful coalitions operating in Scotland and Wales throughout the past decade. Scotland now has a minority Scottish Nationalist government, and this too has been remarkably stable. Unstable government, then, is fundamentally a product of weak leadership rather than any particular electoral system, but there is no denying that where FPTP is combined with a system in which the executive can call an election at any time it likes (as opposed to fixed terms), a hung parliament can be massively destabilising. We saw it in the UK at the end of the 1920s and in 1974, and in recent years we have seen it in Canada. FPTP eschews consensus politics and makes the Russian roulette option all too tempting for embattled Prime Ministers.

The flipside of 'weak government' is a strong parliament and there is now a broad consensus that the latter is a good thing. Strong governments which can force whatever they like through Parliament are prone to making poor legislation. It is the fact that the House of Lords is politically balanced and thus no one party can force through legislation which has lead to its reputation as a

---

* See 'London Assembly: Technical and Turnout', London Elects website.

good scrutiniser of legislation in recent years – not romantic notions about its 'expertise' and 'independence'. As an aside, to answer Louise Christian's concerns about an elected second chamber, in fact crossbenchers have incredibly low participation rates in the Lords while working peers vote on party lines as much as MPs, if not more – an elected, and hence more legitimate, second chamber is likely to be a stronger champion for civil liberties than the present one. Forcing governments to negotiate with Parliament in order to deliver their programmes of action can only be a good thing. And where we have had coalition governments in Scotland and Wales, they have emerged as a result of long, protracted negotiations, debated relatively openly and resulting in coalition documents available for all to see. Contrast that with the way the UK government negotiates with its own backbenchers and interest groups.

The objection that PR gives political parties too much power is a valid one, but not one that applies to all systems. The closed list system which we currently use for European elections certainly gives the voter no choice of candidate. Other 'semi-open' list systems, which allow voters to choose between voting for either a party list or an individual candidate, offer voters the illusion of choice but very little power to effect change, although much depends on which counting method is used. But systems such as STV and the fully open list system (used in Finland) offer the electorate a clear choice of candidates. More to the point, many people who use this argument against PR are supporters of FPTP – the ultimate closed list system. Indeed the closed list nature of FPTP has led to the rise of the 'independent' MP – Martin Bell in 1997 and Richard Taylor in 2001 – where parties stand aside for non-aligned candidates in order to defeat the incumbent.

Nor is there any evidence to suggest that the method that the Conservatives have come up with to tackle this problem – US-style open primaries – has opened up the field. Primaries certainly can lead to greater participation and scrutiny of candidates and this was certainly the case in the 2008 US primaries for the Democratic and Republican presidential candidates. However, participation rates in primaries for congressional candidates are much lower.* Even the Conservatives' relatively high-profile primary for a London mayoral candidate only resulted in 20,000 participants,† fewer than the total number of Conservative Party members in London. It remains a very poor substitute to the increased choice which open list and STV elections offer.

Only the final objection, that PR destroys the 'constituency link' between the MP and their electorate, remains a stumbling block. But even here the picture is more mixed than opponents of PR would have you believe, since many systems of PR do indeed retain a constituency link. The additional member system, used in Scotland, Wales and the London Assembly, does, for one. The experience of STV – which uses multi-member constituencies – in the Republic of Ireland and Northern Ireland has been a *strengthening* of local ties as all the candidates attempt to outbid each other to prove how embedded they are in the constituency. Some, including the former leader of the Ulster Unionists Lord Trimble, have even suggested this has gone too far.‡

At the same time it should be recognised that the single-member constituency link is a modern phenomenon. It was not until the abolition of the remaining multi-member constituencies in the late 1940s that single-member constituencies became universal in the House of Commons. The model of the case-working MP championing local causes is an even more modern phenomenon and one which has become entrenched by the parliamentary expenses system. It has led to many MPs becoming a combination of super-councillor, ombudsman and citizens' advice bureau, and all but ignoring their primary functions as legislators. As it has become the norm over the past two decades, the autonomy of local government has been weakened. Certainly there are advantages to MPs having a sense of place, but is it really

* Adrian Shepherd, 'Participation or Moderation: Should Primary Elections Be Used in the UK?', in *Broadening Participation: Thinking beyond Party Membership* (London: New Politics Network, 2003), pp. 23–6.

† See Brendan Carlin, 'Boris Johnson is Tory choice for London Mayor', *Daily Telegraph*, 1 October 2007.

‡ Hansard, HL Deb, 27 June 2006, vol. 683, col. 1111.

so important – or even desirable – that their area of concern is rooted in just a handful of communities?

Just as the main arguments against PR are beginning to crumble, so are we seeing increased evidence that our electoral system is unsustainable. As Nick Clegg writes in this collection, in both 2001 and 2005 fewer people voted for the 'winning' party than didn't bother voting at all.

Proportional voting systems do not in and of themselves lead to higher participation rates in elections. What we do know, however, is that competitive elections lead to higher turnouts (we can expect the 2009/2010 general election to have a significantly higher turnout than 2005, for example) and that proportional voting systems lead to more competitive elections. International evidence is sketchy due to the low sample sizes and a large number of other factors, but average turnout in countries which use FPTP (67 per cent) tends to be slightly lower than turnout in countries which use list systems (73 per cent).[*]

There has been a string of voting fraud scandals in British elections – at least forty-two since 2000.[†] The pressure to cheat in a winner-takes-all system such as FPTP, where small shifts in the vote can make all the difference, is immense. At the same time, the extreme right has returned to British politics. Although issues such as immigration have risen on the electorate's list of concerns over the past decade, this alone cannot explain the increase in British National Party (BNP) councillors from zero in 1998 to around sixty in 2008. The real secret behind the modern BNP's success has been the exploitation of the electoral system. The BNP have operated by rushing into working-class areas with low participation rates in local politics and exploiting a (very real) sense that local people are being ignored. BNP candidates have even got themselves

[*] See Rafael López Pintor and Maria Gratschew, *Voter Turnout since 1945: A Global Report* (Stockholm: International IDEA, 2002), p. 88. For information, average turnout in countries using STV is 80 per cent but the sample size – two – is too small to be significant.

[†] See Stuart Wilks-Heeg, *Purity of Elections in the UK: Causes for Concern* (York: Joseph Rowntree Reform Trust, 2008), p. 31.

elected by standing in areas where there are fewer candidates than places on the council.*

It is a system ripe for abuse. In Scotland, for example, in the 2003 local elections (which used FPTP) each ward had an average of 3.4 candidates. Sixty-one wards across Scotland had just one candidate, who was therefore elected unopposed. By contrast, using STV in 2007, each voter was offered a choice of 7.4 candidates on average. Not a single candidate in Scotland was elected unopposed,[†] while at the same time in England 533 councillors in primary local authorities were not subject to a ballot. Parish and community councils offer even less choice and are thus open to even greater exploitation. Across Wealden in East Sussex in 2007, for example, there were just 474 candidates for 455 places, or 1.04 candidates for every seat. Several parish councils in that area had fewer candidates than places.[‡]

The spectre of extremist parties is often conjured up by opponents of PR but there is no question that in this respect FPTP has been a gift to the BNP; indeed it is unlikely that without the free rein FPTP has given them in recent years they would be experiencing this resurgence. To be clear, if enough people vote for extremist parties they will be elected under any electoral system. But no PR system would lead to a disgrace like that of the 2006 local elections in Barking & Dagenham, where the BNP were not only overrepresented (getting a quarter of the seats with 17 per cent of the vote) but leapfrogged the more popular Conservative Party (which got just one seat despite gaining 19 per cent of the popular vote). The BNP are now in contention for the Barking parliamentary constituency but even if they win they are highly unlikely to get much more than a third of the popular vote in the constituency.

FPTP was introduced in an era of relatively low literacy rates (the university seats were elected by STV) and at a time of two-

---

* See Dickon Hooper, 'BNP seat in "non-political" town', BBC News website, 30 April 2007.

[†] See Lewis Baston, *Local Authority Elections in Scotland: Report and Analysis* (London: Electoral Reform Society, 2007), p 65.

[‡] See Alex Runswick, 'A Platform for Change', *Voter*, February 2008, p. 14.

party politics. Neither factor applies in 2008. Indeed, as both Helen Margetts and Nick Clegg point out in this collection, over the past fifty years we have been moving towards a system of true multi-party politics. Trends can be reversed, of course, but there is little sign of this happening any time soon. The situation reached such a point in the 2005 general election that the Electoral Reform Society described that set of results as the 'worst election ever'.* With a majority of the votes cast not going to a winning candidate, and even more being cast in areas where there was no real contest, it is hard to disagree with this analysis.

The next general election may yet result in a balanced House of Commons with no party having overall control. As we have seen, the toxic combination of FPTP and executive control over when to call the election leads prime ministers to go for the high-risk option of telling the electorate that they must deliver a workable majority for one of the two main parties. This is, broadly speaking, what happened in both 1929 and 1974. More recently, however, no party gained a majority in the 2004 Canadian federal election and this happened again in 2006.† As Helen Margetts suggests, the level of multi-party politics in the UK is already producing a high level of instability, and this situation is likely to continue and even worsen, no matter how much the main two parties insist otherwise.

If we reach a point where balanced parliaments become the norm rather than the exception then we will be left with all the weaknesses of the FPTP system with none of its alleged benefits. Larger parties will be guaranteed overrepresentation without being able to secure actual parliamentary majorities. Even the strongest defenders of FPTP will no longer be able to deny that it is unfit for purpose.

A written constitution

A written constitution is about more than tidying up our constitutional law, however desirable that may be. A written

---

* *The UK General Election of 5 May 2005: Report and Analysis* (London: Electoral Reform Society, 2005), passim.
† Another Canadian federal election may take place in autumn 2008.

constitution, in the words of the American revolutionary and thinker Patrick Henry, is 'not an instrument for the government to restrain the people, [but] an instrument for the people to restrain the government – lest it come to dominate our lives and interests'. Our present 'flexible', largely uncodified constitution can do no such thing. Within our present settlement, as long as a government can guarantee a bare majority in the House of Commons, it can ultimately do almost anything it likes. And as we have seen, a majority in the House of Commons needn't mean the government has a majority of the popular vote.

Even the most visceral opponents of electoral reform ought to be profoundly troubled by the implications of this. The government's Counter-Terrorism Bill, which proposes extending pre-charge detention to forty-two days, was passed by the Commons in June 2008 with a majority of nine. If the government insists on pressing ahead with this legislation, it will be able to bypass the House of Lords through use of the Parliament Act. This policy was not even in Labour's 2005 manifesto. It may eventually be deemed incompatible with the Human Rights Act but even then the government would not be forced to reconsider. It is simply unacceptable that a right as profound as habeas corpus can be treated with such disdain by the state.

One of the claimed flexibilities of the present system is the doctrine of parliamentary sovereignty, which dictates that no parliament can pass laws that future parliaments cannot change. This is a nice idea in theory but the reality is somewhat different. If the Lisbon treaty were eventually ratified by all twenty-seven European Union member states (which currently looks doubtful due to Ireland's 'no' referendum result in June 2008), a future government determined to reverse it would have two options: renegotiate the treaty, which other member states will be loath to do, or leave the EU. The majority of EU member states factor this in when negotiating European treaties. In France, for instance, European treaties must be ratified by 60 per cent of the members of both houses of parliament in a special joint session. In Germany treaties require the approval of two thirds of both houses of parliament. We have no higher test, meaning that for as long as we remain members of the EU, European law has a higher status within the UK than UK law. The doctrine of parliamentary sovereignty has, in effect, cancelled itself out. This is an absurdity that even the most ardent pro-European should be troubled by.

Conversely, in many areas the doctrine of parliamentary sovereignty has lead to a culture of legislating first and worrying about the consequences later. In the case of local government, this has led to the UK, and England in particular, becoming one of the most centralised developed nations in the world. Without a clear framework spelled out in a written constitution, the state has been free to diminish the autonomy of local government bit by bit, tacitly encouraged by MPs keen to strengthen their 'constituency link'. Far too late, the government now recognises it may have overdone things, yet every proposal to reverse this process comes with strings attached. By failing to limit the control of central government in any way, or even to establish some broad principles outlining the functions of national, regional and local government, the effect is a constitution which presumes that central control is the best option. Even when it does decentralise, as it has done to varying degrees in Scotland, Wales, Northern Ireland and London, it has done so in such a haphazard way as to foment further discontent. By contrast, Spain – a country with a similar patchwork quilt of national, regional and local identities – has the principle of 'self-government' written into its constitution. Like the UK, some regions have greater levels of autonomy than others; unlike the UK, this can be said to be the settled will of the people, as the areas with less autonomy have the right to demand greater powers if they wish.

Slowly but surely, we are starting to see the government wake up to the idea that the time has come to introduce a written constitution. The possibility of a written constitution was floated in the 2007 *Governance of Britain* Green Paper. The secretary of state for justice, Jack Straw, repeated this in a speech in Washington. The head of University College London's Constitution Unit, Professor Robert Hazell, was quick to dismiss this: 'Constitutions don't get written in cold blood. Written constitutions typically follow defeat in war, a revolution, independence or the collapse of the previous system of government. None of those fates is likely to befall the UK. So however

desirable it may be, a written constitution isn't going to happen.'*
It is fair to say that constitutions typically get written in times of
crisis, but Hazell overstates the case in suggesting that it would
need a collapse. Canada, South Africa and France's Fifth Republic
are just three exceptions to this so-called rule. Sometimes a
written constitution is adopted specifically to pre-empt a collapse
in government. The question is: are we reaching a crisis point in
the UK?

I would argue that we do indeed appear to be heading towards
a perfect constitutional storm. Leaving aside the general level of
antipathy towards politics in the UK today, and the collapse of the
two-party system which has been discussed above, there are six
different issues which combined will force us to radically rethink
our political system over the coming decade:

- **Human rights and the rule of law.** Both the Labour and
  Conservative approaches to adopting a Bill of Rights are
  inherently contradictory. On the one hand, they argue for
  human rights legislation over which the public will have a
  greater sense of ownership. On the other hand, both regularly
  object to the role of the courts. As John Jackson writes in this
  collection, the implications of the Constitutional Reform Act
  – committing government and Parliament to abiding by the
  rule of law for the first time in history while leaving the
  definition of that principle for the judiciary to decide – have
  yet to be fully appreciated. We need to resolve both these
  issues once and for all.
- **Privacy and the surveillance society.** The right to privacy
  has been taken for granted by successive governments but
  Labour's full-blown assault on it is unprecedented. Tens of
  thousands of individuals have signed up to NO2ID's pledge
  to refuse to register for an identity card, making it potentially
  the biggest civil disobedience movement the UK has seen
  since the poll tax riots. The use of powers granted to
  government agencies by the Regulation of Investigatory
  Powers Act for frivolous things such as checking to see if

* Quoted in 'Straw's written constitution hint', BBC News website,
13 February 2008.

parents are living in the right school catchment areas*
undermines the idea that these powers are in the public
interest. Repeated instances of government departments,
agencies and contractors losing copies of individuals' personal
data and other information technology fiascos are eroding the
public's confidence in the doctrine of 'transformational
government'. All these trends point towards a backlash and
the public demanding a rolling back of the state's powers to
interfere with our private lives.

- **Devolution and decentralisation.** Scotland, Wales and
Northern Ireland are all moving towards greater autonomy at
varying speeds. Meanwhile in England there is growing
pressure to reverse the centralisation of recent decades and a
small but growing sense of disaffection as predicted by Tam
Dalyell's famous 'West Lothian question'. The general lack of
co-ordination between all these processes potentially
threatens the integrity of the union itself. A referendum on
Scottish independence is likely to bring these issues to a head
and the only solution short of the total dissolution of the UK
would appear to be a structure with federal characteristics,
possibly along Spanish lines.

- **The European Union and globalisation.** The project to
reform EU governance is unlikely to end with Ireland's 'no'
vote rejecting the Lisbon treaty in June 2008. Within the UK,
every new European treaty has further highlighted the
dysfunctional and divisive way in which we negotiate such
things and thus the need for reform. Meanwhile, everything
from climate change and oil through to trade and security
highlights how we increasingly need to adopt global
agreements to advance our interests. Our existing system,
which largely excludes Parliament from such negotiations, let
alone the public, is set to look increasingly flawed.

- **Life after Elizabeth.** The Queen's position is not under
serious threat. But just as many republicans have affection for
the Queen, many monarchists are wary of her heir, the more

---

* See Fay Schlesinger, 'Council uses criminal law to spy on school place
applicants', *Guardian*, 11 April 2008.

activist Prince Charles. Public opinion on the monarchy can shift dramatically, as we saw immediately after the death of Princess Diana in 1997. If the monarchy were to be abolished, a written constitution would be more or less inevitable. But it may be that a written constitution, clarifying and limiting the role of the monarch, is the price that must be paid before the public will accept Charles on the throne.

All six of these factors must be addressed over the next couple of decades, but the existing ad hoc approach is likely to make the situation worse. It would be foolish to consider the state's relationship with its citizens, nations, counties, municipalities, parliament and monarchy in isolation from one another. All of them point towards a need for greater codification and from there it is just a small step towards a fully fledged written constitution. Nevertheless, our political system may be falling about our ears and failing by almost every standard, but the status quo suits constitutional romantics and bureaucrats alike who are likely to do everything they can to thwart reform at every turn.

Ultimately, real power is always taken. It is never given. The process must be led from the bottom up and the final document must be ratified by the people. The Human Rights Act's greatest vulnerability is the notion, encouraged by certain politicians and the tabloid press, that it was imposed on the people. Despite the fact that the Act is designed to protect individuals from the excesses of the state, it has somehow become warped in the imaginations of large sections of the public. Never again can we allow. constitutional reform to be so vulnerable to accusations of elitism.

Such a process will not begin unless there are significant numbers of voices demanding it. Polling evidence suggests that the public broadly agrees with the idea of a written constitution.[*] At the same time, dissatisfaction with the present system is at an all-time high. The trick for Unlock Democracy will be to find ways to capture the public imagination and build a mass movement. Charter 88 successfully did that in the late 1980s and

---

[*] See *State of the Nation 2006* (York: Joseph Rowntree Reform Trust, 2006).

1990s and with the rise of the internet we now have a chance to communicate directly with supporters and build up activist networks in ways that could not have been imagined then.

Although we can never afford to drop our guard against the ever-present forces against democracy, rights and freedoms, we have every reason to be optimistic about the future. Despite all the challenges that the democratic reforms of the past decade present, there is no desire to go back to the pre-1997 constitutional settlement. Even the opponents of the Human Rights Act are unsure how it should be changed and tend to talk about alternatives. There are few who will even publicly defend the status quo; the only question is which direction we go in, and how far we want to go. We can't afford to be defensive and should be looking for every opportunity to move the agenda forward.

Twenty years on from the launch of Charter 88, its broader message remains as vital as ever: 'Only people themselves can ensure freedom, democracy and equality before the law ... Such ends are far better demanded, and more effectively obtained and guarded, once they belong to everyone by inalienable right.' Almost unnoticed, it has transformed political discourse irrevocably. The prospects for democratic reform are far better than they were in 1988. As the breadth of opinion in this collection shows, we are all democratic reformers now. And while its ultimate goals – of a written constitution and institutions which reflect our pluralist democracy – have yet to be realised, they are being openly discussed in the halls of Westminster and Whitehall in a way that in the past was unimaginable. We are immensely proud to be continuing this work.

ARCHIVE

List of materials

The *Guardian* and *Observer* advertisements that helped launch the movement

The original Charter 88

Front cover of *New Statesman*, 2 December 1988

Folk alphabet

Briefing MPs on the day of presentation

'We Can Make It Happen'

A Charter 88 vigil

Charter 88 featured on *Spitting Image*

Cartoon by Jane Monahan

Front cover of *Debating the Constitution*

Cartoons by Tim Sanders

'Ten Lords a-Lending'

Advertisement in the *Guardian*, 30 November 1988.
(Guardian News and Media Ltd)

14   OBSERVER SUNDAY 22 JANUARY 1989

THOUSANDS HAVE SIGNED CHARTER 88 – JOIN US

CHARTER 88

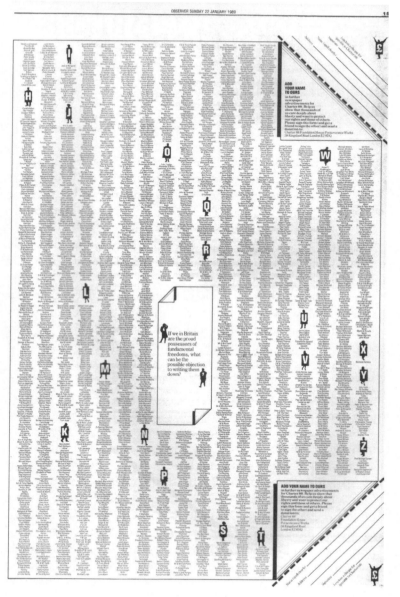

Advertisement in the *Observer*, 22 January 1989.
(Guardian News and Media Ltd)

The original Charter 88

We have been brought up in Britain to believe that we are free: that our Parliament is the mother of democracy; that our liberty is the envy of the world; that our system of justice is always fair; that the guardians of our safety, the police and security services, are subject to democratic, legal control; that our civil service is impartial; that our cities and communities maintain a proud identity; that our press is brave and honest.

Today such beliefs are increasingly implausible. The gap between reality and the received ideas of Britain's 'unwritten constitution' has widened to a degree that many find hard to endure. Yet this year we are invited to celebrate the third centenary of the 'Glorious Revolution' of 1688, which established what was to become the United Kingdom's sovereign formula. In the name of freedom, our political, human and social rights are being curtailed while the powers of the executive have increased, are increasing and ought to be diminished.

A process is underway which endangers many of the freedoms we have had. Only in part deliberate, it began before 1979 and is now gathering momentum. Scotland is governed like a province from Whitehall. More generally, the government has eroded a number of important civil freedoms: for example, the universal rights to habeas corpus, to peaceful assembly, to freedom of information, to freedom of expression, to membership of a trade union, to local government, to freedom of movement, even to the birth-right itself. By taking these rights from some, the government puts them at risk for all.

A traditional British belief in the benign nature of the country's institutions encourages an unsystematic perception of these grave matters; each becomes an 'issue' considered in isolation from the rest. Being unwritten the constitution also encourages a piecemeal approach to politics; an approach that gives little protection against a determined, authoritarian state. For the events of 1688 only shifted the absolute power of the monarch into the hands of the parliamentary oligarchy.

The current administration is not an un–English interruption in the country's way of life. But while the government calls upon aspirations for liberty, it also exploits the dark side of a constitutional settlement which was always deficient in democracy.

The 1688 settlement had a positive side. In its time the Glorious Revolution was a historic victory over Royal tyranny. Britain was spared the rigours of dictatorship. A working compromise between many different interests was made possible at home, even if, from Ireland to India, quite different standards were imposed by Empire abroad. No criticism of contemporary developments in Britain should deny the significance of past democratic achievements, most dramatically illuminated in May 1940 when Britain defied the fascist domination of Europe.

But the eventual victory that liberated Western Europe preserved the paternalist attitudes and institutions of the United Kingdom. These incorporated the popular desire for work and welfare into a post–war national consensus. Now this has broken down. So, too, have its conventions of compromise and tolerance: essential components of a free society. Instead, the inbuilt powers of the 1688 settlement have enabled the government to discipline British society to its ends: to impose its values on the civil service; to menace the independence of broadcasting; to threaten academic freedom in universities and schools; to tolerate abuses committed in the name of national security. The break with the immediate past shows how vulnerable Britain has always been to elective dictatorship. The consequence is that today the British have fewer legal rights and less democracy than many other West Europeans.

The intensification of authoritarian rule in the United Kingdom has only recently begun. The time to reverse the process is now, but it cannot be reversed by an appeal to the past. Three hundred years of unwritten rule from above are enough. Britain needs a democratic programme that will end unfettered control by the executive of the day. It needs to reform a Parliament in which domination of the lower house can be decided by fewer than 40 per cent of the population; a Parliament in which a majority of the upper house is still determined by inheritance.

We have had less freedom than we believed. That which we have enjoyed has been too dependent on the benevolence of our rulers. Our freedoms have remained their possession, rationed out to us as subjects rather than being our own inalienable possession as citizens. To make real the freedoms we once took for granted means for the first time to take them for ourselves.

The time has come to demand political, civil and human rights in the United Kingdom. The first step is to establish them in constitutional form, so that they are no longer subject to the arbitrary diktat of Westminster and Whitehall.

We call, therefore, for a new constitutional settlement which would:

Enshrine, by means of a Bill of Rights, such civil liberties as the right to peaceful assembly, to freedom of association, to freedom from discrimination, to freedom from detention without trial, to trial by jury, to privacy and to freedom of expression.

Subject executive powers and prerogatives, by whomsoever exercised, to the rule of law.

Establish freedom of information and open government.

Create a fair electoral system of proportional representation.

Reform the upper house to establish a democratic, non-hereditary second chamber.

Place the executive under the power of a democratically

renewed parliament and all agencies of the state under the rule of law.

Ensure the independence of a reformed judiciary.

Provide legal remedies for all abuses of power by the state and the officials of central and local government.

Guarantee an equitable distribution of power between local, regional and national government.

Draw up a written constitution, anchored in the idea of universal citizenship, that incorporates these reforms.

Our central concern is the law. No country can be considered free in which the government is above the law. No democracy can be considered safe whose freedoms are not encoded in a basic constitution.

We, the undersigned, have called this document Charter 88. First, to mark our rejection of the complacency with which the tercentenary of the Revolution of 1688 has been celebrated. Second, to reassert a tradition of demands for constitutional rights in Britain, which stretches from the barons who forced the Magna Carta on King John, to the working men who drew up the People's Charter in 1838, to the women at the beginning of this century who demanded universal suffrage. Third, to salute the courage of those in Eastern Europe who still fight for their fundamental freedoms.

Like the Czech and Slovak signatories of Charter 77, we are an informal, open community of people of different opinions, faiths and professions, united by the will to strive, individually and collectively, for the respect of civil and human rights in our own country and throughout the world. Charter 77 welcomed the ratification by Czechoslovakia of the UN International Covenant on Political and Civil Rights, but noted that it 'serves as a reminder of the extent to which basic human rights in our country exist, regrettably, on paper only'.

Conditions here are so much better than in Eastern Europe as to bear no comparison. But our rights in the United Kingdom remain unformulated, conditional upon the goodwill of the government and the compassion of bureaucrats. To create a democratic constitution at the end of the twentieth century, however, may extend the concept of liberty, especially with respect to the rights of women and the place of minorities. It will not be a simple matter: part of British sovereignty is shared with Europe; and the extension of social rights in a modern economy is a matter of debate everywhere. We cannot foretell the choices a free people may make. We are united in one opinion only, that British society stands in need of a constitution which protects individual rights and of the institutions of a modern and pluralist democracy.

The inscription of laws does not guarantee their realisation. Only people themselves can ensure freedom, democracy and equality before the law. Nonetheless, such ends can be far better demanded, and more effectively obtained and guarded, once they **belong to everyone by inalienable right.**

Front cover of *New Statesman and Society*, 2 December 1988.
(*New Statesman*)

The folk alphabet

t was around Guy Fawkes Day in 1988 when Stuart Weir (then editor of *New Statesman and Society*) invited me to a small meeting at the Reform Club in Pall Mall, where Richard Holme inspired us all by stressing the need to create a mythology behind what was to be Charter 88. *New Statesman and Society* was soon to feature Charter 88 for the first time and I was asked to design the front cover for the 2 December issue. Suspecting that textual matter would be the main content for Charter 88 to come, and knowing that *NSS* front cover designs were then treated typographically, I saw the chance to kill two birds with one stone by creating an alphabet as a generic device to animate any given text. The sandwich man was the obvious choice to be mobilised as a demonstrative icon. So, hurriedly, more than fifty silhouettes were required at a common scale to make up the alphabet.

The well-suited, bold capitals on the folk figures, as well as the other typefaces used subsequently in the Charter 88 campaign material, first appeared in the freshly redesigned *NSS* magazine. The folk alphabet was a prime part in a visual kit adopted for much of the literature issued later for the campaign. Twenty years on, I now feel it was a sanguine, and neatly off-the-wall, methodist design response. The last words should come from Dick Hebdige (*NSS*, 1 December 1989): 'The Charter 88 logo with the Letraset lookalike men and women – faceless, ageless and most importantly deracinated – is an inspired solution to the problem of giving an individuated yet anonymously civic image to the campaign for constitutional reform.'

Keith Ablitt

CHARTER 88

We can make it happen in the next ten years.

Briefing MPs on the day they presented Charter 88 as a petition to Parliament. Left to right: Geoffrey Robertson, Ursula Owen, Archy Kirkwood MP, Sarah Spencer, Anthony Barnett, Robin Cook, Salman Rushdie (partially obscured), Stuart Weir, Richard Holme. (Rex Features)

A Charter 88 vigil.

The reaction of the main party leaders to Charter 88, as suggested by *Spitting Image*.

Jane Monahan's cartoon of a Charter 88 gathering in Manchester. (Jane Monahan)

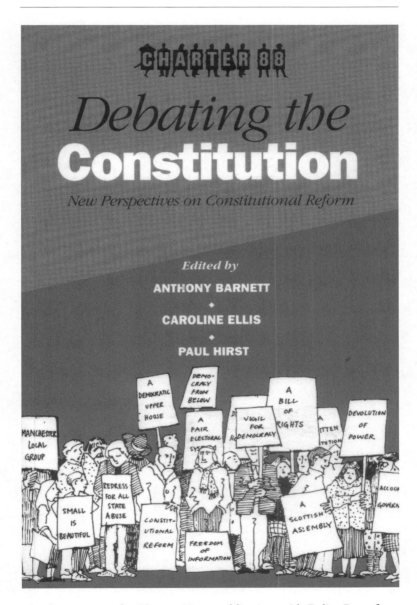

The front cover of a Charter 88 co-publication with Polity Press from 1993. (Polity Press)

Cartoons by Tim Sanders commissioned by *Citizen* magazine in 2003.
(Tim Sanders)

Unlock Democracy's 2006 Christmas card, commissioned from David Shenton. (David Shenton)

Index